CRIME, COMMUNITIES, AND PUBLIC POLICY

CHICAGO ASSEMBLY BOOKS

Creating Jobs, Creating Workers: Economic Development and Employment in Metropolitan Chicago (1990)

Paying for Health Care: Public Policy Choices for Illinois (1992)

Affordable Housing and Public Policy: Strategies for Metropolitan Chicago (1993)

Crime, Communities, and Public Policy (1995)

Paying for State and Local Government (forthcoming)

The Chicago Assembly is a collaborative project of the Center for Urban Research and Policy Studies at the University of Chicago and the Metropolitan Planning Council of Chicago.

CRIME, COMMUNITIES, AND PUBLIC POLICY

EDITED BY

LAWRENCE B. JOSEPH

A CHICAGO ASSEMBLY BOOK

CENTER FOR URBAN RESEARCH AND POLICY STUDIES
THE UNIVERSITY OF CHICAGO

DISTRIBUTED BY UNIVERSITY OF ILLINOIS PRESS

Copyright © 1995 by the University of Chicago. All rights reserved.

ISBN 0-9626755-3-9 (paper)

Published by:

    The University of Chicago
    Center for Urban Research and Policy Studies
    969 E. 60th Street
    Chicago, IL 60637

Distributed by:

    University of Illinois Press
    1325 S. Oak St.
    Champaign, IL 61820

CONTENTS

Preface / *Laurence E. Lynn, Jr., and Deborah C. Stone*   ix

Acknowledgments   xi

Introduction / *Lawrence B. Joseph and Laurence E. Lynn, Jr.*   1

Crime and Community Safety / *Report of the Chicago Assembly*   15

Crime and Communities: Prevalence, Impact, and Programs / *Arthur J. Lurigio*   33

    Comments / *Carolyn Rebecca Block*   77
    Comments / *Robert J. Sampson*   81

Community-Based Crime Prevention: Citizens, Community Organizations, and the Police / *Paul J. Lavrakas*   85

    Comments / *Karen N. Hoover*   123

The Criminal Justice System: Unfair and Ineffective / *Randolph N. Stone*   127

    Comments / *Frances Kahn Zemans*   151

The Future of Corrections: Probation / *Patrick D. McAnany*   155

    Comments / *Norval Morris*   177

Drugs and Violence: Myth and Reality / *Paul J. Goldstein*   181

Youth Gangs: Problem and Policy / *Irving A. Spergel*   201

A Comprehensive Approach to Violence Prevention:
Public Health and Criminal Justice in
Partnership / *Howard Spivak, Deborah
Prothrow-Stith, and Mark Moore*　　　　　　　　　231

   Comments / *Margaret K. Rosenheim*　　　　253
   Comments / *Darnell F. Hawkins*　　　　　　259

The Politics of Street Crime and Criminal Justice /
   Stuart A. Scheingold　　　　　　　　　　　265

   Comments / *Peter M. Manikas*　　　　　　295

Notes on Contributors　　　　　　　　　　　　301

Chicago Assembly Participants　　　　　　　　305

Chicago Assembly Program Committee　　　　311

Chicago Assembly Advisory Board　　　　　　312

TABLES

Lawrence B. Joseph and Laurence E. Lynn, Jr.
1: Prisoners Under Jurisdiction of Federal and State
   Correctional Authorities　　　　　　　　　　4
2: Expenditures for State and Local Justice Systems　5
3: Violent Crime and Property Crime in the
   United States　　　　　　　　　　　　　　　6
4: Violent Crime in the United States, Illinois,
   and Chicago, 1985-1993　　　　　　　　　　8

Arthur J. Lurigio
1: Crime Index Trends in the United States, 1965-1993　38
2: Victimization Levels for Selected Crimes in the
   United States, 1981-1992　　　　　　　　　39
3: Violent Crime Index in Illinois, 1976-1992　　　44
4: Violent Crime Rates in Illinois and the United
   States, 1976-1992　　　　　　　　　　　　45
5: Violent Crime Index Offenses in Illinois,
   Cook County, and Chicago, 1992　　　　　　46
6: Homicides in Chicago, 1969-1994　　　　　　47
7: Property Crime Index in Illinois, 1976-1992　　49

8: Property Crime Index Offenses in Illinois, Cook County, and Chicago, 1992	50
9: Adult Prison Population in Illinois, 1970-1993	60

Paul J. Lavrakas
1: Levels of Crime Prevention and Operational Realms	93

Patrick D. McAnany
1: Illinois Adult Felony Probation Caseload and Adult Prison Population	158
2: Correctional Population in the United States, 1985-1990	161

Stuart A. Scheingold
1: Salience of the Crime Issue in Local Elections, 1948-1978	275
2: The Political Salience of Crime in the United States, 1968-1980, Open-Ended Questions	277
3: The Political Salience of Crime in the United States, Selected Years 1973-1980, Forced-Choice Questions	278

FIGURE

Howard Spivak, Deborah Prothrow-Stith, and Mark Moore
1: Model for Violence Prevention Activities	241

PREFACE:
THE CHICAGO ASSEMBLY

The Chicago Assembly is designed to illuminate important public policy issues facing Chicago and the broader metropolitan region of northeastern Illinois. The project is a collaborative endeavor of the Center for Urban Research and Policy Studies at the University of Chicago and the Metropolitan Planning Council. The major objectives of the Chicago Assembly are to focus attention and stimulate informed discussion on critical policy issues in the Chicago region; to educate government officials, community and civic leadership, and the general citizenry regarding the factual background and the range of policy options in each issue area; to facilitate more effective communication among decision-makers from the public and private sectors, as well as from city, suburban, and statewide entities; and to raise the level and quality of public policy discourse in metropolitan Chicago on a continuing basis.

Each year the Chicago Assembly considers a public policy issue that has critical importance for the Chicago area, as well as broader national implications. In preparation for each annual assembly, the project commissions a set of background papers and commentaries written by leading public policy experts. The background material is distributed to participants in advance of the assembly itself, which includes prominent representatives from government, business, labor, civic groups, community-based organizations, relevant professional groups, and academia. The Chicago Assembly is a working, participatory enterprise, where regional leaders gather for an intensive two-day period to deliberate about fundamental issues *and* to reach some conclusions. Each Chicago Assembly produces a written report, containing findings and recommendations, that is endorsed by participants at a concluding plenary session. The final report is an integrated document reflecting major points of agreement and disagreement among participants. Shortly after the assembly, the report is released for general distribution throughout the Chicago metropolitan area. Subsequently, the Chicago Assembly publishes a book containing the background papers, commentaries, and final report. Finally, the project facilitates various follow-up activities that emerge from each assembly.

This book is a product of the fourth annual Chicago Assembly, "Crime and Community Safety," which was held November 19-20, 1992, in St. Charles, Illinois. The assembly on crime was made possible by grants from the M. R. Bauer Foundation and the John D. and Catherine T. MacArthur Foundation. Continental Bank provided in-kind support for the reproduction of the Chicago Assembly Report.

Laurence E. Lynn, Jr.

Director, Center for Urban
   Research and Policy Studies
University of Chicago

Deborah C. Stone

Executive Director
Metropolitan Planning Council

ACKNOWLEDGMENTS

The essays in this book are revised and updated versions of papers that were originally prepared for the Chicago Assembly on "Crime and Community Safety," held in November 1992. Amy Keller, Courtenay Savage, and Joel Werth provided staff support for that event. The Chicago Assembly Report on "Crime and Community Safety" was developed with the help of a drafting committee consisting of discussion leaders, recorders, and other assembly participants: Joseph P. Beazley, Larry Bennett, Carolyn Rebecca Block, Eduardo Camacho, Thomas R. Fitzgerald, Warren Friedman, Thomas G. Fuechtmann, William A. Geller, Michael Brennan Getty, John P. Heinz, Karen N. Hoover, Suzanne E. Jones, Wayne Kerstetter, Peter M. Manikas, Nancy Martin, Dennis E. Nowicki, Margaret K. Rosenheim, Barbara M. Schleck, James R. Simmons, Ron Tonn, and Wim Wiewel. Courtenay Savage wrote the initial draft of the report.

Jane Lichty, managing editor of *Social Service Review*, served as copy editor for this volume. Nancy Radner helped with background research. Desirae Chambers-Docks and Victoria Jacobs assisted in preparing tables, checking references, and proofreading.

L.J.

INTRODUCTION

Lawrence B. Joseph and Laurence E. Lynn, Jr.

On August 25, 1994, after months of furious debate and political maneuvering, the U.S. Congress passed the Violent Crime Control Act, which was portrayed as "an unprecedented federal venture into crime fighting" (CQ, 1994, p. 2488). The legislation contained an unusual amalgam of "conservative" and "liberal" elements. On the one hand, it authorized federal funding for hiring more police at the local level, as well as for state prison construction. It also applied the death penalty to dozens of new or existing federal crimes and adopted the "three strikes and you're out" rule, which mandates life in prison for three-time violent offenders. On the other hand, the legislation banned the manufacture and possession of certain types of semi-automatic assault weapons and provided federal grants for local crime prevention programs, including domestic violence prevention, midnight basketball leagues for inner-city youths, and drug abuse treatment. Republican opponents of the bill had wanted to cut funding for social programs, increase mandatory minimum sentences for gun and drug offenses, and exclude the ban on assault weapons. Passage of the omnibus anti-crime package was regarded as a major victory for the Clinton administration (Povich, 1994; Masci, 1994).

Several days later in Chicago, 14-year-old Shavon Dean was fatally shot near the front porch of her home in the Roseland community on the city's far south side. She was the unintended victim of gunfire from a semi-automatic pistol aimed at a group of teenagers. Police soon began an intensive search for the prime suspect in the murder, an 11-year-old neighbor and gang member named Robert Sandifer. Just a few days later, Robert Sandifer's slain body was found under a railroad viaduct. He had been killed execution-style, with several shotgun wounds to the head, by other members of his own gang. Two brothers, 14 and 16 years old, were charged with the murder. (A Cook County juvenile court judge later ruled that the younger brother would be tried as an adult.) These two murders received heavy media attention nationwide. Law enforcement officials viewed the Sandifer case as an extreme example of a growing phenomenon of younger and more violent criminals (Warren and Marx, 1994). Robert Sandifer, whose short life was marked by parental abuse and neglect, an extensive juvenile criminal record, and gang membership at the age of nine, quickly became a symbol for the violence and other severe social problems that plague America's inner cities (*New York Times*, 1994; Terry, 1994).

The juxtaposition of these two news stories—the passage of the anti-crime bill and the death of Robert Sandifer—highlighted the huge gap between the politics of crime on Capitol Hill and the harsh realities of violence in urban communities. Most of the provisions of the crime bill were largely symbolic, designed to reassure an anxious and fearful public, with little prospect for actually reducing or preventing crime. Neither building more prisons nor organizing basketball leagues nor banning some assault weapons (while leaving others in circulation) would have salvaged the lives of Shavon Dean and Robert Sandifer.

Crime is an exceptionally complex, seemingly intractable policy problem. Public debate on crime issues is too often distorted by ideological posturing and political symbolism. As one of the contributors to this book puts it: "The political rhetoric of conservatives and liberals is stale, with the right offering more laws but continued disorder and the left offering sweeping visions of reform but few short-term or intermediate remedies. The politics of street crime have not served us well" (Manikas, 1995).

CRIME AND PUBLIC POLICY

Contemporary federal efforts at fighting urban street crime began with the Omnibus Crime Control and Safe Streets Act of 1968. Congress passed the bill in the midst of a tumultuous election year when "law-and-order" was a key campaign issue. The legislation established the Law Enforcement Assistance Administration (LEAA) to channel funds in support of state and local crime control efforts, permitted wiretapping in a wide variety of federal and state criminal cases, and attempted to overturn several Supreme Court decisions involving the rights of the accused. Passage of the measure—which bore little resemblance to the bill originally submitted by President Johnson—was characterized as a major political defeat for the administration and for congressional liberals. The bill was signed reluctantly by the president (CQ, 1969, pp. 323-325).

Introduction

During the 1970s and 1980s, the dominant political response to crime moved further in the direction of various "get tough" policies. Both the federal government and state governments revised their criminal codes and sentencing laws in an effort to keep criminal offenders off the streets. For example, the Comprehensive Crime Control Act of 1984, a top legislative priority of the Reagan administration, required federal judges to follow new, stricter sentencing guidelines in most cases. Other major provisions of the legislation included allowing pretrial detention of certain criminal defendants and instituting harsher penalties for convicted drug dealers (CQ, 1985, pp. 698-701). Similarly, various states enacted a wide range of measures designed to get tough on crime. In Illinois, these initiatives included mandatory minimum prison sentences for serious criminal offenders, creation of new classes of criminal offenses and harsher penalties for existing offenses, reinstitution of the death penalty, preventive detention of some criminal defendants, and automatic transfer of some juvenile offenders to adult criminal court (Vlasak, 1989; Wortham, 1993).

Since the early 1980s, a major focus of anti-crime efforts by federal, state, and local governments has been the "war on drugs." The Anti-Drug Abuse Act of 1988 expanded federal drug interdiction efforts, applied the death penalty to major drug traffickers, and established the Office of National Drug Control Policy, headed by a cabinet-level "drug czar" (CQ, 1990, pp. 748-749). There have been similar efforts at the state and local levels to combat drug trafficking and drug use. As a result, drug-related criminal cases and offenders have flooded court systems and correctional institutions. In Cook County criminal courts, drug offenses represented 14 percent of all felony cases filed in 1978, 43 percent in 1990, and 50 percent in 1993 (ICJIA, 1989, pp. 75, 85; 1991, p. 190).[1] Drug offenders accounted for less than 6 percent of state prison admissions in Illinois in 1983 but more than 27 percent by 1990. There has been a similar trend in state prison systems nationwide (Austin, 1991, p. 16; BJS, 1994, p. 612).

Another significant policy development, related to both changes in sentencing practices and the war on drugs, has been dramatic increases in rates of incarceration. Between 1980 and 1992, the number of inmates in federal prisons grew 277 percent.

---

[1] Unpublished data for 1993 obtained from the Illinois Criminal Justice Information Authority.

For state correctional facilities, the adult prison population grew nearly 200 percent, with a comparable increase in Illinois (see Table 1). In an effort to keep up with burgeoning prison populations, there has been a boom in prison construction at both the federal and state levels. This has been and continues to be an expensive proposition; it costs about $75,000 to build a prison cell and about $25,000 per year to maintain an inmate in a state prison (Blumstein, 1995, p. 403). In 1979, corrections accounted for 25 percent of total criminal justice system expenditures by state and local governments nationwide, compared with 52 percent for police protection. By 1990, the share for corrections had increased to 36 percent, while the share for police protection had dropped to 43 percent (see Table 2).

TABLE 1: Prisoners Under Jurisdiction of Federal and State Correctional Authorities

	U.S. Total	Federal	State	Illinois
1980	319,598	23,778	295,819	11,497
1982	414,362	29,673	384,689	14,293
1985	487,593	35,781	451,812	18,279
1990	743,382	58,838	684,544	27,516
1992	883,656	80,259	803,397	31,640
1993	973,325	89,587	883,738	34,495
Pct. chg. 1980-93	204.5	276.8	198.7	200.0

Note: Data indicate prison populations as of December 31 of each year.

Source: Bureau of Justice Statistics, *Sourcebook of Criminal Justice Statistics—1993* (Washington, D.C.: U.S. Department of Justice, 1994).

TABLE 2: Expenditures for State and Local Justice Systems (in $ millions)

	FY 1979	Pct. Distr.	FY 1990	Pct. Distr.	Pct. Change 1979-90
Police protection	11,864	52.4	27,784	42.8	134.2
Corrections	5,686	25.1	23,504	36.2	313.4
Judicial/legal services	4,752	21.0	13,072	20.1	175.1
Courts	3,011	13.3	7,754	11.9	157.5
Prosecution/legal services	1,384	6.1	3,982	6.1	187.7
Public defense	357	1.6	1,336	2.1	274.3
Total	22,651	100.0	64,918	100.0	186.6

Source: Bureau of Justice Statistics, *Sourcebook of Criminal Justice Statistics—1993* (Washington, D.C.: U.S. Department of Justice, 1994).

CRIME TRENDS

The crime control strategies of the past few decades have been the subject of different interpretations and assessments.[2] There is little evidence, however, that changes in policy have led to significant reductions in crime, especially violent crime. The FBI's crime index, which measures incidents known to the police, escalated rapidly during the 1960s, especially in the latter part of the decade. As shown in Table 3, both the violent crime index (murder, rape, robbery, aggravated assault) and the property crime index (burglary, larceny-theft, motor vehicle theft) more than doubled between 1960 and 1970. The percentage growth for both types of crime was relatively lower during the 1970s, although the growth in numbers of incidents was greater.

---

[2] See, e.g, Jencks, 1991; DiIulio, 1992; Wilson, 1994; Skolnick, 1994.

TABLE 3: Violent Crime and Property Crime in the United States

	Violent Crime Index	Violent Crime Rate	Property Crime Index	Property Crime Rate
1960	288,460	161	3,095,700	1,727
1965	387,390	200	4,352,000	2,249
1970	738,820	364	7,359,200	3,621
1975	1,039,710	488	10,252,700	4,811
1980	1,344,520	597	12,063,700	5,353
1985	1,328,800	557	11,102,600	4,651
1990	1,820,130	732	12,655,500	5,089
1993	1,924,190	746	12,216,800	4,737

Pct. Chg.

1960-65	34.3	24.2	40.6	30.2
1965-70	90.7	82.0	69.1	61.0
1970-75	40.7	34.1	39.3	32.9
1975-80	29.3	22.3	17.7	11.3
1980-85	- 1.2	- 6.7	- 8.0	-13.1
1985-90	37.0	31.4	14.0	9.4
1990-93	5.7	1.9	- 3.5	- 6.9

Violent Crime Index = murder and non-negligent manslaughter, forcible rape, robbery, and aggravated assault.

Property Crime Index = burglary, larceny-theft, and motor vehicle theft.

Crime Rate = Crime Index per 100,000 population.

Source: Bureau of Justice Statistics, *Sourcebook of Criminal Justice Statistics—1993* (Washington, D.C.: U.S. Department of Justice, 1994).

In the first half of the 1980s, there was a small decrease (1.2%) in the violent crime index and a larger decrease (6.7%) in the violent crime rate (the crime index relative to population). The downward trend was more pronounced for the property crime index and property crime rate (see Table 3). The Reagan administration and other proponents of get-tough policies claimed that

Introduction

stronger law enforcement and stiffer sentencing had been successful in reducing crime. Some policy analysts, however, pointed to other factors—especially changes in the age structure of the population, which greatly influences crime rates (Steffensmeier and Harer, 1991).[3] In the latter part of the 1980s, the upward trend resumed, especially for violent crime, which grew 37 percent from 1985 to 1990. In 1992, both the violent crime index and the violent crime rate stood at all-time highs (see Table 3).

Recent crime data indicate a very disturbing trend of higher levels of violent crime committed by youths. From 1984 to 1993, arrests for violent crime among those under age 18 increased 68 percent, compared with 46 percent among adults. Arrests for murder and non-negligent manslaughter increased 168 percent for youths but only 13 percent for adults. Put differently, in 1984, persons under 18 accounted for less than 7 percent of all arrests for those offenses; in 1993, they accounted for 16 percent (FBI, 1994, p. 221). In Chicago, there has also been a trend toward younger victims of crime. In 1994, Chicago had more than 260 homicide victims between the ages of 11 and 20—more than double the number six years earlier. That age group accounted for 28 percent of all homicide victims in 1994, compared with only 18 percent in 1988 (Martin and de la Garza, 1995).

The growth pattern for violent crime since 1985 has been remarkably similar in the nation as a whole, in the state of Illinois, and in the city of Chicago (see Table 4). During that period, Chicago consistently accounted for about three-fourths of violent crime in Illinois, even though the city represents only about one-fourth of the state's population. Likewise, Chicago accounts for more than 90 percent of violent crime in Cook County but less than 55 percent of county residents (Illinois State Police, 1994). Within the city, violent crime is most prevalent in communities with high levels of poverty, joblessness, and drug trafficking. For example, the Pullman police district, where the murders of Shavon Dean and Robert Sandifer occurred, had a homicide rate in 1994 that was more than 50 percent above the citywide rate. Five other districts (out of 25) had even higher homicide rates (Martin and de la Garza, 1995).

---

[3] A disproportionate amount of crime is committed by young males between the ages of 15 and 25. This demographic group represented a growing share of the nation's population in the 1960s and 1970s and a declining share in the early 1980s.

TABLE 4: Violent Crime in the United States, Illinois, and Chicago, 1985-1993

	U.S.	Pct. Chg.	Illinois	Pct. Chg.	Chicago	Pct. Chg.
1985	1,328,800	----	81,450	----	60,399	----
1986	1,489,170	12.1	93,454	14.7	68,819	13.9
1987	1,484,000	- 0.3	92,216	- 1.3	68,494	- 0.5
1988	1,566,220	5.5	93,557	1.5	69,140	0.9
1989	1,646,040	5.1	98,611	5.4	73,326	6.1
1990	1,820,130	10.6	110,575	12.1	82,388	12.4
1991	1,911,770	5.0	119,955	8.5	89,962	9.2
1992	1,932,270	1.1	113,664	- 5.2	83,713	- 6.9
1993	1,924,190	- 0.4	112,260	- 1.2	78,707	- 5.1
Ave. annual pct. chg.:		4.8		4.3		3.7

Violent Crime Index = murder and non-negligent manslaughter, forcible rape, robbery, and aggravated assault.

Sources: Bureau of Justice Statistics, *Sourcebook of Criminal Justice Statistics—1993* (Washington, D.C.: U.S. Department of Justice, 1994); Federal Bureau of Investigation, *Uniform Crime Reports for the United States* (Washington, D.C.: U.S. Department of Justice, various years); Illinois State Police, *Crime in Illinois* (Springfield: Illinois State Police, various years).

CRIME AND COMMUNITIES

The chapters in this book are revised and updated versions of papers that were originally prepared for the fourth annual Chicago Assembly, "Crime and Community Safety." The authors examine crime as both a criminal justice problem and a social problem. They focus on critical issues such as the community context of crime, the effectiveness and practical capacities of the criminal justice system, possibilities for community-based crime prevention, the effects of public policies on crime at the community level, and crime prevention strategies involving collaboration between the criminal justice system and other institutions.

The lead chapter by Arthur Lurigio begins with an overview of crime trends in the nation, in Illinois, and in Chicago. Lurigio then explores the relationship between crime and communities. Following in the tradition of the "Chicago school" of urban sociology, he emphasizes that communities most vulnerable to crime are also communities with high rates of unemployment, large numbers of unstable families, and visible manifestations of social disorder and physical decay. The chapter concludes with a discussion of crime-related public policies at the national, state, and local levels. In Lurigio's view, the most significant of recent policy trends may be community policing, which holds the best promise for joining police and citizens in a concerted effort to improve the quality of neighborhoods.

Paul Lavrakas provides a critical review of major community crime prevention programs and policies during the past 25 years, ranging from projects initiated with federal LEAA funding in the 1970s to community policing endeavors of the 1980s and 1990s. He emphasizes that it is a mistake to view the police as the primary mechanism for crime prevention; citizens must play a central and organized role in preventing crime in their communities. In that sense, all crime *prevention* should be viewed as "community-based." Lavrakas proposes a comprehensive crime prevention strategy that would include, at its core, neighborhood residents, indigenous community institutions, and local law enforcement agencies, but would also require resources and active participation from a host of other public and private entities.

Randolph Stone offers a critical examination of the criminal justice system. He focuses primarily on Cook County, where the system is seriously overloaded with cases and offenders, and scant attention is devoted to the prevention and reduction of crime. Stone also argues that the overriding emphasis on "get tough" measures has resulted in an alarming increase in the incarceration rate of African-American males, with little or no relief from crime in urban communities. His chapter concludes with some proposals for restoring effectiveness and fairness to the process of reducing and controlling crime: developing comprehensive crime prevention strategies at the national, state, and community levels; providing adequate and balanced funding to institutions within the criminal justice system; shifting focus from incarceration to a wide range of community-based, intermediate sanctions; and conscious efforts to minimize racial bias in criminal justice decision-making.

The chapter by Patrick McAnany considers the issue of corrections. McAnany suggests that the growing fiscal and social costs of incarceration will force an impending policy shift away from prisons and jails and toward greater use of probation, as well as "intermediate sanctions" involving some form of community release. His chapter discusses recent data on corrections, the jurisprudence underlying sentencing reform, and changes in the nature of probation that have made it a more clearly punitive sanction. McAnany also examines key policy issues for probation, including the conflict between desert-based and crime-control approaches to sentencing, integration of intermediate sanctions into current sentencing reforms, resources that are critical for effective intermediate sanctions, and the pivotal role of judges.

Paul Goldstein's chapter documents the complex relationship between drugs and violence. After relating some harrowing stories derived from ethnographic studies of street opiate users, Goldstein presents a tripartite conceptual framework for understanding the drugs/violence nexus: "Psychopharmacological violence" involves aggressive behavior that may be associated with the use of certain drugs. In the case of "economic-compulsive violence," drug users may commit robbery or other crimes in order to finance their addiction. "Systemic violence" stems from the conditions of doing business in an illicit market. Limited empirical evidence indicates that public fears about the first two forms of violence are often exaggerated; the most serious form of drug-related violence is systemic violence. Goldstein also suggests that intensified law enforcement efforts have probably contributed to *increased* levels of systemic violence.

Irving Spergel addresses the increasingly prominent problem of youth gangs. He examines the history, contemporary scope, and seriousness of the problem, various models for understanding youth gangs, and different programmatic approaches to reducing the crime, violence, and community fear associated with gang activity. The chapter identifies four basic strategies for dealing with youth gangs: community mobilization (involving grassroots citizen participation and local community organizations), social intervention (including youth outreach), increased social and economic opportunities for inner-city youths, and suppression of gang activity. Spergel calls for "interactive and balanced strategies," with emphasis on a community-mobilization approach, though he also contends that no single approach will be sufficient. The systemic and structural dimensions of the youth gang problem mean that we can expect only limited success.

Howard Spivak, Deborah Prothrow-Stith, and Mark Moore offer a comprehensive approach to violence prevention that in-

Introduction 11

volves collaboration between criminal justice and public health professionals. They present a conceptual framework that identifies three levels of violence prevention activity: primary prevention (efforts directed toward broad public values and attitudes), secondary prevention (intervention focused on high-risk sub-groups), and tertiary prevention (trying to reduce or alleviate the negative consequences of violence). The authors emphasize the inherent limitations of the criminal justice system, which is more reactive than preventive in its basic orientation toward the problem of violence. They contend that the public health community offers an approach that emphasizes identification of risk factors that could become the focus of preventive interventions.

The concluding chapter by Stuart Scheingold examines the politics of street crime. Scheingold questions the conventional view that crime becomes a political issue when an increasingly victimized and frightened public demands action from its political leaders. He contends that public reaction to street crime is driven at least as much by what people *believe* about victimization as by victimization as such. Those closest to street crime—criminal justice professionals and residents of heavily populated urban areas—are less receptive to the simplistic remedies of the "myth of crime and punishment." The paradoxical result is an inverse relationship between politicization of and proximity to street crime. That is, the further politicians are from communities with the most serious crime problems, the easier it is to exploit public fears by advocating exclusively punitive policies to combat crime.

This introduction is followed by the Chicago Assembly Report on "Crime and Community Safety." Participants at the Chicago Assembly included more than 70 regional and state leaders from law enforcement agencies, criminal courts, corrections, community organizations, social service agencies, civic and advocacy groups, and universities. The report reflects consensus among a very diverse group of participants on several major themes: Crime is a difficult and complex public policy problem that is not amenable to "quick-fix" solutions. Although a fair and effective criminal justice system is essential, responsibility for *crime prevention* should not be left to criminal justice institutions alone. Crime prevention must involve long-term policy strategies, as well as short-term crisis intervention in response to immediate crime problems. Finally, comprehensive crime prevention strategies must focus on *communities* and must involve new forms of collaboration between the criminal justice system and other public and private institutions, including community organizations, businesses, educational institutions, youth and family service agencies, mental health centers, substance-abuse treatment agencies, and other human service providers.

REFERENCES

Austin, Jeffrey (1991). "A Record Year for Criminal Justice," *The Compiler* (Illinois Criminal Justice Information Authority), Fall 1991, pp. 15-16.

BJS (1994). *Sourcebook of Criminal Justice Statistics—1993*. Washington, D.C.: Bureau of Justice Statistics, U.S. Department of Justice.

Blumstein, Alfred (1995). "Prisons." In James Q. Wilson and Joan Petersilia, eds., *Crime*. San Francisco: Institute for Contemporary Studies.

CQ (1969). *Congress and the Nation, Vol. II: 1965-1968*. Washington, D.C.: Congressional Quarterly, Inc.

——— (1985). *Congress and the Nation, Vol. VI: 1981-1984*. Washington, D.C.: Congressional Quarterly, Inc.

——— (1990). *Congress and the Nation, Vol. VII: 1985-1988*. Washington, D.C.: Congressional Quarterly, Inc.

DiIulio, John J. (1992). "Crime." In Henry J. Aaron and Charles L. Schultze, eds., *Setting Domestic Priorities: What Can Government Do?* Washington, D.C.: The Brookings Institution.

FBI (1994). *Uniform Crime Reports for the United States, 1993*. Washington, D.C.: Federal Bureau of Investigation, U.S. Department of Justice.

ICJIA (1989). *Trends and Issues 89: Criminal and Juvenile Justice in Illinois*. Chicago: Illinois Criminal Justice Information Authority.

——— (1991). *Trends and Issues 91: Education and Criminal Justice in Illinois*. Chicago: Illinois Criminal Justice Information Authority.

Illinois State Police (1994). *Crime in Illinois, 1993*. Springfield: Illinois State Police.

Jencks, Christopher (1991). "Is Violent Crime Increasing?" *The American Prospect*, Winter 1991, pp. 98-109.

Manikas, Peter (1995). "Comments." In this volume.

Martin, Andrew, and Paul de la Garza (1995). "City Sets Marks for Gun Murders and Slain Youths," *Chicago Tribune*, January 2, 1995.

Masci, David (1994). "$30 Billion Anti-Crime Bill Heads to Clinton's Desk," *CQ Weekly Report*, August 27, 1994, pp. 2488-2493.

New York Times (1994). "'That's a Baby There.'" Editorial, September 9, 1994, p. A26.

Povich, Elaine (1994). "Crime Bill OKd, Health Reform May Be Stalled," *Chicago Tribune*, August 26, 1994, sec. 1, p. 1.

Skolnick, Jerome H. (1994). "Wild Pitch: 'Three Strikes, You're Out' and Other Bad Calls on Crime, *The American Prospect*, Spring 1994, pp. 30-37.

Steffensmeier, Darrell, and Miles D. Harer (1991). "Did Crime Rise or Fall During the Reagan Presidency? The Effects of an 'Aging' U.S. Population on the Nation's Crime Rate," *Journal of Research in Crime and Delinquency*, vol. 28, no. 3 (August 1991), pp. 330-359.

Terry, Don (1994). "In an 11-Year-Old's Funeral, a Grim Lesson," *New York Times*, September 8, 1994, p. A1.

Vlasak, Teresa (1989). "A Bad Problem Just Gets Worse," *The Compiler* (Illinois Criminal Justice Information Authority), Summer 1989, pp. 11-13.

Warren, Ellen, and Gary Marx (1994). "Juvenile Court Proves Crime Has No Age Limit," *Chicago Tribune*, September 18, 1994, sec. 1, p. 1.

Wilson, James Q. (1994). "What to Do About Crime," *Commentary*, September 1994, pp. 25-34.

Wortham, Sarah Dowse (1993). "Juvenile Justice in Illinois: An Overview," *The Compiler* (Illinois Criminal Justice Information Authority), Summer 1993, pp. 4-8.

CRIME AND COMMUNITY SAFETY

Report of the Chicago Assembly

Crime and public safety are issues of central concern for local governments and communities throughout the Chicago metropolitan area and the state of Illinois. Yet, the incidence of crime problems is not the same for different population groups and different communities. Some communities are much more likely than others to be confronted with the reality of crime and its consequences for individuals, families, schools, and businesses. Typically, these same communities are also plagued by myriad social problems such as poverty, unemployment, drug abuse, and social disorganization.

The fourth annual Chicago Assembly, "Crime and Community Safety," was held November 19-20, 1992, in St. Charles, Illinois. More than 70 regional and state leaders participated, including representatives from law enforcement agencies, criminal courts, corrections, community-based organizations, social service agencies, civic and advocacy groups, and universities. Chicago Assembly participants engaged in two days of intensive discussion and deliberation about crime both as a law-enforcement/criminal-justice problem *and* as a social problem. They focused on such critical issues as the community context of crime and the impact of crime on the quality of community life, the effectiveness and practical capacities of the criminal justice system in dealing with crime at the community level, and possibilities for community-based crime prevention and for community interventions to alleviate the social problems that are considered to be among the root causes of crime. Given the diversity of participants and the complexity of crime problems, the Chicago Assembly did not reach consensus on all major issues. There is, however, widespread agreement that crime prevention is too large a task for the criminal justice system alone, that crime prevention must involve broad-based, long-term policy strategies, and that comprehensive crime prevention strategies must involve new forms of collaboration between the criminal justice system and other public and private institutions.

BACKGROUND

CRIME TRENDS

Nationwide, crimes reported to the police escalated rapidly in the latter part of the 1960s and continued to increase, albeit at a slower rate, throughout the 1970s. There was a modest drop in the early 1980s, but growth resumed in the last half of the decade, especially for violent crime. In Illinois, there was a 44 percent increase in the violent crime index (which includes murder, sexual assault, robbery, and aggravated assault) from 1985 to 1991. By contrast, the state's property crime index (burglary, theft, motor vehicle theft, and arson) increased less than 10 percent over the same period (Lurigio, 1995, Tables 1, 3, 7; FBI, 1992, p. 70).

Crime in Chicago

The city of Chicago, with 24 percent of the state's population, accounts for about 40 percent of all reported property crimes in Illinois and about 75 percent of all violent crimes. The violent crime index in Chicago increased 49 percent from 1985 to 1991. In 1991, the violent crime rate in Chicago was 3,251.7 per 100,000 inhabitants, compared with 1,039.2 for Illinois and 758.1 nationwide. Although the violent crime rate in Chicago was much higher than in suburban Cook County as a whole, some suburbs also had very high rates—for example, Harvey (2,552.8) and Chicago Heights (1,753.7) in southern Cook County and Maywood (2,461.4) in western Cook County (Lurigio, 1995; FBI, 1992, pp. 58, 70; Reardon and Lucadamo, 1992, pp. 1, 12).

The number of homicides in Chicago increased by more than 40 percent from 1988 to 1992, when there were 938 murders, the second highest number in the city's history. In 1991, Chicago's homicide rate (33.1 per 100,000 residents) was fourth highest among U.S. cities with populations over one million (ICJIA, n.d.; Lurigio, 1995, Table 6; BJS, 1993). In the same year, more than two-thirds of homicides in the city involved the use of firearms, and 58 percent involved handguns. Between 1987 and 1991, the number of homicides committed with firearms increased 72 percent, while all other homicides declined. The impact of Chicago's murder toll has been most devastating for the city's African-American community, which accounted for 79 percent of all homicide victims and 80 percent of offenders in 1991 (Chicago Police Department, 1992, pp. 14, 19-21).

Crime Among Youth

There has also been an escalation of violent crime among youth. From 1980 to 1990, the juvenile arrest rate for violent crime nationwide increased 27 percent. Juvenile arrest rates rose 87 percent for murder, 64 percent for aggravated assault, and 37 percent for forcible rape. In Illinois, there were 103 juvenile arrests for homicide in 1991, compared with only 39 in 1985 (FBI, 1992, pp. 279-289; Illinois State Police, 1987, 1992).

In some communities, the most visible increases in violent crime have involved youth gangs. The Chicago Police Department has estimated that there are more than 40 youth gangs or major factions and 36,000 gang members in the city. The annual number of street-gang-related homicides in Chicago fluctuated during most of the 1980s but increased steadily from 50 in 1987 to 133 in 1991 (Spergel, 1995; ICJIA, n.d.).

POLICY TRENDS

For well over a decade, the dominant public policy response to crime—at the national, state, and local levels—has been to "get tough" with criminal offenders. This approach has been manifested in numerous ways, including mandatory sentencing legislation, increased rates of incarceration, and the "war on drugs."

Mandatory Sentencing Laws

During the 1970s and 1980s, many states rewrote their criminal sentencing laws. In 1978, Illinois enacted legislation establishing a determinate sentencing system, under which each convicted offender is sentenced to a fixed number of years in prison with no possibility of parole. The state also reclassified the former non-probationable Class 1 felonies into a new category, "Class X," which includes serious offenses such as attempted murder, aggravated criminal sexual assault, and armed robbery. Class X felons receive mandatory prison sentences and are not eligible for alternative sanctions such as probation or conditional discharge. Since

1978, the state legislature has applied mandatory prison terms to many additional offenses, including residential burglary and the manufacture and delivery of certain amounts of illegal drugs (Vlasak, 1989; McAnany, 1995; Illinois Task Force, 1993, p. 95).

Increased Rates of Incarceration

A study released in 1979 showed that the United States had the third highest rate of incarceration in the industrialized world—behind only South Africa and the Soviet Union. In 1991, the U.S. had the *highest* rate of incarceration—426 prisoners per 100,000 population. The U.S. Department of Justice reported that there were more than 755,000 inmates in state and federal prisons at the end of 1990, more than twice the number of ten years earlier (Mauer, 1991; Clark Foundation, 1992, p. 3). Similarly, the adult prison population in Illinois has more than doubled over the past decade, growing from less than 13,000 in 1980 to over 32,000 in 1992 (McAnany, 1995, Table 1; Illinois Task Force, 1993, p. 19). The causes of this trend include longer terms for violent criminal offenders receiving mandatory sentences and increased prosecution of drug-related offenses. Since 1978, the state has built 15 new prisons, for a total cost of more than $560 million in the past decade alone. Nonetheless, overcrowding remains a serious problem: At the end of 1992, Illinois's prison population exceeded the system's design capacity by more than 50 percent and its rated capacity by more than 30 percent (Illinois Task Force, 1993, pp. 5, 19).[1]

The War on Drugs

The war on drugs has had a major impact on criminal justice institutions, including law enforcement agencies, criminal courts, and correctional facilities. During the 1980s, anti-drug policies at the federal, state, and local levels put increasing emphasis on law

---

[1] "Design capacity" refers to the number of inmates that a correctional facility was originally designed to house. "Rated capacity" refers to the maximum population that should be housed based on administrative judgments and sound correctional practices (Illinois Task Force, 1993, p. 19).

enforcement and incarceration. In 1991, there were more than 17,000 felony drug cases filed in Cook County courts, an increase of 160 percent over a seven-year period. In contrast, non-drug felony cases rose only 4 percent (ICJIA, 1991, pp. 188-189). Drug offenses have been a prime target of the movement to mandatory sentencing in Illinois. A repeat offender convicted of selling 1-15 grams of cocaine must be sentenced to a minimum of four years in prison (Stone, 1995). In 1990, the Illinois Department of Corrections admitted more than 4,000 drug offenders, an increase of 65 percent from 1989 and more than seven times the number admitted in 1983 (ICJIA, 1991, pp. 188-189).

FINDINGS AND RECOMMENDATIONS

Crime is a difficult and complex public policy problem; "quick-fix" solutions will not work. A fair and effective criminal justice system is essential, but responsibility for *crime prevention* should not be left to criminal justice institutions alone. Crime prevention must involve broad-based, long-term policy strategies, as well as short-term crisis intervention in response to immediate crime problems. Crime prevention strategies must focus on *communities* and must identify and address the root causes of crime. Each actor in the criminal justice system has a role to play in prevention, and that role should be defined comprehensively. In addition, every component of the community has a responsibility for crime prevention. Community interventions should be part of a larger prevention framework, which must include increased opportunities for employment, more effective schools, early education to prevent drug abuse, and violence-reduction education for children and youth. Comprehensive crime prevention strategies will require new forms of collaboration involving the criminal and juvenile justice systems, other government institutions, community organizations, businesses, educational institutions, youth and family service agencies, mental health centers, substance-abuse treatment agencies, and other human service providers.

COLLABORATIVE CRIME PREVENTION AND COMMUNITY POLICING

Community policing is a collaborative approach to crime prevention that emphasizes cooperation between law enforcement agencies and community residents. In contrast to traditional strategies in which the principal role of the police is to respond to particular crime incidents and service calls, community policing involves an ongoing collaborative effort to identify and deal with a range of problems that may breed crime in a particular neighborhood or community (see Lavrakas, 1995).

There is strong and widespread support among Chicago Assembly participants for the concept of community policing, which must, at minimum, involve an enhanced partnership between police and the community, as well as a more proactive approach to community problem-solving. Community policing has the potential for involving communities in establishing law enforcement priorities, focusing on specific community problems, mobilizing community support for public safety, and fostering public respect for the law.

Examples of Community Policing in Metropolitan Chicago

In 1991, the Illinois Criminal Justice Information Authority awarded grants to create and expand community policing programs in the cities of Joliet and Aurora. The Evanston Police Department has also adopted community-oriented policing strategies. In 1993, the City of Chicago instituted community policing in five neighborhoods (Austin, Englewood, Marquette Park, Morgan Park, and Rogers Park); it plans eventually to expand the program citywide (Vlasak, 1992; Jones, 1993).

According to the Joliet Police Department, Neighborhood-Oriented Policing (NOP) has had a significant impact since the program was initiated in April 1991. The impact is most perceptible, although difficult to measure, in the attitudes of police officers and community residents in those neighborhoods where NOP has been implemented. The police officers who have been involved report increased satisfaction with their work, and several have attested to a "professional rebirth." In addition, the communities in which these teams operate have become possessive of "their" neighborhood police officers. The success of NOP has led to demands by community residents for expansion of this style of policing into other neighborhoods in Joliet.

Challenges for Community Policing

The media and the general public must be educated about the complexities involved in community policing if they are to recognize its value as a long-term investment. Measuring the effects of community policing may be difficult, especially in the short term. Neither police nor community residents can be expected to solve the myriad of historic and entrenched social problems facing many communities. However, community policing offers the possibility of an ongoing collaborative effort to address specific crime-related problems and to enhance community safety. To be effective, community policing programs must confront a number of planning and implementation challenges:

- Community policing programs must recognize differences among communities in expectations, resources, and organizational capacities. Successful community policing efforts should also take into account the racial and ethnic composition of communities.

- Effective community policing must be aware of differences and conflicts *within* communities that may make it difficult for community leadership to emerge and for key issues to be identified. Some residents may be resistant to community policing because they fear an increase in police power to intervene in community problems. Others may believe that they have fulfilled their civic obligations by paying taxes and that crime prevention is the sole responsibility of the police department.

- Challenges for community policing may be presented by conventional police department structures and systems and by officer resistance to both a change in policing philosophy and a shift in emphasis from incident-response to problem-solving. Community policing may require changes in recruitment and training, incentive systems, supervisory approaches, research and planning capabilities, and dispatching and deployment policies.

- Many Chicago Assembly participants emphasize that community policing must be a genuinely collaborative undertaking, not something imposed on the community by police departments. Some communities may object to community policing unless they are involved in planning, implementation, and evaluation of the program. Effective implementation of community policing requires collaborative training that involves both the police and community participants. In addition, there should be adequate funding for the "community side" of community policing.

- Mobilizing resources to address community problems may require going outside particular communities themselves, especially those communities with the highest levels of serious crime and the lowest levels of problem-solving resources. Community crime prevention efforts therefore need cooperation and support from elected officials and from government agencies other than police departments.

THE CRIMINAL JUSTICE SYSTEM

The principal goal of the criminal justice system should be to dispense justice and protect the public. To achieve this goal, the system must provide justice for both victims of crime and criminal defendants. It must also enhance safety and security, as well as the perception of safety and security. At the same time, criminal justice institutions are limited in their capacity for crime *prevention*. In attempting to deal with problems created by the broader social order, the criminal justice system is suffering from institutional and fiscal strain, with agencies competing for scarce public funds. More resources must be invested in supplements to the criminal justice system, as well as in alternatives to current processes within the system, including early intervention, aftercare, and the reduction of recidivism.

Coordination within the Criminal Justice System

The criminal justice system in Illinois is comprised of independently elected and appointed officials (police, prosecutors, public defenders, corrections officials) with diverse agency missions and constitutionally mandated responsibilities. A report on criminal justice in Cook County has characterized the system as decentralized and highly fragmented, with key components funded by different levels of government (Manikas, Trossman, and Doppelt, 1989, p. xvii; Manikas et al., 1990). The Cook County Criminal Justice Coordinating Council was established in 1990 to deal with interagency problems that affect the criminal justice system (e.g., conditions for the pretrial detention population at Cook County Jail). The Coordinating Council is composed of key public officials from Cook County and the City of Chicago (Manikas, Trossman, and Doppelt, 1989, p. 2).[2] Such efforts ought to be encouraged in order to improve coordination among criminal justice agencies and make more efficient use of tax revenue.

Sentencing

The movement in criminal justice policy toward mandatory and determinate sentencing has gone too far and should be reassessed, particularly for non-violent crimes. Because of mandatory sentencing laws, discretion now lies almost entirely with prosecutors, who decide what charges will be brought against a criminal defendant. A greater degree of discretion in sentencing should be reintroduced in the criminal justice process—particularly for judges, whose use of discretion can be reviewed through the appellate courts. The legislature must ensure that judges have an adequate choice of resources available to make their use of discretion in sentencing meaningful and effective. Such resources would include intermediate sanctions (e.g., intensive probation, mandatory substance-abuse treatment, community service, restitution) as well as better background information about individual offenders.

Corrections

Correctional systems—which encompass jails, prisons, probation, and parole—can be said to have several different goals: retribution, deterrence, incapacitation, rehabilitation (ICJIA, 1990, p. 181). Chicago Assembly participants believe that rehabilitation should remain a major objective of corrections. A larger proportion of public safety funds should be directed toward both prevention services and the rehabilitation of individuals already in the criminal justice system.

At any given time, there are more than 20,000 released inmates on supervision in Illinois (Illinois Department of Corrections, 1992, p. 71). The vast majority of convicted offenders eventually return to their home communities, most of them in a

---

[2] The Coordinating Council includes the Chief Judge of the Circuit Court, the President of the Cook County Board of Commissioners, the Clerk of the Circuit Court, the Cook County Sheriff, the State's Attorney, the Public Defender, and the Chief Probation Officer, as well as the Superintendent of the Chicago Police Department.

short period of time. These individuals need to be reintegrated into the community. PreStart, a program initiated in 1991 by the Illinois Department of Corrections, is a step in the right direction. PreStart is designed to reduce recidivism by providing pre-release training and post-release services for ex-offenders (Morison, 1992, pp. 6-8; Illinois Department of Corrections, 1992, pp. 69-71, 119-124). A critical issue is adequacy of resources for the program, especially for substance-abuse treatment and for job training and placement.

Case management: Adult offenders, as well as more serious juvenile offenders, are likely to have considerable social liabilities that interfere with their integration into the community (including successful employment). Therefore, comprehensive case management services are recommended for individuals on probation and mandatory supervised release. Case management involves conducting systematic needs assessments and coordinating services available to individuals with complex, multiple problems and needs. Working across different agencies and institutions is often required to bring an individual all the services he or she needs. These services may include substance-abuse treatment, vocational and remedial education, job counseling and placement, and mental health treatment.

Community corrections: Some Chicago Assembly participants contend that community policing should be supplemented by community-based corrections. One innovative example is Project Safeway, a community-based probation program on Chicago's West Side. Project Safeway involves a working partnership between the Cook County Adult Probation Department, not-for-profit service providers, and the community. It is a "full-service" model of probation: The Safer Foundation offers programs in employment, educational, and life-management skills, while Treatment Alternatives for Special Clients (TASC) provides a range of services for substance-abuse treatment and prevention. A community advisory council is designed to maintain and strengthen the project's links to the community.

DRUGS AND CRIME

The relationship between drugs and crime is more complex than citizens and policymakers often realize. Data compiled for the

Drug Use Forecasting program of the National Institute of Justice show a high prevalence of drug use (especially of cocaine) by male arrestees in Chicago. Between 1987 and 1992, the proportion of arrestees testing positive for cocaine was generally in the range of 50-60 percent. At the same time, those charged with drug-related offenses were most likely to test positive for drug use, whereas those charged with violent crimes were least likely to use cocaine or other illegal drugs (TASC, 1992).[3]

Drugs and violence may be linked in several different ways: The ingestion of certain drugs may be associated with aggressive or violent behavior ("psychopharmacological violence"), although the extent of causality is unclear. Alternatively, some drug users may commit crimes such as robbery in order to finance their addiction ("economic-compulsive violence"). Some of the available empirical evidence suggests that the most serious violence involving drug users and dealers stems from the conditions of doing business in an illicit market ("systemic violence") (Goldstein, 1995).

Over the past decade, law enforcement agencies at the federal, state, and local levels have been preoccupied with the "war on drugs." As a result, both criminal courts and correctional facilities have been inundated with drug offenders. The war on drugs has not, however, eliminated illicit drug consumption or significantly reduced drug abuse by persons at high risk of committing criminal acts. Nor has it reduced the violence associated with the economics of illicit drug production and distribution.

Law Enforcement

Many communities are plagued by severe drug problems and need protection from the violent and criminal conduct of drug abusers and traffickers. Law enforcement is one of several means of achieving this protection. Law enforcement efforts and resources should distinguish between entrepreneurial sellers and those who sell drugs to support their own addiction, as well as between sellers and users and between casual users and hardcore addicts.

---

[3] Data covering 1987-1992 show cocaine use by two-thirds of those charged with drug-related crimes, about 55 percent of those charged with property crimes, and less than half of those charged with violent crimes.

At the same time, some Chicago Assembly participants also believe that law enforcement efforts in the "war on drugs" have concentrated disproportionately on individuals from minority groups and have not brought about an increased sense of security, either in minority communities or in other communities.

Drug-Abuse Prevention and Treatment

The principal mechanism through which substance-abusing offenders in Illinois can obtain treatment is the Alcoholism and Other Drug Dependency Act.[4] Under certain limited circumstances, an individual convicted of a non-violent crime can elect to be treated as an addict and, if mandated by the court, can receive up to five years' probation while undergoing treatment by a designated agency. Treatment Alternatives for Special Clients (TASC) is currently the sole agency designated by the Department of Alcoholism and Substance Abuse to provide such services.

Effective drug treatment efforts have been constrained by mandatory sentencing statutes. In most cases, judges do not have the discretion to sentence drug offenders to treatment programs. Most drug offenders must be sentenced to prison, where there is limited access to treatment resources. Only three state prisons in Illinois currently have in-house drug treatment programs. These programs accommodate only 154 beds, whereas the state's total prison population now exceeds 32,000.

More emphasis should be placed on drug-abuse prevention and treatment both before and after an individual enters the criminal justice system, as well as through different stages of the criminal justice process. More public resources should be directed to prevention and treatment efforts and to the improvement of treatment methodologies, and better use should be made of treatment programs that have proved to be effective.

---

[4] *Illinois Revised Statutes*, Chapter 111½, par. 6351-6361-3.

YOUTH AND CRIME

Juvenile Justice

The juvenile justice system in Illinois is designed to provide individualized treatment and guidance for juveniles who are involved in relatively minor incidents, as well as to incapacitate dangerous juvenile offenders (ICJIA, 1990, pp. 217-218). The juvenile courts do not currently have the resources to deal effectively with the growing problems of youth gang members and other juvenile offenders. Between 1975 and 1985, for example, Cook County Juvenile Court expenditures did not keep pace with inflation. From 1985 to 1991, the number of juvenile court petitions filed in Cook County increased 55 percent, while inflation-adjusted expenditures for the court rose by only 15 percent.[5] The juvenile justice system must have increased public resources for more effective supervision of juvenile offenders sentenced to probation and for more individualized treatment of cases.

A growing number of first-time juvenile offenders in Illinois are being tried as adults. Since 1982, state law has required that juveniles (aged 15 or over) charged with murder, armed robbery, or aggravated criminal sexual assault be transferred to adult criminal court. In 1986, automatic transfers were mandated for certain drug or weapons violations committed in or near a school. Beginning in 1990, juveniles charged with drug offenses on public housing property received mandatory transfers. For example, a 15-year-old first-time offender charged with selling drugs near his home in the suburbs would be processed through the juvenile justice system, whereas a similar offender charged with selling drugs within 1,000 feet of a public housing project would be tried as an adult criminal defendant. In 1991, Cook County had more than 500 mandatory transfers from juvenile court to adult criminal court, compared with only 145 in 1984 (ICJIA, 1990, p. 220; Stone, 1995). Policies that mandate automatic transfers from juvenile court to criminal court should be reassessed, particularly for non-violent offenders.

---

[5] Data from the Illinois Criminal Justice Information Authority.

Youth Intervention Strategies

Crime prevention efforts that focus on youth must address a broad range of issues, including targeting school dropouts, drug-resistance and gang-resistance education, and training in conflict-resolution skills. There must be more resources for and collaboration among youth service agencies in local communities throughout Illinois, as well as greater collaboration among all relevant public and private agencies dealing with at-risk youth.

Youth intervention strategies should target those at risk of becoming involved in criminal activity. Once identified for early intervention, troubled youths can be referred by youth officers, schools, and parents to a community-based social service agency. A prevention program can reach out to the youth and his or her family, conduct a needs assessment, and provide access to services that meet individual and family needs. Types of services may include individual and family counseling, tutoring, advocacy, and treatment for learning, emotional, and physiological problems.

Collaborative Efforts Focusing on Youth

A number of Chicago Assembly participants identified specific examples of collaborative efforts focusing on youth who are at risk of becoming involved in serious crime. Although the effectiveness of each program is still to be determined, these efforts represent a policy direction supported by most Chicago Assembly participants.

• The State of Illinois recently enacted the Serious Habitual Offender Comprehensive Action Program (SHOCAP), a multidisciplinary, interagency case-management and information-sharing system involving juvenile justice agencies, schools, and social service providers. SHOCAP is designed to enable relevant agencies to make more informed decisions regarding the early identification and treatment of habitual juvenile offenders. Each county in the state may establish a SHOCAP committee to intensify supervision of serious juvenile offenders and to enhance early intervention strategies and rehabilitation efforts.

• One local effort at comprehensive, community-based violence prevention is the Englewood Consortium on Chicago's South Side. The Englewood Consortium seeks to recombine existing resources and leverage additional resources to address problems of youth who may be at risk of gang, street, or family violence. The coalition includes youth and family service agencies, community health organizations, cultural organizations, educational institutions, community development organizations, and state and local elected officials.

- An example of service collaboration from another state is Virginia's Comprehensive Services for At-Risk Youth and Families, which has restructured the state's service delivery for youth with emotional and/or behavioral problems. Key components include interagency collaboration at both the state and local levels, involving program areas such as youth and family services, mental health, substance-abuse treatment, education, and juvenile corrections; consolidation of state categorical funding streams into a pool that is allocated to localities on a formula basis; demonstration projects to create and expand community-based services through an interagency approach; and training and technical assistance for local communities as they reconfigure their service systems.

A SOCIAL CIVILITY SYSTEM

One of the working groups at the Chicago Assembly developed a conceptual framework, derived from the field of public health, for developing comprehensive crime prevention strategies.[6] A "social civility system" (or "community order and justice system") constitutes a societal effort to produce order and justice. It incorporates prevention and treatment as well as traditional criminal justice functions. The system encompasses all agencies and activities that affect the occurrence of, reactions to, and consequences of "incivilities," ranging from minor to the most severe.

The social civility system has three overlapping components: *Primary prevention* involves the activities of institutions such as families, schools, and religious organizations in fostering and encouraging responsible behavior. It may also include efforts to strengthen support systems for families and other community institutions. *Secondary prevention* involves reactions to "lesser incivilities," that is, problems that are not yet severe. This may include, for example, informal police intervention and community services that focus on troubled youth and other "high-risk" individuals. *Tertiary prevention* involves responses to "marked inci-

---

[6] For a similar approach, see Spivak, Prothrow-Stith, and Moore, 1995. See also Lavrakas, 1995.

vility" (e.g., violent crime) and includes the traditional functions of the criminal justice system (police, courts, corrections, etc.) in investigating and punishing criminal behavior.

Incivility has traditionally been addressed by emphasizing tertiary prevention, which is extremely expensive and, inevitably, meets with limited success. Yet, all individuals who wind up needing tertiary intervention started out as potential candidates for primary and secondary prevention. These "earlier" approaches are likely to be both more effective and less expensive. The future success of the social civility system will depend, in part, on increased emphasis on primary prevention; this must be reflected in resource allocation as well as in policy statements. Instead of expanding the responsibilities of the criminal justice system, we should be expanding coordination among various institutions in the social civility system.

CONCLUSION

Collaborative approaches to crime prevention require the support and cooperation of the public. Without involvement of the larger community, efforts to control or prevent crime will have little success. Better public understanding of the criminal justice system, as well as a redirection of public debate about criminal prevention policies, is critical. The local media need to be better informed about crime prevention and criminal justice issues and about successful programs and policies. There must be an informed and ongoing public discussion in order to avoid the temptation of "quick fixes" to control crime and to change perceptions that new public policy strategies may be a threat to community safety. Public officials, criminal justice professionals, and community leaders and organizations must all recognize their responsibility to contribute to this public education effort, which is a key prerequisite for reducing crime and its devastating impacts on both individuals and communities.

REFERENCES

BJS (1993). *Sourcebook of Criminal Justice Statistics—1992*. Washington, D.C.: Bureau of Justice Statistics, U.S. Department of Justice.

Chicago Police Department (1992). *1991 Murder Analysis.* Chicago: Detective Division, Chicago Police Department.

Clark Foundation (1992). *Americans Behind Bars.* New York: Edna McConnell Clark Foundation, March 1992.

FBI (1992). *Uniform Crime Reports for the United States, 1991.* Washington, D.C.: Federal Bureau of Investigation, U.S. Department of Justice.

Goldstein, Paul (1995). "Drugs and Violence: Myth and Reality." In this volume.

ICJIA (1990). *Trends and Issues 90: Criminal and Juvenile Justice in Illinois.* Chicago: Illinois Criminal Justice Information Authority.

_____ (1991). *Trends and Issues 1991: Education and Criminal Justice in Illinois.* Chicago: Illinois Criminal Justice Information Authority.

_____ (n.d.). "Chicago Homicide Project." Chicago: Illinois Criminal Justice Information Authority, Chicago Police Department, and Loyola University of Chicago.

Illinois Department of Corrections (1992). *Human Services Plan. Fiscal Years 1991-1993.* Springfield, August 1992.

Illinois State Police (1987). *Crime in Illinois, 1986.* Springfield: Illinois State Police.

_____ (1992). *Crime in Illinois, 1991.* Springfield: Illinois State Police.

Illinois Task Force (1993). *Final Report.* Chicago: Illinois Task Force on Crime and Corrections, March 1993.

Jones, Richard (1993). "Daley Hopes New Cops Will Add Spark for Community Policing," *Chicago Tribune*, May 6, 1993, sec. 3, p. 3.

Lavrakas, Paul (1992). "Community-Based Crime Prevention: Citizens, Community Organizations, and the Police." In this volume.

Lurigio, Arthur J. (1995). "Crime and Communities: Prevalence, Impact, and Programs." In this volume.

Manikas, Peter M., Mindy S. Trossman, and Jack C. Doppelt (1989). *Crime and Criminal Justice in Cook County: A Report of the Criminal Justice Project.* Chicago: Criminal Justice Project of Cook County; Evanston, Ill.: Center for Urban Affairs and Policy Research, Northwestern University.

Manikas, Peter, John P. Heinz, Mindy S. Trossman, and Jack C. Doppelt (1990). *Criminal Justice Policymaking: Boundaries and Borderlands: Final Report of the Criminal Justice Project.* Chicago: Criminal Justice Project of Cook County; Evanston,

Ill.: Center for Urban Affairs and Policy Research, Northwestern University.

Mauer, Marc (1991). "Americans Behind Bars: A Comparison of International Rates of Incarceration." Washington, D.C.: The Sentencing Project, January 1991.

McAnany, Patrick (1995). "The Future of Corrections: Probation." In this volume.

Morison, Kevin (1992). "Getting a New Start on Their Future," *The Compiler* (Illinois Criminal Justice Information Authority), Winter 1992.

Reardon, Patrick T., and John Lucadamo (1992). "Crime Up 10% in Cook Suburbs," *Chicago Tribune*, November 8, 1992, sec. 1.

Spergel, Irving (1995). "Youth Gangs: Problem and Policy." In this volume.

Spivak, Howard, Deborah Prothow-Stith, and Mark Moore (1995). "A Comprehensive Approach to Violence Prevention: Public Health and Criminal Justice in Partnership." In this volume.

Stone, Randolph (1995). "The Criminal Justice System: Unfair and Ineffective." In this volume.

TASC (1992). "An Analysis of Chicago Drug Use Forecasting Results: Trends in Use and Usage by Index Offense Charge." Chicago: Illinois Treatment Alternatives for Special Clients, November 1992.

Vlasak, Teresa (1989). "A Bad Problem Just Gets Worse," *The Compiler* (Illinois Criminal Justice Information Authority), Summer 1989, pp. 11-13.

―――― (1992). "Walking the Beat in Joliet, Illinois," *The Compiler* (Illinois Criminal Justice Information Authority), Winter 1992, pp. 13-15.

CRIME AND COMMUNITIES: PREVALENCE, IMPACT, AND PROGRAMS

Arthur J. Lurigio[*]

Crime has been a prominent feature of the American landscape for most of the 20th century. Criminal victimization and fear of crime are inescapable aspects of contemporary urban life. In January 1994, a *Los Angeles Times/CBS News* poll showed that crime was the number one concern of Americans nationwide, ranking ahead of health care, the economy, unemployment, the federal budget deficit, and drug abuse (Winters, 1995). And in a 1993 survey, nearly 40 percent of America's middle- and high-school students reported that they knew someone personally who had been injured or killed by a gun (Romer, 1993). Despite its ubiquitous nature, however, the nation's crime problem cannot be easily explained or alleviated. The causes of crime are quite diverse, and changes in criminal justice programs or policies have a scant effect (if any) on overall crime rates. Nonetheless, law enforcement agencies throughout America have been waging an unrelenting campaign against crime since the late 1960s.

This chapter presents an overview of crime in the nation, in the state of Illinois, and in the city of Chicago. The first section presents data on crime trends at the national, state, and local levels. The second section explores the broader impact of crime on communities and considers some of the neighborhood characteristics that promote or discourage crime. The final section discusses crime-related public policy at the national, state, and local levels.

---

[*] The author expresses his sincere appreciation to Carolyn Block, Andrea Kushner, and Jeff Travis of the Illinois Criminal Justice Information Authority for providing useful statistics on crime in Chicago and Illinois. They helped immensely in the preparation of this chapter.

A DESCRIPTION OF CRIME TRENDS

There are two primary sources of data on the nature and extent of crime in the United States: the Uniform Crime Reports (UCR) and the National Crime Victimization Survey (NCVS). Since 1930, law enforcement agencies throughout the country have voluntarily reported crimes to the Federal Bureau of Investigation (FBI) for inclusion in a national database called the UCR. The UCR is the best recognized and most widely publicized official source of crime statistics (Siegel, 1989). Almost 16,000 city, state, and county law enforcement agencies submit crime information to the UCR program. UCR data are compiled from crimes that become known to the police through patrols, investigations, or victim/witness reports. To assure uniformity in reporting, the FBI has written standardized definitions of the offenses and terminology used in the program, which are provided to participating agencies (Schmalleger, 1995).

UCR statistics focus on eight categories of crime known as the Crime Index. This includes four categories of violent crime (murder, sexual assault, robbery, and aggravated assault) and four categories of property crime (burglary, larceny, motor vehicle theft, and arson). The solving of index crimes is the touchstone that the public and the media usually use to evaluate the effectiveness of police performance (Territo, Halsted, and Bromley, 1992). UCR clearance rates are based on the proportion of reported crimes that have been solved through arrests. A UCR reporting system for all law enforcement agencies in Illinois became mandatory in 1972. These agencies report crime in their local jurisdictions to the Illinois State Police, which compiles the Illinois Uniform Crime Reports (ICJIA, 1990).

The NCVS, which began in 1973, collects data by interviewing a representative sample of approximately 50,000 households encompassing some 100,000 persons and asking them about their recent experiences as victims of crime during a specific period. The purpose of NCVS is to learn more about reported and unreported crime and about incidents of criminal victimization. It measures six of the eight UCR index crimes, excluding homicide and arson. Unlike the UCR, it does not include crimes against businesses and counts only offenses against persons age 12 or older and against their households. No attempt is made to verify self-reported NCVS crimes by comparing them to official UCR (police) statistics. The NCVS also provides descriptive information such as victim and offender characteristics; the setting, time, and circumstances of the offense; the occurrence of injury; and the economic consequences of the victimization (BJS, 1988).

The UCR and NCVS are both limited in their capacity to yield measures of the "true" amount of crime. The most serious shortcoming of the UCR is its concentration on reported and recorded crimes. The majority of crimes, excluding murder and auto theft, are grossly underreported. For example, NCVS data showed that only 38 percent of the victimizations occurring in 1990 were ever reported to the police (BJS, 1992). Victims fail to report crimes for a variety of reasons, such as a belief that the police cannot do anything about the crime, a fear of retaliation, or an unwillingness to become involved in the legal process (Schmalleger, 1995). The UCR undercounts crime in another way by recording only the most serious offense in an episode involving multiple crimes. In addition, the UCR database may contain inaccuracies stemming from a deliberate manipulation of arrest data by law enforcement officials hoping to improve their agency's public image and success rate (Siegel, 1989). For example, an audit of Chicago Police Department cases in 1982 found that 41 percent of the 2,386 cases studied had been incorrectly classified; it was determined that the department had systematically "downgraded" certain crimes or had falsely concluded that others were "unfounded" (Skogan and Gordon, 1982).

The NCVS also has measurement problems. For example, it does not collect information on the "victimless crimes" of illegal gambling, prostitution, or drug use. Because it is based on a random sample of American households, the NCVS is susceptible to sampling errors. A disclaimer on the first page of the NCVS acknowledges: "Details about the crimes come directly from the victims, and no attempt is made to validate the information against police records or any other source." Similar to the UCR, the NCVS employs a hierarchical counting system in which only the most serious crime is recorded in any series of offenses perpetrated against the same individual. Furthermore, NCVS data may be affected by respondent-associated errors: false or exaggerated reports, faulty memories, misinterpretations of events, or a reluctance to report crimes committed by relatives or spouses.

The UCR and NCVS serve different purposes, count crime differently in some instances, and suffer from different types of measurement errors; hence, any attempt to present an accurate portrait of crime in America should draw on both sources. As Wilson and Petersilia (1995) point out, news accounts concerning crime trends may vary depending on whether they are based on

UCR or NCVS data. During the 1980s, for example, the UCR reported that rates of rape and assault had increased, whereas the NCVS reported that the rates of these two crimes had decreased. This discrepancy may be explained by the greater willingness of rape and assault victims to report their crimes to the police.

Crime in the Nation

According to crime historians, the crime rate in America steadily decreased from the turn of the century to the 1920s. During the Prohibition era, violent criminal gangs fought ruthlessly for control of illegal drugs and alcohol. At that time, drive-by shootings were common, and violent crime rates grew to unprecedented heights in crowded urban ghettos (Zucchino, 1994). After Prohibition, the crime rate decreased and leveled off until the 1940s, when it fell dramatically because large numbers of young males—the "crime prone" segment of the population—left to fight World War II. With their return to civilian life, birthrates skyrocketed, creating a "baby boom." In the 1960s, "baby boomers" became teenagers, and crime increased at a faster pace and to higher levels than at any time since the late 1930s (Schmalleger, 1995; Schrag, 1971). The period following World War II has been characterized as "an age of crime [during which] every category of serious crime has risen drastically from a base that was already high" (Friedman, 1993, p. 451). In 1950, the number of crimes reported to the police was 1.8 million; 40 years later it climbed to 14 million (Baird, 1993). The overall crime rate in America in 1980 was 215 percent higher than it was in 1960; the violent crime rate was 270 percent higher (ALEC, 1995).

Several factors other than changes in the age distribution of our population can account for the marked growth in crime in the period after World War II (Baird, 1993). One key factor is that America became increasingly urbanized during much of that period. Crime is typically much more prevalent in urban environments than in rural areas and small towns.

The rise in crime may be partially due to improvements in crime reporting and tracking capabilities as well as the public's greater willingness to report crime. In the late 1960s and early 1970s, the Law Enforcement and Assistance Administration invested millions of dollars to upgrade the country's crime reporting technology.

Fundamental changes in the workplace and in job opportunities in the United States may also have contributed to the rising levels of crime. Since the 1970s, the number of low-skill manufacturing jobs have dwindled, making it extremely difficult for people without college degrees to find decent-paying positions. Most of the employment prospects for these individuals are in low-paying service industry work. The lack of job opportunities has increased the likelihood of crime and violence, especially among young, inner-city residents.

Finally, the structure of the American family has changed dramatically since the 1950s. During the past 20 years, the number of single-parent families has risen 137 percent. The ability of the family to nurture and supervise children has been seriously compromised. All these developments to one extent or another have played a role in America's crime problem.

National Crime Statistics

Table 1 shows the dramatic and rapid increases that occurred in the UCR crime index and crime rate between 1965 and 1975. During this ten-year period, both the crime index and crime rate more than doubled. The precipitous growth in crime persisted throughout the late 1970s until 1981. The crime index grew at a more moderate pace in the late 1970s and actually declined in the early 1980s. From the late 1980s through 1992, UCR data overall showed declines in property crime and increases in violent crime.

NCVS data show that 1981 was a peak year for criminal victimization. There were 41.5 million victimizations in 1981, compared with 33.6 million in 1992 (see Table 2). At the beginning of the 1980s, one of every three American households was victimized by at least one violent crime or theft; at the end of the decade, the prevalence dropped to one in four. From 1981 to 1992, the total rate of victimization declined 19 percent. Over the same period, personal thefts decreased 23 percent, and household crimes decreased 22 percent. The rates of personal theft and household crime in 1992 were the lowest ever recorded by the NCVS for these offenses (BJS 1994a). The trend has been somewhat different for violent crimes, which decreased 9 percent from 1981 to 1990 but then increased by 10 percent from 1990 to 1992.

TABLE 1: Crime Index Trends in the United States, 1965-1993

	Crime Index	Pct. Change	Crime Rate	Pct. Change
1965	4,739,400	----	2,449	----
1966	5,223,500	10.2	2,671	9.1
1967	5,903,400	13.0	2,990	11.9
1968	6,720,200	14.0	3,370	12.7
1969	7,410,900	10.3	3,680	9.1
1970	8,098,000	9.3	3,984	8.3
1971	8,588,200	6.1	4,165	4.5
1972	8,248,800	- 3.9	3,961	- 4.9
1973	8,718,100	5.7	4,154	4.9
1974	10,253,400	18.0	4,850	16.8
1975	11,292,400	10.0	5,299	8.9
1976	11,349,700	0.4	5,287	- 0.3
1977	10,984,500	- 3.3	5,078	- 4.6
1978	11,209,000	2.0	5,140	1.7
1979	12,249,500	9.1	5,566	8.3
1980	13,408,300	10.3	5,950	6.9
1981	13,423,800	0.1	5,858	0.1
1982	12,974,400	- 3.3	5,604	- 5.9
1983	12,108,600	- 6.7	5,175	- 7.6
1984	11,881,800	- 1.9	5,031	- 2.8
1985	12,431,400	4.6	5,207	3.5
1986	12,211,900	6.3	5,480	5.2
1987	13,508,700	2.2	5,550	1.3
1988	13,923,100	3.1	5,664	2.1
1989	14,251,400	2.4	5,741	1.4
1990	14,475,600	1.6	5,820	1.4
1991	14,872,900	2.7	5,898	1.3
1992	14,438,200	- 2.9	5,660	- 4.0
1993	14,141,000	- 2.1	5,483	- 3.1

Crime Index = murder and non-negligent manslaughter, forcible rape, robbery, aggravated assault, burglary, larceny-theft, and motor vehicle theft.

Crime Rate = Crime Index per 100,000 population.

Sources: Bureau of Justice Statistics, *Sourcebook of Criminal Justice Statistics—1993* (Washington, D.C.: U.S. Department of Justice, 1994); Federal Bureau of Investigation, *Uniform Crime Reports for the United States, 1993* (Washington, D.C.: U.S. Department of Justice, 1994).

TABLE 2: Victimization Levels for Selected Crimes in the United States, 1981-1992

Number of Victimizations (in 1,000's)

	Total	Violent Crimes	Personal Theft	Household Crimes
1981	41,454	6,582	15,863	19,009
1982	39,756	6,459	15,553	17,744
1983	37,001	5,903	14,657	16,440
1984	35,544	6,021	13,789	15,733
1985	34,864	5,823	13,474	15,568
1986	34,118	5,515	13,235	15,368
1987	35,336	5,796	13,575	15,966
1988	35,796	5,910	14,056	15,830
1989	35,818	5,861	13,829	16,128
1990	34,404	6,009	12,975	15,419
1991	35,497	6,587	12,885	16,025
1992	33,649	6,621	12,211	14,817
Pct. change 1981-92	-18.8	0.6	-23.0	-22.1

Source: Bureau of Justice Statistics, *Sourcebook of Criminal Justice Statistics—1993* (Washington, D.C.: U.S. Department of Justice, 1994).

Three major factors might explain the general decline in criminal victimization rates, as measured by NCVS, since 1981. The first factor is the continued emphasis on strenuous crime control policies, which were promoted by the Reagan and Bush administrations (Siegel, 1989). Throughout the 1980s, sweeping revisions in sentencing legislation and a proliferation of stricter laws led to a higher percentage of offenders being sent to prison for longer terms and with fewer hopes for parole (Irwin and Austin, 1987; Skogan, 1990).

The second factor is a decrease in the size of the adolescent and young adult populations, which are the most crime-prone age groups in the United States. A rise in the crime rate is expected to occur in the next few years when the children of baby boomers will be reaching the age range of 16 to 25 (Siegel, 1989). By the turn of the century, the number of Americans under the age of 18 will increase from 60 million (their current population size) to more than 70 million (Krauss, 1994).

The third factor is a shift in household location and size. For the past two decades, urban residents in the United States have increasingly been moving to suburban and rural areas. For example, in the years 1975 to 1985, the percentage of households in urban areas decreased from 32 percent to 29 percent, while the percentage of suburban and rural households increased from 68 percent to 71 percent. In addition, the average size of American households has been declining. Households with fewer persons are less likely to record one of their members as a crime victim in the NCVS, which counts the number of households affected by crime in its annual report. One-person households accounted for 21 percent of all households in 1975; in 1991 they accounted for 25 percent of all households. At the same time, the percentage of households with six or more persons declined from 7 percent to 3 percent. Therefore, the population shifted from households more likely to experience criminal victimization (i.e., larger households in urban areas) to households less likely to experience criminal victimization (i.e., smaller households in suburban and rural areas) (Bastian, 1992).

Perhaps the most compelling of these factors explaining the recent downturn in criminal victimization is age. Research has never established clear relationships between crime and emigration patterns or criminal justice policies (Baird, 1993). But the association between age and crime is strong and well known. It is invariant over time, place, gender, and type of crime, and it cannot be explained away by other variables that correlate with age (Farrington, 1986). In short, unlike the other two factors—crime control policies and household changes—age appears to have a clear and direct effect on crime (Hirschi and Gottfredson, 1983). For example, the decline in homicides from 1980 to 1985 in America can be attributed mainly to the fact that the number of youth between 10 and 17 peaked in 1980. In that year, they represented 14 percent of the total U.S. population but accounted for 41 percent of arrests for UCR property crimes and 22 percent of all arrests for UCR violent crimes (Greenwood, 1995).

Fear of Crime

Although criminal victimization in general has decreased or leveled off in recent years, fear of crime in America appears to be on the rise. For example, a Gallup poll taken in 1993 found that twice as many Americans, when compared with those interviewed in 1981, reported that they frequently feared being murdered (Dorning, 1995). What can account for the inconsistency between the apparent risk of victimization (which has gone down) and fear of crime (which seems to be going up)? One explanation is the explosion of crime coverage on television and in newspapers, which has been unrelenting and widespread. People's perceptions of crime and their own vulnerability to victimization are shaped largely from the images they see on the nightly news and on popular television programs that depict real crimes or that re-enact actual crime scenes very graphically.

The Center for Media and Public Affairs in Washington, D.C., reported that the number of crime stories aired on the three major networks' evening news shows more than doubled from 1992 to 1993 (Buckman, 1994). The stories that receive the most media attention are usually sensational, grisly, or random acts of violence. More mundane crimes never make it into print or on the airwaves. The nightly news programs are usually followed by a heavy dose of violent TV programming, which broadcasts "an average of six to eight acts of violence per hour in prime time, and an average of two murders each night" (McQueen, 1992, p. 249). These vivid images have a significant impact on citizens' fears. In contrast, crime statistics are pallid; most individuals do not know how to interpret crime rates, which simply do not have the power to evoke the same visceral reactions as a drive-by shooting or a double homicide. Politicians have fueled people's fears by making crime a front-line issue in elections at every level.

Americans may also be feeling more fearful of crime because of recent episodes of random violence that have occurred in seemingly safe locations under everyday circumstances—for example, a string of murders of foreign tourists in Florida, the massacre of patrons at a Denny's restaurant, the shooting deaths of passengers on a Long Island commuter train, and the terrorist bombing of the World Trade Center. These incidents cause individuals to experience vicarious victimization, which heightens fear of crime (Skogan, 1990). In particular, it is easy for people to "put themselves in the shoes" of the victims of these crimes and difficult for them to imagine avoiding these situations in their own daily lives. A handful of heinous crimes, which get saturated coverage in the media, can seem like a crime epidemic (Zucchino, 1994).

Americans' escalating fearfulness is not entirely groundless. A recent FBI report indicated that the proportion of homicides in America involving strangers is rising. In 1992, more than half of all murders appeared to have been committed by individuals who were strangers to the victims. This was the first time that the figure has exceeded 50 percent since the FBI began collecting these data in 1965. Furthermore, the number of homicides committed during the course of other felonies, mostly robberies, increased 47 percent from 1985 to 1992. At the same time, carjackings, which terrorize an auto-dependent American public, occurred at a rate of more than one per week. Police have attributed the trend in stranger-on-stranger violence to many factors, including "the trade in illegal drugs, the growth of urban gangs, and the younger ages of gang members; a general loosening of social strictures against aggressive behavior; the proliferation of weapons and the greater firepower of guns now on the streets" (Dorning, 1995, pp. 1, 12).

Recent data on juvenile arrests indicate that juvenile crime in America is becoming more serious. Between 1980 and 1990, the proportion of all homicide arrests involving juveniles rose from 10 percent to 14 percent. And between 1984 and 1992, the number of persons under the age of 15 who were arrested for homicide increased by 50 percent, and the rate for those 16 to 20 more than doubled (Krauss, 1994). Several reasons have been advanced to explain the recent trends in violent crime by juveniles, including "increasing involvement in street-level drug selling; the increased availability and lethality of firearms; and the glorification of violence in the movies, videos, and rap music" (Greenwood, 1995, p. 97).

National Crime Characteristics

The risk of criminal victimization varies according to place of residence, age, gender, income, and educational level. For example, rural residents are substantially less vulnerable to violent crime than are urban residents. Between 1987 and 1989, people in rural areas constituted 25 percent of the nation's population but accounted for only 16 percent of the country's violent victimizations. During that time, the average annual overall rate of violent crime (robbery, rape, assault) among city dwellers was 92 percent higher than among rural residents and 56 percent higher than among suburban residents (BJS, 1992).

Violent crime is more likely to strike men, younger persons, people in lower income brackets, and African-Americans. In 1992, African-American males had the highest rate of violent victimization, followed by African-American females, White males, and White females (BJS, 1994a, p. 25). African-Americans are seven times more likely than Whites to be homicide victims (BJS, 1994b, p. 385). Younger people are also more likely to be victims of crime. Persons under 25 years of age have the highest rates of violent victimizations (BJS, 1994a, p. 23). Those between the ages of 25 and 34 are the most likely homicide victims; homicide rates fall dramatically after age 44 (BJS, 1988). In short, Americans with the greatest likelihood of being murdered are young, African-American males living in extremely poor neighborhoods.

Crime in Illinois and Chicago

Violent crime: In 1992, Illinois's violent crime rate of 977 per 100,000 residents was the sixth highest in the nation behind Florida, New York, California, Maryland, and Louisiana (BJS, 1994b, p. 366). Table 3 presents summary data on violent crime in Illinois from 1976 through 1992. The state's violent crime index was fairly constant until 1983, when it rose nearly 25 percent. An even more significant increase occurred in 1984, when violent crime jumped 33 percent. Similarly, prior to 1983, Illinois's violent crime rate was below the national average; after 1983, it was significantly higher than the national rate (see Table 4). This marked shift in the 1983-84 period can be partially explained by a change in crime recording practices, particularly by the Chicago Police Department. Since the mid-1980s, the violent crime index in Illinois has continued to rise, increasing 38 percent from 1985 to 1992 (see Table 3).

TABLE 3: Violent Crime Index in Illinois, 1976-1992

	Crime Index	Pct. Change	Crime Rate	Pct. Change
1976	52,426	----	466.9	----
1977	50,731	- 3.2	451.2	- 3.3
1978	53,800	6.0	478.4	6.0
1979	53,531	- 0.5	476.7	- 0.4
1980	55,787	4.2	490.6	2.9
1981	50,647	- 9.2	443.6	- 9.6
1982	50,832	0.4	452.8	2.1
1983	63,186	24.3	551.8	21.8
1984	84,281	33.3	736.4	33.4
1985	83,467	- 1.0	729.3	- 1.0
1986	94,517	13.2	825.8	13.2
1987	93,823	- 0.8	819.8	- 0.7
1988	95,148	1.4	823.9	0.5
1989	100,780	5.9	867.6	5.3
1990	112,024	11.2	980.0	13.0
1991	121,260	8.2	1,060.8	8.3
1992	115,193	5.0	1,007.8	- 4.9

Violent Crime Index = murder and non-negligent manslaughter, forcible rape, robbery, and aggravated assault.

Violent Crime Rate = Violent Crime Index per 100,000 population.

Source: Illinois Uniform Crime Reports.

TABLE 4: Violent Crime Rates in Illinois and the United States, 1976-1992

	Illinois	U.S.	Difference
1976	466.9	459.6	7.3
1977	451.2	466.6	- 15.4
1978	478.4	497.8	- 19.4
1979	476.7	548.9	- 72.2
1980	490.6	596.6	-106.0
1981	443.6	594.3	-150.7
1982	452.8	571.1	-118.3
1983	551.8	537.7	14.1
1984	736.4	539.2	197.2
1985	729.3	556.2	173.1
1986	825.8	617.3	154.5
1987	819.8	609.7	210.1
1988	817.0	637.2	179.8
1989	867.6	663.7	203.9
1990	980.0	731.8	248.2
1991	1,060.8	758.1	302.7
1992	1,007.8	757.5	250.3

Violent Crime Index = murder and non-negligent manslaughter, forcible rape, robbery, and aggravated assault.

Violent Crime Rate = Violent Crime Index per 100,000 population.

Difference = Illinois rate minus U.S. rate.

Sources: Illinois Uniform Crime Reports; Federal Bureau of Investigation, *Uniform Crime Reports for the United States*, 1986, 1990.

The most common violent crimes in Illinois are robbery and aggravated assault, representing 93 percent of all the violent crimes reported in the state. Both crimes increased in the early 1970s and then leveled off into the early 1980s. From 1982 to 1984, robbery and assault rose sharply as a result of changes in police reporting practices, which also affected the overall violent crime index (see Table 3). Similar to robbery and assault, homicide in Illinois increased rapidly in the early 1970s. During the late 1970s, the number of murders declined across the state and then grew slowly until 1982, when it fell again and then leveled off for most of the rest of the decade (ICJIA, 1990, p. 49). Beginning in 1989, the number of homicides in Illinois again grew significantly.

Violent crimes are most common in Illinois's large municipalities (including Chicago), followed by its smaller cities and towns and its rural areas. The city of Chicago accounts for about one-fourth of the state's population but more than two-thirds of its violent crime. Hence, violent offense patterns in the city largely determine the state's violent crime trends. As shown in Table 5, for example, more than 70 percent of Illinois's murders and more than 80 percent of its reported robberies in 1992 occurred in Chicago.

Table 6 shows homicide trends in Chicago from 1969 to 1994. The number of Chicago homicides in 1991, 1992, and 1994 were among the four highest ever recorded. (The record for Chicago remains 970 homicides in 1974.) However, the 1992 murder rate of 33.1 per 100,000 residents was the highest in the city's history. That year, Chicago's homicide rate ranked third among cities with populations over a million—behind Detroit and Dallas, ahead of Los Angeles, Houston, New York, Philadelphia, and San Diego (BJS, 1994b, p. 368).

TABLE 5: Violent Crime Index Offenses in Illinois, Cook County, and Chicago, 1992

	Murder	Sexual Assault	Robbery	Aggravated Assault
Illinois	1,319 (100%)	6,768 (100%)	47,707 (100%)	59,399 (100%)
Cook County	1,027 (78%)	3,827 (57%)	41,767 (88%)	45,518 (77%)
Chicago	939 (71%)	3,245 (48%)	38,449 (81%)	41,080 (69%)

Source: Illinois Criminal Justice Information Authority.

TABLE 6: Homicides in Chicago, 1969-1994

	No. of Homicides	Pct. Change
1969	715	----
1970	810	13.3
1971	824	1.7
1972	711	-13.7
1973	864	21.5
1974	970	12.3
1975	818	-15.7
1976	814	- 0.5
1977	823	1.1
1978	787	- 4.4
1979	856	8.8
1980	863	0.8
1981	877	1.6
1982	668	-23.8
1983	729	9.1
1984	741	1.6
1985	666	-10.1
1986	744	11.7
1987	691	- 7.1
1988	660	- 4.5
1989	742	12.4
1990	849	14.4
1991	927	9.2
1992	941	1.5
1993	847	-10.0
1994	930	9.8

Source: *Chicago Tribune*, analysis of Chicago Police Department records.

Chicago had several other chilling homicide trends in the early 1990s. There were more youthful victims than ever before. In 1994, 30 percent of the city's homicide victims were between the ages of 11 and 20, compared with only 16 percent in 1974. Another significant trend was the growing proportion of murders involving firearms—69 percent in 1992, 74 percent in 1993, and 74 percent in 1994, compared with only 54 percent in 1987. In addition, the use of sophisticated weapons such as semi-automatic pistols became more commonplace. Finally, more homicides in Chicago were committed in public places such as streets, sidewalks, alleys, and parks. In 1993, 61 percent of homicides were in public places, compared with only 42 percent ten years earlier (Recktenwald, 1992, 1993; Recktenwald and Papajohn, 1994; Martin and de la Garza, 1995).

Property crime: The most common property crimes in Illinois (in order of frequency) are theft, burglary, motor vehicle theft, and arson. In contrast to violent crime, the property crime index has been relatively stable. As shown in Table 7, statewide property crimes rose only 8 percent from 1976 to 1992. Also unlike violent index crimes, the majority of reported property index crimes (except for motor vehicle theft) in Illinois are committed outside of Chicago (see Table 8). At the same time, the property crime rate is generally higher in Chicago and other large municipalities than it is in either small municipalities or rural areas. From 1976 to 1982, however, Chicago had a lower property crime rate than other large municipalities. In addition, while property crime rates increased or remained constant throughout most of the state from 1986 to 1987, Chicago's rate decreased 7 percent, before rising again to its 1984-86 levels and then increasing steadily through 1991. The disparities in property crimes between Chicago and the rest of the state may be attributable to differences in crime reporting behavior rather than to real differences in property offense rates. That is, residents in Chicago may be less likely to report property crime when compared with those living in the predominantly suburban or rural areas of Cook County and the rest of the state (ICJIA, 1990).

TABLE 7: Property Crime Index in Illinois, 1976-1992

	Property Crime Index	Pct. Change	Property Crime Rate	Pct. Change
1976	508,290	----	4,526.5	----
1977	496,822	-2.2	4,418.1	-2.4
1978	495,863	-0.2	4,416.4	-0.2
1979	520,416	5.0	4,628.6	4.9
1980	542,717	4.3	4,773.5	3.1
1981	514,128	-5.2	4,502.6	-5.7
1982	519,378	1.0	4,595.7	2.1
1983	535,001	3.0	4,672.2	2.0
1984	534,313	-0.1	4,668.4	-0.1
1985	537,303	0.6	4,694.6	0.6
1986	555,567	3.4	4,854.1	3.4
1987	538,060	-3.2	4,701.2	-3.1
1988	559,012	3.9	4,840.8	3.0
1989	563,737	0.8	4,853.1	0.2
1990	568,089	0.8	4,969.9	2.4
1991	586,741	3.3	5,133.1	3.3
1992	551,122	-6.1	4,821.5	-6.5

Property Crime Index = burglary, theft, motor vehicle theft, and arson.

Property Crime Rate = Property Crime Index per 100,000 population.

Note: Arson data were not collected as part of the Illinois property crime index until 1980.

Sources: Illinois State Police; Illinois Criminal Justice Information Authority.

TABLE 8: Property Crime Index Offenses in Illinois, Cook County, and Chicago, 1992

	Burglary	Theft	Motor Vehicle Theft	Arson
Illinois	123,176 (100%)	352,623 (100%)	71,203 (100%)	4,120 (100%)
Cook County	68,649 (56%)	190,159 (54%)	58,201 (82%)	2,392 (58%)
Chicago	49,048 (40%)	119,700 (34%)	44,990 (63%)	1,853 (45%)

Source: Illinois Criminal Justice Information Authority.

COMMUNITIES AND CRIME

Neighborhood Characteristics and Crime: The Chicago School

Some of the earliest and most seminal research on the relationship between communities and crime was performed by University of Chicago sociologists in the 1920s and 1930s. The work of Clifford Shaw and Henry McKay was particularly influential in creating the "Chicago school" of urban sociology, which explored the effects of communities on crime and attempted to explain crime within the context of the changing urban environment. Specifically, they examined the association between levels of crime and the physical, social, and cultural characteristics of neighborhoods. According to Shaw and McKay, the ultimate causes of crime were found in the ecological conditions (e.g., social and physical environment) of the city itself. Their research refuted the notions that crime was a product of psychological or biological differences or that it was inextricably linked to any specific racial or ethnic groups (Shaw and McKay, 1931; Siegel, 1989).

Shaw and McKay found that crime tends to be concentrated in the inner city or slum areas (i.e., locations adjacent to the central city) and decreases with movement away from the central city. They referred to these distinct areas as "interstitial areas" and "zones of transition," where many immigrants were newly settled. Moreover, they observed that in most cities, crime rates were quite stable over long periods of time. In other words, neighborhoods had specific enduring features of their social and economic structures that made them more or less susceptible to crime. For example, Shaw and McKay reported that communities with high crime and delinquency rates in 1900 also had high crime rates in 1940, despite changes in ethnic composition (Shaw and McKay, 1942).

In Shaw and McKay's model, high crime rates are explained primarily by the concept of "social disorganization," which occurs when the family and immediate community can no longer function as effective socializing or control agents. Shaw and McKay contended that disorganization arose from the urbanization process, which increased the mobility and heterogeneity of neighborhood residents, caused cultural conflict, and disrupted the local social control mechanism that keeps communities safe and orderly (Shaw and McKay, 1942).

Crime is only one of several consequences of diminished social control. Shaw and McKay reported that neighborhoods with serious crime problems also exhibited other problems such as juvenile delinquency, mental illness, large numbers of families on relief (welfare), school truancy, high rates of tuberculosis, and low rates of homeownership (Shaw and McKay, 1942). In short, Shaw and McKay offered a well-documented and elaborate description of both yesterday's slums and today's underclass neighborhoods, which remain centers of crime, drug use, and other social pathologies.

The centerpiece of Shaw and McKay's theories was that neighborhood disintegration and deterioration are the fundamental causes of crime and urban problems. Hence, solutions to these problems could be achieved by physically renovating the slums and developing social interventions that draw on community resources and institutions. The efforts of Shaw and McKay have set the stage for numerous crime-related community action and treatment programs (Siegel, 1989).

Research on Communities and Crime

Many of the relationships posited by Shaw and McKay and their contemporaries are still relevant. Social ecology researchers and theorists have continued the Chicago tradition of criminology. Similar to their predecessors, they study crime and communities by focusing on macro-level variables such as employment opportunities, housing conditions, social inequality, and family structures. A selective review of social ecology and related research suggests a number of community-level variables that are associated with crime.

(1) Relative deprivation may be a direct cause of crime. That is, crime is higher in underclass neighborhoods that are located near wealthy areas. Blau and Blau (1982) note that the visible and stark contrast in living conditions fuels underclass residents' sense of social injustice and anger, which leads to hostility and criminal behavior. Block (1979) found that the proximity of poor and affluent neighborhoods was the best predictor of crime rates in Chicago.

(2) Urban environments and their attendant economic and social conditions are criminogenic. For example, McGahey (1987) reported that neighborhoods in New York with few legitimate employment opportunities had high rates of property crime, drug sales, and other illegal activities. Sampson (1987) observed that areas with high-density populations create impersonal environments that increase the risk of criminal victimization. Messner and Tardiff (1986) found a strong relationship between homicide rates and the percentage of a neighborhood's households with broken families and poverty-level incomes. Community areas in Chicago with the highest crime rates also have relatively higher levels of single-parent households, unemployment, families on welfare, and drug use.

(3) Areas that border neighborhoods undergoing racial change experience higher crime rates because their residents condone law-breaking behaviors that are designed to keep out racial minorities (Heitgerd and Bursik, 1987). Marquette Park is an example of this phenomenon from Chicago's recent past. During the period when this community's neighboring areas were changing in their racial composition, Marquette Park's violent crime rate increased. Several violent interracial altercations in the neighborhood became flashpoints of racial tension.

(4) Demographic composition and demographic trends are related to neighborhood crime. High-crime communities are home

to relatively large numbers of single elderly persons, unattached youth, female-headed households with children, and unstable families (Reiss, 1987). The percentage of African-Americans in a neighborhood is positively and strongly related to rates of violence. The independent effect of racial composition on violence, however, has not been established (Sampson, 1985, 1995). Communities characterized by high population turnover *and* high levels of poverty have higher violent crime rates than both more affluent areas with rapid population turnover and poor but stable communities (Smith and Jarjoura, 1988). Gentrification leads to minor reductions in personal crime rates (McDonald, 1987). The "yuppified" areas in some Chicago neighborhoods, such as Lincoln Park and Lake View, have experienced only modest declines in violent crime.

(5) Neighborhoods with high levels of social disorder (e.g., public drinking and drug use, corner gangs, street prostitution, panhandling, verbal harassment of women, open gambling) and physical decay (e.g., vandalism, trash in vacant lots, boarded-up buildings, stripped and abandoned cars) have significantly higher crime rates and fear of crime. These signs are collectively referred to as "incivilities" (Hunter, 1978) and may be indirectly linked to crime through their effect on the fears of residents (Skogan, 1987, 1989). For example, Taylor and Gottfredson (1987) propose a causal sequence in which incivilities lead to fear of crime, which leads to lower levels of informal social control, which lead to more crime and more fear. Similarly, Wilson and Kelling (1982) suggest that fear of crime causes community residents to be less vigilant, more suspicious of their neighbors, and less likely to get involved in collective anti-crime activities. Consequently, the neighborhood becomes "vulnerable to criminal invasion." Some neighborhoods may attract criminals if the areas are already stigmatized as sites for drugs and street prostitution (Stark, 1987; Wilson and Kelling, 1982). The appearance of incivilities in Chicago neighborhoods covaries with crime in a regular and predictable pattern. For example, areas with the highest crime rates on the West Side and Near South Side of the city are characterized by more garbage, gangs, abandoned buildings, and empty lots when compared with those on the Northwest and Southwest sides of the city, which have the lowest crime rates.

The Impact of Drugs on Communities

Drug sales and the variety of crimes they spawn have affected every major American city. Drugs have had an especially devastating impact on poor communities and are both a symptom and a causal factor in the continued decline of those areas. Some researchers argue that drugs in inner-city communities have created a criminal underclass that is heavily involved in drug distribution, sales, and consumption. Members of this underclass often engage in violent and disruptive behaviors that have had a devastating impact on the poor (Johnson, Williams, Dei, and Sanabria, 1990). Scholars have compared the psychological consequences of living in underclass neighborhoods to the effects of living in a war zone (Garbarino, Kostelny, and Dubrow, 1991). Not surprisingly, in a 1988 national survey of poor households, 40 percent of the respondents identified "illegal drugs and drug problems" as the "number one" issue facing the nation (Lavrakas, 1988). Similarly, a national survey of law enforcement executives revealed that citizens in their jurisdictions considered drug trafficking the country's principal crime problem (Lavrakas and Rosenbaum, 1989).

Researchers have extensively documented the relationship between drugs and crime and their link to neighborhood disintegration (Gandossy et al., 1980). Citizens typically perceive visible drug sales and use as signs of social disorder and degeneration (Skogan, 1990). Indeed, when residents become acutely aware of active drug dealers and prospering "drug houses," they conclude that citizens and the police have lost control over the streets. Residents soon begin to view their community as an inadequate environment in which to raise children or to establish businesses.

Drug sales provide poorly educated, unemployable, and impoverished youths with a steady "job" that is easy to learn and highly profitable, with relatively low risk of arrest and incarceration (Johnson, Kaplan, and Schmeidler, 1990). Moreover, drug habits commonly force young men and women into prostitution or drug sales. Hence, an entire generation of inner-city inhabitants is being lured away from mainstream employment and into the drug trade, which leads many to prison or premature death.

Michael Tonry (1994) argues that African-Americans bore the brunt of the Reagan-Bush "war on drugs" because drug arrests are easier to make in socially disorganized, inner-city neighborhoods than they are in middle-class, suburban areas. Drug enforcement in poor, minority communities is also easier because of the public nature of drug sales; drug dealers in disorganized neighborhoods are more likely to sell outdoors to strangers. Hence, undercover operations are much more successful in poor communities than they could ever be in middle-class communities. Moreover, penalties for drug crimes since the mid-1980s have become steadily harsher and more likely to lead to incarceration, and drug laws have created further racial disparities by punishing the dealers of crack cocaine more severely than those who sell powder cocaine (i.e., the so-called 100-to-1 rule that equates one gram of crack cocaine with 100 grams of powder). Crack dealers are more likely to be poor and African-American. Tonry sums up the situation in this way:

> The people who launched the drug wars knew all these things—that the enemy troops would be mostly young minority males, that an emphasis on supply-side antidrug strategies, particularly use of mass arrests, would disproportionately ensnare young minority males, that the 100-to-1 rule would disproportionately affect Blacks, and that there was no valid basis for believing that any of these things would reduce drug availability or prices (Tonry, 1994, p. 488).

Community Crime Prevention

Many criminal justice experts have noted that perhaps the best hope for curtailing drugs and crime in inner-city neighborhoods lies with the cooperation and involvement of local residents (Lavrakas, 1985; Rosenbaum, 1988). Community crime prevention programs usually operate under aegis of local police departments and community organizations and are designed to mobilize citizens for the purposes of preventing, detecting, or reporting criminal offenses. The fundamental philosophy of community crime prevention is that the most effective means of combating crime must involve residents in proactive interventions aimed at reducing or precluding the opportunity for crime in their neighborhoods. In practice, this involvement translates into a wide range of activities, including resident patrols, citizen crime-reporting networks, block-watch programs, home security surveys, property-marking projects, police-community councils, and a variety of plans for changing the physical environment.

Community crime prevention is grounded in two basic theoretical models. The first involves informal social control. This model suggests that reductions in crime and in the fear of crime are by-products of various processes that include vigorous enforcement of social norms, clearer delineation of neighborhood boundaries and identities, and establishment of a stronger sense of community and increased social interaction. These models reflect what Podolefsky and DuBow (1981) describe as a "social problem" approach to community crime prevention, which seeks to reduce crime through the amelioration of the social conditions that breed criminal activity.

Community crime prevention projects are also rooted in an "opportunity reduction" model of crime prevention, which emphasizes the deterrence value of designing or modifying the physical environment to enhance the security of commercial and residential settings and of encouraging residents to adopt measures to minimize their vulnerability to crime. The latter is often achieved through formal, anti-crime educational campaigns sponsored by the media, law enforcement officials, and citizen groups. In addition, opportunity reduction may involve fostering a closer relationship between local police and citizens by restructuring the deployment of patrol officers to increase their contact with community residents.

In general, evidence supporting community crime prevention theory or programs has been mixed. Rosenbaum (1987) argues that the most reliable data on community crime prevention programs come from experiments that examine whether programs can be "implanted" in neighborhoods that do not already have them. These studies show that even when vigorous attempts are made to recruit area residents to join block-watch groups, overall participation levels are low. Community anti-crime programs are not likely to arise spontaneously or to be successfully implanted in neighborhoods characterized by poverty and by high levels of crime and disorder (Greenberg, Rohe, and Williams, 1985). Participation in community organizations in general, and in crime prevention programs in particular, is more likely in communities where residents are middle-income, are well educated, and own their own homes, as well as in communities that already are relatively free of crime and disorder (Skogan, 1989; Greenberg, Rohe, and Williams, 1982). In addition, studies indicate that community crime prevention projects are most effective when they have adequate funding and technical assistance, when they are supported by the police, and when they are planned and implemented with substantial police involvement (Lewis, Grant, and Rosenbaum, 1988).[1]

PUBLIC POLICY AND CRIME

The federal government began to pursue its first clearly articulated anti-crime policies in late 1960s, during the Johnson administration. The "war against crime" was launched in the wake of the President's Commission on Law Enforcement and Administration of Justice, which issued a report in 1967 that thoroughly described the nature and extent of the crime problem and placed it in the context of urban discord and blight. Policy was heavily influenced by academics and other pundits who advocated causal analyses of crime. They strongly believed that crime in America would never be eradicated unless the country confronted its social and economic root causes, such as poverty, racism, and social inequality. In the words of the commission:

> Warring on poverty, inadequate housing, and unemployment is warring on crime. A civil rights law is a law against crime. Money for schools is money against crime. . . . Every effort to improve life in America's inner cities is an effort against crime (President's Commission on Law Enforcement, 1967, p. 6).

The crime policies of the Johnson era were primarily formulated to attack the slum conditions that fostered crime and despair in the inner city. One such program was Mobilization for Youth, based in New York City (Siegel, 1989). The project had several objectives: to educate teachers to handle problem youth, to create job prospects for young persons through neighborhood job centers, to organize neighborhood councils and associations, to establish counseling services for neighborhood families, and to deploy street workers to interact with local gangs. Other programs designed to combat crime by alleviating poverty and enriching education and employment opportunities included the Job Corps, VISTA, Head Start, and Upward Bound.

By the 1970s, during the Nixon, Ford, and Carter administrations, the view that crime was caused by remediable social conditions had come under considerable fire. Critics observed that

---

[1] Community policing will be discussed later in this chapter.

crime continued to grow despite improvements in employment, education, and income levels. In short, crime rates were paradoxically rising at the same time that the plight of the disadvantaged was improving. Also, crime was simultaneously increasing in most other Western nations. Hence, detractors noted that attempts to attribute crime to shortcomings in America's institutions were both misguided and misinformed. Finally, several academic studies of offender programs seemed to suggest that "nothing works" and that rehabilitation was a failure (Lipton, Martinson, and Wilks, 1975).

The "Get Tough" Movement

By 1980, with the election of President Ronald Reagan, public attitudes shifted further toward advocating tough penalties for criminals and away from interventions dealing with social problems and neighborhood deterioration. The Attorney General's Task Force on Violent Crime proclaimed,

> We are not convinced that a government, by the invention of new programs or the management of existing institutions, can by itself recreate those familial and neighborhood conditions, those social opportunities, and those personal values that in all likelihood are the prerequisites of tranquil communities (U.S. Department of Justice, 1981, pp. 2-3).

Thus, along with public opinion, the federal government turned away from social action programs and toward ways to deal more swiftly and harshly with offenders, that is, to "get tough" with criminals.

The "get tough" movement in criminal justice included such reforms as mandatory minimum sentences, determinate sentencing, sentencing enhancements, the abolition of early release of prisoners. As a consequence of these policy changes, the prison population in America reached unprecedented levels. From 1980 to 1992, the number of incarcerated Americans increased 160 percent, and spending on prison construction, operations, and maintenance nearly doubled, reaching $25 billion in 1992 (Clark Foundation, 1993). The National Institute of Justice characterized prison and jail overcrowding in the 1980s "as the most serious problem facing the criminal justice system" (BJS, 1988).

In 1992, 40 states and the District of Columbia were operating under court orders to relieve prison overcrowding. At the

Crime and Communities 59

start of 1993, the nation's 900 state and 70 federal prisons held about 883,000 inmates; at the end of the year, the population exceeded 948,000. The 1993 incarceration rate in federal and state prisons of 351 per 100,000 was three times the incarceration rate that had prevailed for more than 50 years (Blumstein, 1995, p. 388). Although it is difficult to establish a direct link between penalties and crime, conservatives argued that the tough crime control strategies of the 1980s incapacitated career criminals and deterred potential criminals, thereby lowering the crime rate (Siegel, 1989).

Getting Tough in Illinois

Illinois has become one of many states with a prison crowding problem. The precipitous growth of Illinois's prison population can be traced to two sweeping policy changes enacted in 1978 (ICJIA, 1989). The first change was the institution of a determinate sentencing structure that resulted in offenders spending longer terms in prison compared with those previously sentenced for the same crimes. In addition, offenders sentenced to life imprisonment became ineligible for release except through executive clemency (Vlasak, 1989). The second change was the creation of a new class of felonies known as Class X offenses, which included serious crimes such as aggravated sexual assault, attempted murder, and armed robbery. According to Illinois law, Class X felons are not eligible for probation or conditional discharge and must serve their sentences in prison. Since 1978, Class 1 crimes such as residential burglary and aggravated battery of a senior citizen have also carried mandatory prison sentences. More generally, since the late 1970s, the Illinois General Assembly has periodically changed the state's criminal statutes to create new offenses and to increase penalties for existing offenses. These changes have led to a substantial increase in the number of persons imprisoned in Illinois (Vlasak, 1989).

Table 9 presents the size of the adult prison population in Illinois from 1970 to 1993, which more than quadrupled. Increases beginning in 1974 are a function of more felons being sentenced to prison and for longer periods when compared with previous years. Following the implementation of determinate sentencing, the prison population continued to grow steadily. The sharpest increases appeared from 1988 to 1993, when the prison population burgeoned. In just five years, the number of inmates increased by more than 13,000, or 64 percent. By 1993, Illinois prisons were housing more than 30,000 inmates in a system designed to hold only about 20,000 (IDOC, 1994; Vangeloff, 1993).

TABLE 9: Adult Prison Population in Illinois, 1970-1993

	Prison Population	Pct. Change
1970	7,326	----
1971	6,579	-10.2
1972	6,196	- 5.8
1973	6,100	- 1.5
1974	6,707	10.0
1975	8,237	22.8
1976	10,054	22.1
1977	10,982	9.2
1978	10,733	- 2.3
1979	11,749	9.5
1980	12,458	6.0
1981	13,917	11.7
1982	13,895	- 0.2
1983	15,432	11.1
1984	16,854	9.2
1985	18,279	8.5
1986	19,456	6.4
1987	19,850	2.0
1988	21,081	6.2
1989	24,712	17.2
1990	27,516	11.3
1991	29,115	5.8
1992	31,640	8.7
1993	34,495	9.0

Source: Illinois Department of Corrections.

According to the Illinois Department of Corrections, a key factor in the growth of the state's prison population has been the steady increase in new admissions of drug offenders. In 1984, there were 683 drug offenders in Illinois state prisons. By 1993, there were 6,954. During the same time period, the number of inmates sentenced for violent crimes grew from 9,714 to 18,532. Because violent offenders receive longer sentences, they contribute greatly to the size of the prison population (IDOC, 1991, 1994).

The jail system in Illinois has also been strained by the drug problem. Jail overcrowding in Illinois is most pronounced in Cook County, the state's largest county, where the average daily jail population is greater than the average for all other counties combined (IDOC, 1987). The population at the end of 1994 soared to nearly 10,000 offenders in a facility with a capacity to hold approximately 8,500.

The influx of Cook County drug cases has been overwhelming. From 1978 to 1987, felony drug cases increased 140 percent; from 1988 to 1989 alone, drug cases soared 77 percent (ICJIA, 1989). By 1991, more than 17,000 felony drug cases were filed in Cook County—an increase of 160 percent in only seven years. During the same period, non-drug felony filings had risen only 4 percent (ICJIA, 1991).

The Utility of Incarceration

The question of whether stiffer penalties really deter criminals or reduce crime through incapacitation is difficult to address. To date, research has been unable to clearly establish the deterrent effect of incarceration. Some studies have shown that for deterrence to work, the certainty of punishment is more crucial than the severity of punishment. After all, if the likelihood of punishment is low, then the dread of even the most serious penalties will be slight (Blumstein, Cohen, and Nagin, 1978). Other investigations have revealed that "formal" sanctions, which are meted out by the criminal justice system, have less impact on crime than "informal" sanctions, which are administered by family, friends, and the larger community (Tittle, 1983). Although many scholars agree that putting criminals (especially repeat, violent offenders) in prison for longer terms will probably reduce the crime rate, they cannot reach a consensus on the magnitude of the reduction or the costs involved in implementing such a policy. One study found that to cut crime by a mere 10 percent, California would have to increase its prison population by 157 percent, New York by 263 percent, and Massachusetts by 310 percent (Blumstein, Cohen, and Nagin, 1978).

Most reasoned assessments of deterrence point to its limitations. Research suggests that lengthy imprisonment and the death penalty have little deterrent effect (if any) on crime (Clark Foundation, 1993). In 1978, the U.S. Department of Justice funded the National Academy of Sciences Panel on Research on Deterrent and Incapacitative Effects. Its task was to examine the available evidence on the impact of criminal sanctions. The panel concluded: "In summary, we cannot assert that the evidence warrants an affirmative conclusion regarding deterrence" (Blumstein, Cohen, and Nagin, 1978). Fifteen years later, the National Research Council issued a major report, *Understanding and Preventing Violence*, with similar conclusions. Increasing the prison population has had apparently very little effect on violent crime: ". . . if tripling the average length of incarceration per crime [between 1975 and 1989] had a strong preventive effect, then violent crime rates should have declined in the absence of other relevant changes" (Reiss and Roth, 1993, p. 6).

Outside the United States, other countries have repudiated the claims that harsher punishments result in major reductions in crime or improvements in public safety (Tonry, 1994). For example, an official policy statement of the British government, based on a three-year study, expressed skepticism about the preventive effects of sanctions:

> Deterrence is a principle with much immediate appeal. . . . But much crime is committed on impulse, given the opportunity presented by an open window or an unlocked door, and is committed by offenders who live from moment to moment; their crimes are as impulsive as the rest of their feckless, sad, or pathetic lives. It is unrealistic to construct sentencing arrangements on the assumption that most offenders will weigh up the possibilities in advance and base their conduct on rational calculation (Home Office, 1990, p. 97).

Similarly, the Canadian Sentencing Commission (1987) concluded: "Deterrence cannot be used, with empirical justification, to guide the imposition of sanctions." Six years later, the Committee on Justice and the Solicitor General stated that "the United States affords a glaring example of the limited effect that criminal justice responses may have on crime. . . . If locking up those who violate the law contributed to safer societies then the United States should be the safest country in the world" (Standing Committee on Justice and the Solicitor General, 1993, p. iv).

According to Blumstein (1995), any rational strategies regarding the use of prisons in America must take into account the following key facts:

- The massive growth in prison populations between the mid-1970s and mid-1990s has had no demonstrable effect on crime rates.
- The growth in the use of prisons for drug offenders has had no demonstrable effect on drug selling or drug abuse.
- Money devoted to prison operations (about $20,000 per prisoner per year) is diverted from other efforts (e.g., education, economic development, and rehabilitative programs) that may diminish the future call for more prisons.
- Prisons are ineffective in rehabilitating adults.
- Lengthy prison sentences do little to deter the crimes of underclass individuals, who are the primary occupants of prisons (Blumstein, 1995, pp. 416-417).

The Violent Crime Control Act of 1994

On September 13, 1994, in an elaborate outdoor ceremony rife with political symbolism, President Clinton signed into law the Violent Crime Control Act of 1994. He hailed it as the "toughest, largest, smartest federal attack on crime in the history of our country." Conservative critics called it a "social-welfare boondoggle."

The cost of the crime bill was $32.2 billion over six years and was to be financed by a Crime Trust Fund. The largest share of the money was earmarked for state and local law enforcement ($11.1 billion), followed by state and local prisons ($10.5 billion), crime prevention programs ($7.6 billion), federal law enforcement and courts ($2.8 billion), and drug treatment ($1.3 billion). The major highlights of the crime bill included:

- Adding 100,000 new police on the streets with a focus on community policing;
- Banning the sale and possession of 19 types of semi-automatic assault-style weapons;
- Expanding the number of crimes eligible for the federal death penalty;

- Providing life sentences for anyone convicted of three violent crimes—"three strikes and you're out";
- Building new prisons—with money first going to states with the highest violent crime rates and the rest to states that require inmates to serve at least 85 percent of their sentences before parole;
- Establishing drug courts that place non-violent drug offenders into treatment programs that include drug testing and counseling;
- Ordering convicted sexual offenders to be registered with state law enforcement officials for ten years after release from prison;
- Requiring the adult prosecution of 13-year-olds charged with some violent crimes such as murder, armed robbery, and rape;
- Supporting police, prosecutors, and victim advocates in their efforts to fight crimes against women.

Critics of the crime bill have discussed its limitations (DiIulio, Smith, and Saiger, 1995; Drug Policy Foundation, 1994). First, the impact of "three strikes and you're out" will probably be negligible because only a small number of repeat offenders are processed through the federal courts. Based on 1991 statistics, only 5 percent of commitments to federal prison were for violent crimes. If one-tenth of these were for a third offense—a high estimate given the recidivism rates of federal prisoners—then only one-half of one percent of the federal prisoners sentenced in 1991 would have been affected by the three-strikes provision. Furthermore, the bill equates a violent felony with any drug felony regardless of its seriousness. Thus, a relatively minor drug offense could have the same status as a first-degree murder or criminal robbery.

Second, the crime bill imposes the death penalty for 60 additional offenses, most of which rarely occur (e.g., murder at a U.S. international airport, train sabotage where death results, and genocide). Federal executions are also a rarity; the last time a federal prisoner was executed was in 1963.

Third, the funding for law enforcement requires local jurisdictions to institute community policing (see next section) but does not specify how to design or implement such programs or how to assess their performance. Most important, the bill's widely touted addition of 100,000 new police officers on the streets would, in practice, translate into far fewer officers because of shift demands and days off. In addition, the money for policing must be allocated across hundreds of jurisdictions, which will further dilute the measure's impact on high-crime areas (DiIulio, Smith, and Saiger, 1995, p. 461). Police departments that accept federal money to hire new staff must promise to assume, within six years, the full costs for funding the positions.

Fourth, while the bill prohibits the sale and possession of 19 semi-automatic assault-style weapons, it leaves in circulation thousands more of similar firearms. For example, 650 types of semi-automatic rifles used by hunters and target shooters are exempted from the new regulation.

Finally, to receive funding for prisons, states must pass "truth-in-sentencing" laws, which require inmates to serve at least 85 percent of their sentences in confinement. Many states have been reluctant to adopt truth-in-sentencing policies because of the prohibitive costs of building new prisons, which would surely be necessitated by the passage of these laws. Some state leaders have already indicated that they will forego applying for prison-related funds to avoid these inevitable future expenditures.

Community Policing

While federal and state governments have been preoccupied with "get tough" policies regarding crime, the most significant public policy trend at the local level has been community policing. Community-oriented policing is meant to provide a linkage between citizens and law enforcement. It is designed to put police "back on the streets" through foot patrols, which allow them to have direct contact with residents to discuss routine neighborhood annoyances such as inadequate street lighting, trash cleanup, and rowdy teenagers. Community policing attempts to achieve a working partnership between officers and citizens, not only to combat crime, but to find feasible solutions to everyday problems that plague neighborhoods.

Community-oriented policing was recently implemented throughout the city of Chicago. Chicago's Alternative Policing Strategy (CAPS) is the most sweeping policy innovation in the city's law enforcement since the early 1960s. It demands an entire revamping of police structure and operations, including changes in the way officers are trained and deployed. It also requires a decentralization of the policing function. Most important, community policing necessitates a change in the basic philosophy of policing in Chicago: from a squad-patrol orientation to a foot-patrol orientation; from reactive, incident-driven responses to proactive, problem-driven responses; from part-time, short-term district assignments to full-time, long-term district assignments. Hence, the full-scale implementation of community policing will be expensive and time-consuming.

The CAPS program was initially implemented in five prototype districts that were chosen to reflect the diversity of Chicago's neighborhoods. At the planning stage, Chicago's community policing program had six basic features:

(1) *Neighborhood orientation.* CAPS gives special attention to the residents and problems of specific neighborhoods, which demands that officers know their beats (i.e., crime trends, hot spots, and community organizations and resources) and develop partnerships with the community to solve problems.

(2) *Increased geographic responsibility.* CAPS involves organizing police services so that officers are responsible for crime control in specific areas. A new district organizational structure using rapid-response cars to handle emergency calls allows newly created beat teams to engage in community policing activities. The beat teams share responsibility for specific areas under the leadership of a supervisory beat sergeant.

(3) *Structured response to calls for police service.* A system of differential responses to citizen calls frees beat-team officers from the continuous demands of 911 calls. Emergency calls are handled primarily by rapid-response sector cars, whereas nonemergency and routine calls are handled by beat officers or by telephone call-back contacts. Sector officers also attend to community matters, and sector and beat teams rotate so that all officers participate in community policing.

(4) *Proactive problem-oriented approach.* CAPS focuses on the causes of neighborhood problems rather than on discrete incidents of crime or disturbances. Attention is given to the long-term prevention of these problems and to the signs of community disorder and decay that are associated with crime (e.g., drug houses, loitering youths, and graffiti).

(5) *Community and city resources for crime prevention and control.* CAPS assumes that police alone cannot solve the crime problem and that they depend on the community and other city agencies to achieve success. Hence, part of the beat officer's new role is to broker community resources and to draw on other city agencies to identify and respond to local problems. The mayor's

office ensures that municipal agencies are responsive to requests for assistance from beat officers.

(6) *Emphasis on crime problem analysis.* CAPS requires more efficient data collection and analysis to identify crime patterns and to target areas that demand police attention. Emphasis is placed on crime analysis at the district level, and beat information is recorded and shared among officers and across watches.

CONCLUDING REMARKS

As discussed in the opening of this chapter, crime is a complicated problem that defies easy solutions. Crime has been a pressing national concern for nearly 30 years, and every indication suggests that the problem in the United States will not be alleviated in the near future. If anything, there is reason to be pessimistic. The unacceptably high levels of joblessness and the broader economic factors of the late 1980s, which created even greater disparities in income and living arrangements, will probably continue through much of the current decade. This chronic social inequality in America has bred violence and has fueled our homicide statistics (Blau and Blau, 1982). Poverty and unemployment have likewise been important contributors to crime. Brenner (1976), for example, found that a 1 percent increase in unemployment accounts for 6 percent of the robberies, 9 percent of the drug offenses, and 4 percent of the homicides committed in any given year. Hence, as long as these social and economic conditions persist, we should expect no immediate or dramatic changes in crime at any level.

Tough national, state, and local policies on crime have thrown the criminal justice system into a major crisis because of institutional crowding. According to most studies, stiffer prison sentences have had no real or favorable impact on crime or violence. In fact, population groups, states, and regions of the country with the highest rates of imprisonment also have the highest rates of violent crime (Currie, 1985, chap. 3). Furthermore, sentencing more drug dealers and users to prison has not appreciably influenced drug abuse or sales in Illinois or Chicago.

While more money was being poured into criminal justice programs, less was being given to social programs. Health, employment, and educational interventions for low-income families have been cut, even though the number of poor families has not diminished. Studies have shown that such programs can significantly reduce delinquency rates (Currie, 1985). Notwithstanding these dire observations, a few modest recommendations, which draw from Sampson (1995), are offered to prevent crime in local communities.

(1) Community residents should be empowered to combat crime in manageable target areas or locations. Community crime prevention programs must remain focused at the apartment or block level. Citizens should be asked to be responsible only for the patrol or surveillance of a circumscribed territory in which they are invested. Furthermore, to keep citizens committed to crime prevention activities, any anti-crime strategies should be part of a larger community reform agenda and must include the input and assistance of the police.

(2) Attempts to mobilize residents against crime should focus on poorer neighborhoods where informal mechanisms to control disorder are weakest. Contrary to previous studies, Lurigio and Davis (1992) reported that residents in underclass communities can be successfully organized to combat drug trafficking on their streets.

(3) Social action programs must become a cornerstone of local crime policy. Returning to projects that attempt to address the root causes of crime is essential. Experience has shown that law enforcement without social services and prevention can only have a transient effect on crime.

(4) Community-oriented policing should be vigorously pursued. It offers the best promise for joining the police and citizens in a concerted effort to improve the quality of neighborhoods. Community policing may have its greatest benefit in poor areas of the city, where trust in the police is minimal and where participation in the justice process is low.

(5) Law enforcement efforts should target places where criminal activity is concentrated (i.e., in so-called "hot spots" of crime). With computer mapping techniques and statistical clustering procedures, police can identify, patrol, and intervene in those areas where crime and disorder have a high probability of occurring and can thereby reduce opportunities for crime (Block, 1992).

(6) Collective neighborhood strategies to rid communities of incivilities should be encouraged. These efforts would involve cleaning up graffiti and trash and confronting objectionable activities such as public drinking and prostitution. Neighborhood clean-up interventions can increase public perceptions of safety and can send a message to potential criminal offenders that residents care

about their neighborhood and would be willing to protect it from crime by confronting strangers, intervening in a crime, or calling the police.

(7) Policies should be adopted to foster neighborhood stability. These include resident management of public housing, tenant buy-outs, and low-income housing tax credits. Also, attempts should be made to de-concentrate poverty by eliminating segregated housing projects that have become urban ghettos for the disadvantaged and minorities. Creating scattered site, low-income housing and dispersing concentrated public housing projects are two important steps toward this end.

REFERENCES

ALEC (1995). *What Has Happened to America's Criminal Justice System.* Washington, D.C.: American Legislative Exchange Council.

Baird, Chris (1993). *The "Prisons Pay" Studies: Research or Ideology?* San Francisco: National Council on Crime and Delinquency.

Bastian, Lisa D. (1992). *Crime and the Nation's Households, 1991.* Washington, D.C.: U.S. Department of Justice.

BJS (1988). *Reported Update on Criminal Victimization in the United States.* Washington, D.C.: Bureau of Justice Statistics, U.S. Department of Justice.

——— (1992). *Criminal Victimization in the United States, 1990.* Washington, D.C.: Bureau of Justice Statistics, U.S. Department of Justice.

——— (1994a). *Criminal Victimization in the United States, 1992.* Washington, D.C.: Bureau of Justice Statistics, U.S. Department of Justice.

——— (1994b). *Sourcebook of Criminal Justice Statistics—1993.* Washington, D.C.: Bureau of Justice Statistics, U.S. Department of Justice.

Blau, Judith, and Peter Blau (1982). "The Cost of Inequality: Metropolitan Structure and Violent Crime," *American Sociological Review*, vol. 47, no. 1 (February 1982), pp. 114-129.

Block, Richard (1979). "Community, Environment, and Violent Crime," *Criminology*, vol. 17, no. 1 (May 1979), pp. 46-57.

——— (1992). "Hot Spots and Iso-crimes in Law Enforcement Decision-making." Paper presented at the Convention on

Police and Community Responses to Drugs, University of Illinois at Chicago.

Blumstein, Alfred (1995). "Prisons." In James Q. Wilson and Joan Petersilia, eds., *Crime*. San Francisco: Institute for Contemporary Studies.

Blumstein, Alfred, Jacqueline Cohen, and Daniel Nagin (1978). *Deterrence and Incapacitation*. Report of the National Academy of Sciences Panel on Research on Deterrent and Incapacitative Effects. Washington, D.C.: National Academy Press.

Brenner, Harvey (1976). "Estimating the Social Costs of National Economic Policy." In *Achieving the Goals of the Employment Act of 1946*, vol. 1, paper no. 5. Washington, D.C.: Joint Economic Committee, U.S. Congress (94th Congress, 2nd Session), October 26, 1976.

Buckman, Rebecca (1994). "Critics Say Media Heightens the Public's Fear of Crime," *Indianapolis Star*, August 22, 1994.

Canadian Sentencing Commission (1987). *Sentencing Reform: A Canadian Approach*. Ottawa: Canadian Government Publishing Office.

Clark Foundation (1993). *Americans Behind Bars*. New York: Edna McConnell Clark Foundation.

Currie, Elliott (1985). *Confronting Crime: An American Challenge*. New York: Pantheon.

DiIulio, John J., Steven K. Smith, and Aaron J. Saiger (1995). "The Federal Role in Crime Control." In James Q. Wilson and Joan Petersilia, eds., *Crime*. San Francisco: Institute for Contemporary Studies.

Dorning, Michael (1995). "Lower Murder Rate Small Comfort to America," *Chicago Tribune*, January 17, 1995.

Drug Policy Foundation (1994). "The Crime Bills: Spending Your Money on More of the Same," *Drug Policy Newsletter*, July/August, 1994. Washington, D.C.: Drug Policy Foundation.

Farrington, David P. (1986). "Age and Crime." In Michael Tonry and Norval Morris, eds., *Crime and Justice: An Annual Review of Research*. Chicago: University of Chicago Press.

Friedman, Lawrence M. (1993). *Crime and Punishment in American History*. New York: Basic Books.

Gandossy, Robert P., Jay R. Williams, Jo Cohen, and Henrick J. Harwood (1980). *Drugs and Crime: A Survey and Analysis of the Literature.* Washington, D.C.: National Institute of Justice.

Garbarino, James, Katherine Kostelny, and Nancy Dubrow (1991). *No Place to Be a Child.* Lexington, Mass.: Lexington Books.

Greenberg, Stephanie, William Rohe, and Jay R. Williams (1982). *Safe and Secure Neighborhoods: Physical Characteristics and Informal Territorial Control in High and Low Crime Neighborhoods.* Washington, D.C.: National Institute of Justice.

——— (1985). *Informal Citizen Action and Crime Prevention at the Neighborhood Level: Synthesis and Assessment of the Research.* Washington, D.C.: National Institute of Justice.

Greenwood, Peter W. (1995). "Juvenile Crime and Juvenile Justice." In James Q. Wilson and Joan Petersilia, eds., *Crime.* San Francisco: Institute for Contemporary Studies.

Heitgerd, Janet, and Robert Bursik (1987). "Extra-Community Dynamics and the Ecology of Delinquency," *American Journal of Sociology,* vol. 92, no. 4 (January 1987), pp. 775-787.

Hirschi, Travis, and Michael Gottfredson (1983). "Age and the Explanation of Crime," *American Journal of Sociology,* vol. 89, no. 3 (November 1983), pp. 552-584.

Home Office (1990). *Protecting the Public.* London: H. M. Stationery Office.

Hunter, Albert J. (1978). "Symbols of Incivility: Social Disorder and Fear of Crime in Urban Neighborhoods." Paper presented at the annual meeting of the American Society of Criminology, Dallas, Texas.

ICJIA (1989). *Trends and Issues 1989: Criminal and Juvenile Justice in Illinois.* Chicago: Illinois Criminal Justice Information Authority.

——— (1990). *Trends and Issues 1990: Criminal and Juvenile Justice in Illinois.* Chicago: Illinois Criminal Justice Information Authority.

——— (1991). *Trends and Issues 1991: Education and Criminal Justice in Illinois.* Chicago: Illinois Criminal Justice Information Authority.

——— (1992). "The State of Violent Crime, *The Compiler* (Illinois Criminal Justice Information Authority), Spring 1992, pp. 16-17.

IDOC (1987). *Statistical Presentation of the Illinois Department of Corrections.* Springfield: Illinois Department of Corrections.

_____ (1991). *Statistical Presentation of the Illinois Department of Corrections.* Springfield: Illinois Department of Corrections.

_____ (1994). *Statistical Presentation of the Illinois Department of Corrections.* Springfield: Illinois Department of Corrections.

Irwin, John, and James Austin (1987). *It's About Time: Solving America's Prison Crowding Problem.* San Francisco: National Council on Crime and Delinquency.

Johnson, Bruce D., Mitchell Kaplan, and James Schmeidler (1990). "Days with Drug Distribution: Which Drugs? How Many Transactions? With What Returns?" In Ralph Weisheit, ed., *Drugs, Crime, and the Criminal Justice System.* Cincinnati: Anderson.

Johnson, Bruce D., Terry Williams, Kojo Dei, and Harry Sanabria (1990). "Drug Abuse in the Inner City: Impact on Hard-Drug Users in the Community." In Michael Tonry and James Q. Wilson, eds., *Crime and Justice: A Criminal Review of Research.* Chicago: University of Chicago.

Krauss, Clifford (1994). "No Crystal Ball Needed on Crime," *New York Times,* November 13, 1994.

Lavrakas, Paul J. (1985). "Citizen Self-Help and Neighborhood Crime Prevention Policy." In Lynn A. Curtis, ed., *American Violence and Public Policy.* New Haven, Conn.: Yale University Press.

_____ (1988). *Richard Clark and Associates: A 1988 Survey of Black Americans.* Evanston, Ill.: Northwestern University Survey Laboratory.

Lavrakas, Paul J., and Dennis P. Rosenbaum (1989). *Crime Prevention Beliefs, Policies, and Practices of Chief Law Enforcement Executives: Results of a National Survey.* Evanston, Ill.: Northwestern University Survey Laboratory.

Lewis, Dan A., Jane Grant, and Dennis P. Rosenbaum (1988). *The Social Construction of Reform.* New Brunswick, N.J.: Transaction Books.

Lipton, Douglas, Robert Martinson, and Judith Wilks (1975). *The Effectiveness of Correctional Treatment: A Survey of Treatment Evaluation Studies.* New York: Praeger.

Lurigio, Arthur J., and Robert C. Davis (1992). "Taking the War on Drugs to the Streets: The Perceptual Impact of Four Neighborhood Drug Problems," *Crime and Delinquency,* vol. 38, no. 4 (October 1992), pp. 522-538.

Lynch, James (1995). "Crime in International Perspective." In James Q. Wilson and Joan Petersilia, eds., *Crime*. San Francisco: Institute for Contemporary Studies.

Martin, Andrew, and Paul de la Garza (1995). "City Sets Marks for Gun Murders and Slain Youths," *Chicago Tribune*, January 2, 1995.

McDonald, Scott C. (1987). "Does Gentrification Affect Crime Rates." In Albert Riess and Michael Tonry, eds., *Communities and Crime*. Chicago: University of Chicago Press.

McGahey, Richard (1987). "Economic Conditions, Organization, and Urban Crime." In Albert Reiss and Michael Tonry, eds., *Communities and Crime*. Chicago: University of Chicago Press.

McQueen, Michael (1992). "Political Paradox: People with the Least to Fear from Crime Drive the Crime Issue," *Wall Street Journal*, August 12, 1992.

Messner, Steven T., and Kenneth Tardiff (1986). "Economic Inequality and Levels of Homicide: An Analysis of Urban Neighborhoods," *Criminology*, vol. 24, no. 2 (May 1986), pp. 297-317.

Podolefsky, Aaron, and Fred DuBow (1981). *Strategies for Community Crime Prevention*. Springfield, Ill.: Charles C. Thomas.

President's Commission on Law Enforcement and Administration of Justice (1967). *The Challenge of Crime in a Free Society*. Washington, D.C.: U.S. Government Printing Office.

Recktenwald, William (1992). "922 Homicides Made 1991 Year to Forget," *Chicago Tribune*, January 1, 1992, sec. 1, p. 1.

─────── (1993). "Grim Look at 1993's Homicides," *Chicago Tribune*, December 30, 1993.

Recktenwald, William, and George Papajohn (1994). "Murder No Longer Private Undertaking, Reports Say," *Chicago Tribune*, May 24, 1994.

Reiss, Albert J., Jr. (1987). "Why Are Communities Important in Understanding Crime?" In Albert J. Reiss and Michael Tonry, eds., *Communities and Crime*. Chicago: University of Chicago Press.

Reiss, Albert J., Jr., and Jeffrey A. Roth, eds. (1993). *Understanding and Preventing Violence*. Washington, D.C.: National Academy Press.

Romer, Roy (1993). "Guns in the Hands of Kids," *Vital Speeches of the Day*, November 1993.

Rosenbaum, Dennis P. (1987). "The Theory and Research Behind Neighborhood Watch: Is It a Sound Fear and Crime Reduction Strategy?" *Crime and Delinquency*, vol. 33, no. 1 (January 1987), pp. 103-134.

─────── (1988). "Community Crime Prevention: A Review and Synthesis of the Literature," *Justice Quarterly*, vol. 5, no. 3 (September 1988), pp. 323-395.

Sampson, Robert J. (1985). "Neighborhood and Crime: The Structural Determinants of Personal Victimization," *Journal of Research in Crime and Delinquency*, vol. 22, no. 1 (February 1985), pp. 7-40.

─────── (1987). "Personal Violence by Strangers: An Extension and Test of the Opportunity Model of Predatory Victimization," *Journal of Criminal Law and Criminology*, vol. 78, no. 2 (Summer, 1987), pp. 327-356.

─────── (1995). "The Community." In James Q. Wilson and Joan Petersilia, eds., *Crime*. San Francisco: Institute for Contemporary Studies.

Schmalleger, Frank (1995). *Criminal Justice Today*. Englewood Cliffs, N.J.: Prentice Hall.

Schrag, Clarence (1971). *Crime and Justice: America Style*. Rockville, Md.: Center for Studies of Crime and Delinquency, National Institute of Mental Health.

Shaw, Clifford R., and Henry D. McKay (1931). *Social Factors in Juvenile Delinquency*. Washington, D.C.: U.S. Government Printing Office.

─────── (1942). *Juvenile Delinquency and Urban Areas*. Chicago: University of Chicago Press.

Siegel, Larry J. (1989). *Criminology*. St. Paul, Minn.: West.

Skogan, Wesley G. (1987). "Fear of Crime and Neighborhood Change." In Albert J. Reiss and Michael Tonry, eds., *Communities and Crime*. Chicago: University of Chicago Press.

─────── (1989). "Communities, Crime, and Neighborhood Organization," *Crime and Delinquency*, vol. 35, no. 3 (July 1989), pp. 437-457.

─────── (1990). "Crime in the American States." In Virginia Gray, Herbert Jacob, and Robert Albritton, eds., *Politics in the American States*. Chicago: University of Chicago Press.

Skogan, Wesley G., and Andrew C. Gordon (1982). "Issues in the Recording of Crime: Comments on the Chicago Police Department's Unfounding and Multiple Clearance Audit Report." In *Crime in Illinois*. Springfield: Illinois Department of Law Enforcement.

Smith, Douglas A., and G. Roger Jarjoura (1988). "Social Structure and Criminal Victimization," *Journal of Research in Crime and Delinquency*, vol. 25, no. 1 (February 1988), pp. 27-52.

Standing Committee on Justice and the Solicitor General (1993). *Crime Prevention in Canada: Toward a National Strategy*. Ottawa: Canada Communication Group.

Stark, Rodney (1987). "Deviant Place: A Theory of the Ecology of Crime," *Criminology*, vol. 25, pp. 893-909.

Taylor, Ralph B., and Stephen Gottfredson (1987). "Environmental Design, Crime, and Prevention." In Albert Reiss and Michael Tonry, eds., *Communities and Crime*. Chicago: University of Chicago Press.

Territo, Leonard, James B. Halsted, and Max L. Bromley (1992). *Crime and Justice in America: A Human Perspective*. New York: West.

Tittle, Charles R. (1983). "Social Class and Criminal Behavior: A Critique of the Theoretical Foundation," *Social Forces*, vol. 62, no. 2 (December 1983), pp. 334-358.

Tonry, Michael (1994). "Racial Politics, Racial Disparities, and the War on Crime," *Crime and Delinquency*, vol. 40, no. 4 (October 1994), pp. 475-494.

U.S. Department of Justice (1981). *Attorney General's Task Force on Crime and Violence in America*. Washington, D.C.: U.S. Department of Justice.

Vangeloff, Kenneth (1993). "Full House: Not a Winning Hand," *The Compiler* (Illinois Criminal Justice Information Authority), Winter 1993, pp. 4-5.

Vlasak, Teresa (1989). "A Bad Problem Just Gets Worse," *The Compiler* (Illinois Criminal Justice Information Authority), Summer 1989, pp. 11-13.

Wilson, James Q., and George L. Kelling (1982). "Broken Windows: The Police and Neighborhood Safety," *Atlantic Monthly*, August 1982, pp. 29-38.

Wilson, James Q., and Joan Petersilia (1995). "Introduction." In James Q. Wilson and Joan Petersilia, eds., *Crime*. San Francisco: Institute for Contemporary Studies.

Winters, Paul A., ed. (1995). *Crime and Criminals: Opposing Viewpoints*. San Diego: Greenhaven Press.

Zucchino, David (1994). "Today's Violent Crime Is an Old Story with a New Twist," *Philadelphia Inquirer*, October 30, 1994.

COMMENTS

Carolyn Rebecca Block

As Arthur Lurigio concludes in his detailed overview, "crime is a complicated phenomenon that defies easy solutions." However, a growing body of literature suggests that levels of criminal activity and victimization can be explained, and successful strategies for crime reduction and prevention developed, if we target our efforts in three ways: (1) focus on specific types of offenses that have different characteristics and require different prevention strategies, (2) focus on specific neighborhoods in which the risk of victimization is especially high for a given type of offense, and (3) focus crisis intervention and long-term prevention strategies on the specific groups who are at the highest risk of becoming victims or becoming offenders.

Crime is not random. It occurs disproportionately in some neighborhoods and among certain population groups, and it is concentrated in spurts or peaks at specific points of time. Moreover, the nature of crime often varies radically across these vulnerable neighborhoods, population groups, and high-activity periods. To take street-gang activity as an example, fights over colors or signs are frequent in some gangs, while such symbolic "face maintenance" is relatively rare in street gangs less threatened by competition. One outbreak of lethal street-gang violence may be characterized by an escalating pattern of retribution and revenge, while another spurt may be associated with a drug-business expansion into new territory.

Lurigio's review underscores the common observation that violent crimes and property crimes follow distinct characteristic patterns. They often vary sharply across geographic areas, across time in the same area, and across vulnerable populations. Violent crimes and property crimes also relate differently to descriptive and explanatory variables. Moreover, strongly suggests that violence that begins as interpersonal confrontation (expressive violence) and violence that begins as a predatory attack (instrumental violence) also follow distinctive patterns. In an expressive violent confrontation, violence itself is the assailant's primary goal; although other motives may be present, they are secondary. In contrast, the primary purpose of an act of instrumental violence is not to hurt, injure, or kill, but to acquire money or property. The two poles of the expressive/instrumental continuum respond differently, often in opposite directions, to changes in the social fabric. It is not surprising, then, that research studies that assume crime or violence is monolithic may fail to find significant explanatory patterns or may find conflicting patterns. Statistical anomalies in criminological research may well be the result of comparing a sample, area, or time period that is high in instrumental violence to another that is not.

To understand the "total situation" of crime and to develop successful intervention strategies, we must take into account both time and place. Chicago is a city of neighborhoods, and it has a long and rich history of studies of crime in those neighborhoods, beginning with Shaw and McKay's classic studies of delinquency and continuing with William Julius Wilson's studies of neighborhoods of the "truly disadvantaged" (Shaw and McKay, 1942; Wilson, 1987). While crime is not the major emphasis of Wilson's work, the community areas that he identifies as the most disrupted and impoverished are the same as those having the highest average annual rate of homicide over the 25 years from 1965 to 1989 (Wacquant and Wilson, 1989; Block and Block, 1991). However, the risk of becoming a victim or becoming an offender is not uniform across these neighborhoods. Certain neighborhoods are at very high risk for property versus violent crime, and for specific forms of violence (instrumental vs. expressive), but not at high risk for other types of crime. For example, neighborhoods in which graffiti battles and violent territorial defense between rival street gangs are frequent are not necessarily the same as the neighborhoods in which street-gang-motivated drug offenses are common.

The roles of victim and offender, as well as time and place, in crime cannot be understood in a vacuum but must be seen in light of the total situation. The occurrence of crime requires not only a motivated offender, but also a vulnerable and attractive victim and a situation that provides an opportunity for the offender and does not provide protection for the victim (Felson, 1987). If this total situation is not taken into account, we are in danger of either blaming the victim or placing all responsibility on the offender.

Two other ideas—victim precipitation and subcultural deviance—suffer from the same limited perspective. Both approaches blame the victim. For example, victim precipitation blames the homicide victim for being killed, and subcultural deviance blames some groups of people for being killed more often than other groups. We must avoid the trap of blaming the victim, yet not ignore the empirical evidence that violent acts attract violence and that average levels of violence differ sharply from group to group and from place to place.

If, in an attempt to avoid blaming the victim, we go too far in the other direction, we may fall into an equally dangerous trap: blaming only the "wicked offender." Both "wicked offender" and "blame the victim" viewpoints are simplistic and inaccurate; they may be true in some cases, but they are not true in general. For example, conventional wisdom regarding violence focuses on the unusual case, such as an attack committed by a stranger to gain drugs or money, and ignores the majority of violent attacks, which begin as an argument in which both parties, and often bystanders as well, participate. While instrumental attacks are more rational and involve some choice on the part of the offender, in many expressive confrontations, the person at risk of becoming the offender and the person at risk of becoming the victim are the same person. Routine activities can bring participants together in situations in which the identity of the victim is determined more by chance or happenstance (presence of a weapon, deflection of a blow, availability of medical treatment, presence of others capable of defusing the situation) than by a wicked offender's design.

A myopic belief in the "wicked offender" theory of crime, like blaming the victim, can have serious public policy consequences. In the rush to identify and treat potential offenders or render them harmless, we may ignore other social, situational, or "target-hardening" strategies that would, in the end, prevent more property crime or save more lives.[1] Both blaming the victim and blaming only the wicked offender contain traps for the unwary. To avoid these pitfalls, we need a situational, targeted approach to the explanation of crime patterns and the development of intervention strategies.

---

[1] Target-hardening, usually applied to the avoidance of property crime, can be similarly applied to include strategies to make potential victims of violence less of a target, e.g., the "McGruff" and "Officer Friendly" educational campaigns, the use of the Campbell Danger Assessment (Campbell, 1986), or the "safe home" strategies in use by domestic violence support organizations.

The reduction of violence and other criminal offenses requires two steps: identifying the problem and targeting prevention efforts on that specific problem. Neither of these can be accomplished by the police alone, nor can they be accomplished by any other community agency working alone. To identify the problem, we must identify neighborhoods and population groups that are especially vulnerable to a specific type of crime, using both community and criminal justice information. Then, we must focus crisis intervention and long-term prevention strategies on that specific problem, drawing on the entire spectrum of community and law-enforcement resources.

REFERENCES

Block, Richard, and Carolyn Rebecca Block (1991). "Homicide Syndromes and Vulnerability: Violence in Chicago Community Areas over 25 Years," *Studies on Crime and Crime Prevention: Annual Review*, vol. 1, no. 1 (1991), pp. 81-87.

Campbell, Jacquelyn C. (1986). "Nursing Assessment for Risk of Homicide with Battered Women," *Advances in Nursing Science*, vol. 8, no. 4 (July 1986), pp. 36-51.

Felson, Marcus (1987). "Routine Activity and Crime Prevention in the Developing Metropolis," *Criminology*, vol. 25, no. 4 (November 1987), pp. 911-931.

Shaw, Clifford R., and Henry D. McKay (1942). *Juvenile Delinquency and Urban Areas*. Chicago: University of Chicago Press.

Wacquant, Loïc J. D., and William Julius Wilson (1989). "Poverty, Joblessness, and the Social Transformation of the Inner City." In Phoebe H. Cottingham and David T. Ellwood eds., *Welfare Policy for the 1990s*. Cambridge, Mass.: Harvard University Press.

Wilson, William Julius (1987). *The Truly Disadvantaged: The Inner City, the Underclass, and Public Policy*. Chicago: University of Chicago Press.

COMMENTS

Robert J. Sampson

Arthur Lurigio has performed a great service by bringing together in one chapter a concise overview of crime in the Chicago area and the United States at large. Among other important issues, Lurigio's chapter demonstrates the importance of taking a community-level perspective on crime and violence. As current evidence shows, crime is not randomly distributed among urban communities—it is concentrated in certain areas. Much like researchers in the 1920s found in Chicago, these areas tend to be characterized by poverty, residential instability, family disruption, anonymity and mistrust, and weak surveillance of teenage youth (Sampson and Lauritsen, 1994).

Given these facts, I applaud Lurigio's call for policy solutions from a community-level perspective. As he correctly notes, "get tough" policies have failed us. Indeed, just as demographers were wrong in their prediction that crime would fall in the 1980s as the baby-boom generation turned older, so too it appears that crime-control advocates are wrong in their prediction that the crime problem can be solved by simply locking up more of the population. Recognizing the need for a more comprehensive approach to crime policy, Lurigio argues for a different direction: community crime prevention, mobilization of local residents, social action programs to rebuild communities, and community policing.

Although I might quarrel with the effectiveness of these specific programmatic plans, a community-level perspective on crime does have constructive implications for public policy. The reason is that many of the community-level correlates of crime (e.g., residential instability, concentration of poverty and family disruption, high-density public housing projects, attenuation of social networks) are determined, both directly and indirectly, by the policy decisions of public officials.

Take, for example, municipal code enforcement and local governmental policies toward neighborhood deterioration. In *Making the Second Ghetto*, Hirsch (1983) documents how lax enforcement of city housing codes played a major role in accelerating the deterioration of inner-city Chicago neighborhoods. More recently, Daley and Meislin (1988) have argued that inadequate city policies with regard to code enforcement and repair of city properties led to the systematic decline of New York City's housing stock and, consequently, entire neighborhoods. When considered in conjunction with the practices of redlining and disinvestment by banks and "block-busting" by real estate agents (Skogan, 1986), local policies toward code enforcement have indirectly contributed to crime through neighborhood deterioration, forced migration, and instability.

Even the provision of municipal services such as public health and fire safety—decisions also made with little if any thought to crime and violence—appears to be implicated in the social disintegration of poor communities. As Wallace and Wallace argue, based on an analysis of the "planned shrinkage" of New York City services in recent decades: "The consequences of withdrawing municipal services from poor neighborhoods, the resulting outbreaks of contagious urban decay and forced migration which shred essential social networks and cause social disintegration, have become a highly significant contributor to decline in public health among the poor" (Wallace and Wallace, 1990, p. 427). They go on to describe how the loss of social integration and networks from planned shrinkage increases behavioral patterns of violence that themselves become "convoluted with processes of urban decay likely to further disrupt social networks and cause further social disintegration" (ibid., p. 427). This pattern of destabilizing positive feedback noted by Skogan (1986) appears central to an understanding of the role of governmental policies in fostering the downward spiral of high-crime areas.

Decisions by government on public housing paint a similar picture. Bursik (1989) has shown how the construction of new public housing projects in Chicago in the 1970s increased rates of population turnover, which in turn were related to increases in crime independent of racial composition. More generally, Skogan (1986, p. 206) notes how urban renewal and forced migration contributed to the wholesale uprooting of many urban communities, especially the extent to which freeway networks driven through the hearts of many cities in the 1950s destroyed viable, low-income communities.

Perhaps most disturbing, Wilson (1987) documents the negative consequences of policy decisions to concentrate minorities and the poor in public housing. Opposition from organized community groups to the building of public housing in their neighborhoods and the decision by local governments to neglect the rehabilitation of existing residential units (many of them single-family homes) led to massive, segregated housing projects that have become ghettos for the minorities and disadvantaged. Hence, the social transformation of the inner city, triggered in large part by governmental policy, has resulted in the disproportionate concentration of the most disadvantaged segments of the urban Black population in a few areas. When linked to the effects of concentrated urban poverty and family disruption among Blacks on crime and violence (Sampson and Lauritsen, 1994), governmental housing policies become relevant to crime-control policy.

What thus seem to be "non-crime" policies—for example, where or whether to build a housing project, enforcement of municipal codes, reduction in essential municipal services, rehabilitation of existing residential units, dispersion of the disadvantaged—can have important indirect effects on crime. Namely, many community characteristics implicated in crime—such as residential instability, concentration of poor, female-headed families with children, multi-unit housing projects, and disrupted social networks—appear to stem rather directly from planned governmental policies at local, state, and federal levels.

On the positive side, the implication of this community-level perspective is that there are in fact policy-manipulable options that may help reverse the tide of community social disintegration. Among others that we might add to Lurigio's list are *resident management of public housing* (to increase stability), *tenant buyouts* (to increase homeownership and commitment to locale), *rehabilitation of existing low-income housing* (to preserve area stability, especially single-family homes), *dispersion of public housing* (vs. concentration), and *strict code enforcement* (to fight deterioration). Recent examples suggest that such policies are viable and in fact have stabilizing effects on communities and hence potential for crime reduction.[1]

Although such an approach is currently unpopular, we need to take a renewed look at social policies that focus on *prevention*, as opposed to reactive crime-control approaches that ignore the community context of crime. Community policing is a potential exception because it recognizes the need for formal agents of social control to come together with local residents in promoting community social cohesion. If nothing else, I hope that Lurigio's chapter forces readers to question received wisdom on crime-con-

---

[1] See, e.g., the programs described in Sampson, 1990.

trol policy and focus more directly on similar efforts to achieve community social organization. The additional policy suggestions I have made are by no means complete, but they are consistent with Lurigio's call for merging informal and (non-repressive) formal social control efforts at the community level.

REFERENCES

Bursik, Robert (1989). "Political Decision-Making and Ecological Models of Delinquency: Conflict and Consensus." In Steven F. Messner, Marvin D. Krohn, and Allen E. Liska, eds., *Theoretical Integration in the Study of Deviance and Crime*. Albany: State University of New York Press.

Daley, Suzanne, with Richard J. Meislin (1988). "New York City, the Landlord: A Decade of Housing Decay," *New York Times*, February 8, 1988, p. A1.

Hirsch, Arnold R. (1983). *Making the Second Ghetto: Race and Housing in Chicago, 1940-1960*. Chicago: University of Chicago Press.

Sampson, Robert J. (1990). "The Impact of Housing Policies on Community Social Disorganization and Crime," *Bulletin of the New York Academy of Medicine*, vol. 66, no. 5 (September-October 1990), pp. 526-533.

Sampson, Robert J., and Janet L. Lauritsen (1994). "Violent Victimization and Offending: Individual-, Situational-, and Community-Level Risk Factors." In Albert J. Reiss, Jr., and Jeffrey A. Roth, eds., *Understanding and Preventing Violence, Vol. 3: Social Influences*. Washington, D.C.: National Academy Press.

Skogan, Wesley (1986). "Fear of Crime and Neighborhood Change." In Albert J. Reiss, Jr., and Michael Tonry, eds., *Communities and Crime*. Chicago: University of Chicago Press.

Wallace, Rodrick, and Deborah Wallace (1990). "Origins of Public Health Collapse in New York City: The Dynamics of Planned Shrinkage, Contagious Urban Decay, and Social Disintegration, *Bulletin of the New York Academy of Medicine*, vol. 66, no. 5 (September-October 1990), pp. 391-444.

Wilson, William Julius (1987). *The Truly Disadvantaged: The Inner City, the Underclass, and Public Policy*. Chicago: University of Chicago Press.

COMMUNITY-BASED CRIME PREVENTION: CITIZENS, COMMUNITY ORGANIZATIONS, AND THE POLICE

Paul J. Lavrakas

On July 21, 1992, as the lead-in to the major in-depth story of that night's *CBS Evening News,* Dan Rather announced: "It's the job of the police to protect us from crime and to make us safe in our neighborhoods." Had this pronouncement been advanced 25 years ago, few might have questioned its validity. But since the enactment of the Omnibus Crime Control and Safe Streets Act of 1968, several billion dollars have been spent on crime prevention programming, research, and evaluations in order to expand our concept of how public safety from crime is attained and maintained. Unfortunately, Mr. Rather, his writers, and producers—along with many other journalists—appear not to have kept abreast of major policy developments in the fight against crime. That this out-dated perspective—one of holding the police primarily or even exclusively responsible for achieving public safety—is still held by so many in the 1990s is somewhat discouraging to someone who has been writing about a "new view" of crime prevention and policing since the 1970s.

HISTORICAL PERSPECTIVE

Yet, this "new view" is not really new at all. Instead, it represents an adaptation of the ancient approach to public and private safety updated for the socio-political context and problems faced by many developed nations in the late 20th century.

As human societies developed, it was implicit in the behavior of most individuals that *they* were at least partially, if not primarily, responsible for their own safe daily existence and for that of their families and communities. The checkered history of White settlers in our own American West, less than 100 years ago, is one of individual responsibility for private and public safety, including a tradition of vigilante "justice" (see Brown,

1978). Let it not be thought that this tradition of citizens contributing to their own safety has been without problems and abuses; but, as will be discussed later in this chapter, the fact that citizen participation in the "co-production" of individual, household, and community safety has not always led to positive outcomes does not diminish its tremendous potential for positive benefits (see Clotfelter, 1977; Percy, 1979).

As societies evolved toward more advanced stages (i.e., they became more politically and economically developed), formal mechanisms for addressing issues of safety were instituted and, eventually, politicized (see Jacob and Lineberry, 1982; Kelling and Moore, 1988). As police and other law enforcement officials were empowered with responsibilities for "keeping the peace," the notion that citizens *qua* citizens could and should play a central and explicit role in contributing to public and private safety appears to have been forgotten or ignored (Lavrakas, 1985). Although a definitive historical analysis does not exist, a plausible explanation for this development is that the magnitude of problems that threatened individual and community safety was small enough that law enforcement personnel could handle them well enough to meet the expectations of governments (i.e., politicians) and a majority of the citizenry—at least until the 1960s in the United States. Concerns about uncontrolled vigilante action may have contributed to this increased and willing dependency on the police. This led to a climate in which the identification and promotion of a proper role for citizens and social institutions (e.g., schools and churches) in society's responses to crime was largely ignored. As this occurred, many citizens apparently came to believe that they had no direct role in contributing to individual, household, or community safety, other than paying taxes to maintain their local police departments. In fact, for many years, the police and politicians told voters that this was the way things worked (see Lavrakas, 1985).

Unfortunately, the magnitude of our crime problems became so large that the mechanisms that many had assumed responsible for crime prevention were shown to be wholly inadequate to the task. To make this observation is not to question the almost exclusive responsibility of the police to react to instances of unlawfulness, to restore the peace, and to support the criminal justice system through investigations and arrests. But many politicians, policymakers, criminologists, and others appear not to recognize the critical distinction between *reacting to crimes* and *preventing crime*.

It has been my position for more than a decade that the police should *not* be viewed as the primary mechanism through which crime can be *prevented,* although they should play a central role (see Lavrakas, 1985). This follows, in part, from my assumption that as a free society, we are—and, one hopes, will be able to remain—*unwilling* to hire so many police officers as to saturate our public and private areas to stop all or even most instances of criminality from occurring. If we do not want to live in a highly militarized and restricted society that relies on its police to "prevent" crime, then very significant changes must occur in how our leaders and citizens think about *crime prevention.*

Many are to blame for the situation that presently exists in this and other developed countries, including the police, politicians, and the public. The police did not perceive and/or acknowledge soon enough their limitations in the struggle to prevent crime. To this day, too many rank-and-file police personnel are ignorant about how crime is likely to be prevented, even though many of these same individuals tout themselves as "crime prevention experts" (especially when they moonlight or after they retire and seek employment in the private security field). On the other hand, a majority of police chiefs and sheriffs appear to have begun to "see the light" by acknowledging the need for collaboration with a host of other agencies and institutions outside their departments to marshal a viable comprehensive local crime prevention effort (see Lavrakas and Rosenbaum, 1989).

Politicians and government bureaucrats, even more than the police, must assume blame for the poor state of affairs in which we find our nation *vis-à-vis* crime. Too often they have relied exclusively on an unquestioned maintenance of the status quo in responding to crime problems, which has mostly meant increasing resources for the police and other criminal justice system institutions (see Jacob and Lineberry, 1982). As unfortunate and foolish as it is, we have allowed too many politicians to claim that their policies have reduced crime when, for example, even a small drop in reported crime occurred during their time in office. It is unclear whether it is more tragic that the public has sanctioned this unjustified political rhetoric or that so many politicians have been willing to make these unfounded claims.

Given this assessment of our nation's policy toward crime prevention in last half of this century, I believe what is needed is a radical departure from the "business as usual approach" of placing the burden of responsibility and expectation on our police to *prevent* crime.

To begin reasoned deliberations about what is needed one should have a framework to conceptualize what "prevention of crime" and "crime prevention" really mean. Many major community-based crime prevention initiatives have been planned in the absence of such a guiding framework, which in turn has been partially responsible for their relative lack of success.

THEORETICAL FRAMEWORK FOR COMMUNITY-BASED CRIME PREVENTION

Steven Lab noted that prior to his own textbook, *Crime Prevention: Approaches, Practices, and Evaluations*, first published in 1988, no scholarly treatise had been devoted exclusively to the topic of crime prevention (Lab, 1992). Granted there were some books entitled "crime prevention" (e.g., Washnis, 1976), but these were limited mostly to what the police did to react to crime and encourage citizens to secure their homes. Thus, despite what many may assume, there has not been a long history of critical thinking about what "preventing crime" really means.

Lavrakas and Bennett (1988) described a theoretical framework for guiding the implementation of citizen and community anti-crime measures. This framework consisted of a hierarchy similar to the public health model of prevention, which differentiated among primary, secondary, and tertiary levels of preventive action. Although Lab (1992) and Brantingham and Faust (1976) advanced a "conceptual model of crime prevention" with similarly labeled levels, the substance of their model was quite different from the Lavrakas and Bennett framework, which follows.

Primary Prevention: Addressing the "Root Causes" of Crime

Primary crime prevention is *proactive and preventive in the most basic sense,* in that it encompasses strategies that occur prior to anyone even contemplating the commission of a crime. Primary prevention includes *all efforts that strive to keep individuals from developing into criminal offenders.* It aims at many of the "root causes" of crime, such as poverty, lack of education, discrimination, hatred, the need for immediate gratification, and anomie (see Silberman, 1978; Currie, 1985; Wilson and Herrnstein, 1985).

Examples of primary crime prevention include efforts to raise the educational level of all members of society so as to make them qualified for non-criminal employment. Job-training programs, in particular ones targeted at raising the marketable skill levels of members of the underclass, should be regarded as primary crime prevention (see Curtis, 1988). Companion to these efforts are programs that strive to provide equal opportunities for employment to all qualified individuals. In this vein, affirmative action programs meant to redress past hiring inequities are a form of primary crime prevention to the extent that they succeed in developing positive social behaviors in program participants.

Beyond government-sponsored programs, but no less important, are the myriad efforts of other institutions. Religious denominations strive to impart and nurture prosocial moral values to their members and the society at large. Schools offer education and recreation programs to turn children away from crime. Health care professionals provide services that promote the physical and mental well-being of the populace. A multitude of voluntary service organizations try to help those who are unable, at least temporarily, to help themselves lead better lives.

Primary crime prevention is the most important level at which the war on crime and drugs must be fought. Unfortunately, American politicians and other decision-makers have not provided the necessary vision to move the country in this needed direction. To date there has been no truly comprehensive and coordinated effort to marshal a primary-level crime prevention campaign in which the police, although very important, are one of the players in a large cast of characters.

In terms of motivations for the public to participate in primary crime prevention measures, past research has found that fear of crime and/or past experiences with criminal victimization do not serve as effective motivators (Lavrakas and Bennett, 1988; Lavrakas and Herz, 1982; Lavrakas et al., 1980). Rather, it is *public-minded* motives, such as a sense of civic duty, compassion, altruism, and/or "parenting" beyond one's own immediate family, that explain why many citizens voluntarily choose to get involved.

Secondary Prevention: Reducing Opportunities for Victimization

Crime prevention at a secondary level refers to *proactive measures that prevent specific instances of, or opportunities for, potential threat from developing into instances of actual criminal victimization.* Secondary crime prevention measures are important as they are based on the realistic premises that the potential for crime is ever present and measures can and should be taken to strengthen the "resistance" of individuals and property from being victimized. Secondary crime prevention measures strive to minimize the likelihood that specific criminal acts will be initiated at a particular time and in a particular place.

It should be noted that a valid criticism of all secondary-level measures is that they may merely "displace" crime from one time or place to another (see Maltz, 1972). Unlike primary crime prevention measures, secondary-level measures do not attack the forces and motives that lead individuals to commit crimes except in the crudest sense by "reducing opportunities" for crime. (It is in this latter context that secondary crime prevention measures include all those that have been labeled *opportunity-reduction* strategies.) It is assumed that if the risk of apprehension and punishment is great enough, would-be offenders will be deterred from committing specific crimes. To the extent that there are few low-risk opportunities for crime, it is theorized that potential criminals will be diverted away from crime and toward activities that enhance society, and it is in this sense that some regard opportunity reduction as primary crime prevention (see Lab, 1992).

Examples of secondary crime prevention abound: When individuals voluntarily restrict their behavior, such as staying in their homes at night rather than going out to shop, they are eliminating the chance that they will be present in the outdoor neighborhood environment and "available" to fall victim to robbery or assault. This is secondary-level crime prevention because it is proactive and intended to minimize the likelihood that an individual will become a crime victim.

When residents "target-harden" their homes through the use of locks, security systems, and such, they are engaging in secondary crime prevention. By creating physical barriers to would-be offenders, target-hardening strategies aim to increase the effort and risk involved in the commission of a crime and thereby deter the would-be offender away from a specific target. Increasing the amount and intensity of outdoor lighting also is meant to reduce the perceived opportunity for committing an easy crime in as much as it increases the chances of being observed by someone who might call the police. The use of timers and indoor lighting to give the appearance of home occupancy is thought to create a psychological barrier to the would-be burglar who does not want to confront a resident.

Organized community-level strategies such as Neighborhood Watch and citizen patrols are also forms of secondary crime prevention. Here, the intent is to increase the level of surveillance performed by law-abiding citizens to discourage offenders from finding easily victimized targets. These strategies are also thought to signal a higher degree of social control on the part of residents, which is presumed to further deter would-be offenders.

It is important to note that secondary crime prevention efforts are what many law enforcement personnel have regarded as measures that define crime prevention. The police often have been given free reign to act as our crime prevention experts, even though few have been very thoughtful about what *prevention* means. At the same time, our nation's leaders have not put forth a truly comprehensive crime prevention and reduction plan in which the police are given an important but not exclusive role. Thus, it is not surprising that the police have chosen to define "crime prevention" within rather narrow limits of those responses in which they have had direct involvement. Secondary crime prevention measures are likely to be an important part of any comprehensive crime prevention plan. However, a frequent mistake has been to limit community-based crime prevention programs to measures that attack crime only on a secondary level (see Currie, 1985; Curtis, 1985; Lavrakas, 1985).

Regarding motives for citizen participation in secondary crime prevention, many do so for *private-minded* reasons. For example, deploying target-hardening measures at home is highly related to homeownership and the urge to protect one's "castle" (Lavrakas, 1981). On the other hand, citizen participation in some secondary crime prevention measures, such as those that are deployed throughout a neighborhood (e.g., patrols, informal watches, and such), are motivated by both private-minded and public-minded reasons (e.g., altruism).

Tertiary Prevention: Reducing the Severity of Victimization

There are other responses to crime that are *purely reactive* in that they strive to minimize the severity of loss when specific crimes are threatened or initiated. (An example in the public health field of tertiary prevention would be surgery, radiation, or chemotherapy for a cancer victim *after* the disease is manifest.) Tertiary crime prevention measures include self-protection strategies such as martial arts training or carrying a weapon. These measures typically do not manifest themselves until after the onset of threat—nowadays people do not carry handguns in plain sight to signal potential offenders that they are well armed. Such tertiary measures are preventive only in the sense that they may reduce severity of harm to the potential victim (although, in some cases, victims are harmed when their own weapons are turned against them).

Whistle-STOP, a community anti-crime program developed in Chicago in the 1970s, is a tertiary-level prevention effort. Carrying a high-pitched whistle to blow if one is threatened, or if one witnesses someone being victimized, does nothing to reduce the likelihood of a specific criminal victimization attempt but may "prevent" the offender from succeeding. Personal injury and personal property insurance serve the purpose of "loss reduction." That is, insurance is preventive at a tertiary level because, at best, it reduces the severity of financial loss to criminal victimization.

Motivations for citizens to take tertiary crime prevention measures are entirely self-serving and, thus, private-minded. As they do not lessen the likelihood that an individual will be motivated to attempt a crime (either at a primary or secondary level), they do not reduce the prevalence of crime in a community and are not linked to public-minded motivations.

Policy Implications

Table 1 presents a summary of the levels of prevention and the realms—individual, household, community/neighborhood, and societal—within which they might operate. Anyone developing a comprehensive crime prevention program must rely heavily on the potential impact that law-abiding citizens can have on the amount of crime that exists in a given area. Otherwise, a program would require far too many tax dollars to develop the political support necessary to see its approval and implementation. In American society, the resources that must be mustered to make meaningful headway in the war on crime and drugs are so massive that the only hope is to tap the volunteer potential of the citizenry. This amount of untapped resources will dwarf the amount of tax dollars that our governing bodies can provide (see Lavrakas, 1989).

To improve the chances of increasing citizen participation in crime prevention, a comprehensive plan must take into account the levels of crime prevention and the varied motives that lead citizens to become (and stay) involved. The discussion that has been presented in this section is meant to acquaint the policy-oriented reader with the complexities that must be considered.

TABLE 1: Levels of Crime Prevention and Operational Realms

PRIMARY CRIME PREVENTION: Addressing the causes of crime (Root-Causes Strategies)

Purpose: Strengthening non-criminal values, motivations, and opportunities within society

Individual:	Informal one-on-one assistance to needy individuals Good parenting
Household:	Tax-deductible donations to social service organizations
Neighborhood:	Local school and church programs to divert youth from crime
Societal:	Government-funded job-training and job-placement programs Media campaigns to promote prosocial values Equal opportunity legislation

SECONDARY CRIME PREVENTION: Reducing opportunities for committing crimes (Opportunity-Reduction Strategies)

Purpose: Minimize the likelihood that specific criminal acts will be initiated

Individual:	Self-imposed behavioral restrictions to avoid personal victimization (Risk-Avoidance)
Household:	Target-hardening of homes with locks, bars, alarms, lights, dogs, etc.
Neighborhood:	Increase surveillance of public and private space via organized programs such as Neighborhood Watch or civilian patrols
Societal:	Increase police presence on street Close down drug houses Increase likelihood and severity of punishment for convicted offenders Media campaigns to promote citizen participation in Neighborhood Watch

TABLE 1 (continued)

TERTIARY CRIME PREVENTION: Reduce severity of loss/harm for specific victimization attempts (Loss-Reduction Strategies)

Purpose: Minimize the severity of damage when a specific criminal act is threatened or initiated

Individual:	Carry concealed weapon in public Self-defense training
Household:	Purchase personal property insurance Keep weapon in home
Neighborhood:	Organized neighborhood Whistle-STOP program
Societal:	Government-sponsored low-cost home insurance NRA advertising campaign to promote responsible gun ownership

COMMUNITY-BASED CRIME PREVENTION PROGRAMMING

Many community-based crime prevention programs have been initiated since the mid-1970s—a time when the U.S. Department of Justice's Law Enforcement Assistance Administration (LEAA) was at the high watermark of its annual budget, spending approximately $1 billion a year. In establishing LEAA, in the Omnibus Crime Control and Safe Streets Act of 1968, Congress stated that "crime is essentially a local problem that must be dealt with by state and local governments if it is to be controlled effectively." The legislation went on to specify that funds should be spent at the local level to encourage the participation of the citizenry in crime prevention within the neighborhoods.

In the past two decades, federal, state, and local funding has been provided to a wide range of community-based anti-crime efforts. Unfortunately, these programs too often have not been adequately planned and/or implemented (see Lavrakas, 1985; Lavrakas and Bennett, 1988), nor have they often been fully or even adequately evaluated (see Rosenbaum, 1986; 1988b). Thus, it is not surprising that there have been relatively few meaningful documented impacts associated with the billions of dollars in public- and private-sector funding received by community-based crime prevention programs.

A common theme in almost all of these major anti-crime initiatives has been the important role that community organizations and local institutions are hypothesized as playing in helping to conceptualize and implement local crime prevention efforts, in part, through their ability to mobilize the "voluntary potential" of the local citizenry. Ideally, the local police and indigenous community organizations should be the two central players, along with other public- and private-sector agencies and institutions, in mobilizing and sustaining comprehensive efforts to *prevent* crime at the local level (see Lavrakas, 1985). For the policymaker considering the planning and implementation of a comprehensive crime prevention effort within a municipality or other geo-political region, it is instructive to review the programmatic history of the field in its nearly 20 years of existence.

Crime Prevention Through Environmental Design (CPTED)

Stemming from the writings of Jacobs (1961), Angel (1969), Newman (1972), and Jeffrey (1976), LEAA placed a high priority on exploring the "defensible space" theory of preventing crime through modifications of the physical environment. Millions of dollars were invested in four demonstration sites: residential areas in Minneapolis and Hartford; a commercial area in Portland, Oregon; and a school system in Broward County, Florida.

The CPTED process was hypothesized to prevent crime by creating three "forces" thought to inhibit the opportunity perceived by criminals for successfully committing a crime (Tien, Reppetto, and Hanes, 1976; Kaplan et al., 1978). In this sense, CPTED is secondary crime prevention along the lines discussed earlier in this chapter. Design changes that created *access control*, such as redirecting traffic flow with one-way streets and cul-de-sacs, were thought to encourage the use of public spaces by "legitimate" citizens and discourage potential criminal offenders from entering the spaces. Changes to the environment that promoted *natural surveillance,* such as increasing the number and intensity of city street lights, were reasoned to discourage offenders by increasing the risk that they would be seen and reported to the police and, also, to provide the non-criminal public with a heightened sense of security and confidence when out and about in public spaces. Finally, changes that represented *activity support,* such as public benches and picnic tables along well-landscaped attractive city sidewalks, were thought to increase the sheer number of legitimate users of the environment, thereby discouraging potential offenders and trouble-makers from engaging in "unseemly" and/or criminal behavior (see Wilson, 1976).

As is the case with many of community-based anti-crime programs, the CPTED demonstrations were not easily implemented. In fact, the Minneapolis residential site and the Broward County school site were basically program failures, in that few of the planned changes to the respective environments occurred within the multi-year time frame of the programs.

In the Portland commercial site, the mayor's office and many local agencies worked together during an eight-year period (1974-81) to secure federal and other funds to bring about a number of changes in the physical environment along a three-mile commercial/residential strip (Lavrakas, Normoyle, and Wagener, 1978; Kushmuk and Whittemore, 1981). These changes were associated with the redesign of major thoroughfares (e.g., increased lighting, new pavement and sidewalks, new see-through bus shelters) and a coordinated program between the police and a local business organization to significantly increase target-hardening at commercial establishments. The evaluations of this demonstration concluded that two of the three ultimate goals of the program were achieved: there was a modest decrease in commercial crime and a modest increase in the economic health of the local business community, whereas fear of crime remained basically unchanged (Lavrakas and Kushmuk, 1986).

More impressive were the successes experienced in the Hartford residential site (Fowler and Mangione, 1986). In 1973, an interdisciplinary group of experts began to assess the crime problems in the Hartford target neighborhood. The outcome of this intensive planning process was an integrated attack on crime that included: (1) modifying the physical environment (e.g., radically changing traffic flow within the area); (2) changes in the delivery of police services (e.g., creation of a decentralized team of officers permanently assigned to the area); and (3) efforts to organize residents to improve their own neighborhood (e.g., creation of a police advisory committee to discuss local problems and priorities). During the six-year study of the evolving program (1973-79), it was determined that informal social control increased appreciably, burglary and robbery rates decreased relative to the rest of the city, and fear of crime and concern about crime also decreased compared to the rest of Hartford.

A major lesson of the Hartford and Portland CPTED demonstration programs is that a very considerable amount of time, effort, and funding is required to mount a multi-agency comprehensive crime prevention campaign that is likely to do some good. Also of note was the careful planning that was done *prior* to any program implementation in both programs. In both cities, the police and citizens, through their participation in community organizations, worked together to accomplish with the aid of many other local agencies what none could have hoped to achieve on its own.

Community Anti-Crime Programming (CACP)

The Crime Control Act of 1976 mandated federal funds for the creation of the Office of Community Anti-Crime Programs to oversee the distribution of $30 million for the "development and operation of programs designed to reduce and prevent crime" and for "crime prevention programs in which members of the community participate . . . including but not limited to 'blockwatch' and similar programs." Priority was to be given to "public-minded" initiatives intended to produce collective responses at the neighborhood level, rather than "private-minded" ones that do not result in neighborhood organizing efforts. Of note, this was the first time that the federal government provided funding *directly* to community organizations to fight crime rather than channeling the monies through state or local government criminal justice agencies.

Although admirable in its intent, CACP was a bureaucratic and political failure (Lewis, 1979; McPherson and Silloway, 1981). The crucial lesson learned from this *program* failure was the importance of providing adequate technical assistance, rather than simply providing money, to community organizations. Furthermore, to be successful, the technical assistance needed to be provided in a way that gave the local organizations the information needed to make their own decisions about how best to combat crime in their neighborhoods, while allowing them to remain in control of their destiny, instead of imposing a "top-down" fix (see Lavrakas and Bennett, 1988).

Beat-Rep Program in Chicago

In 1977, a grassroots-spawned, community-based, neighborhood surveillance program, "Beat-Rep," which operated in a few of Chicago's police districts, was selected to receive federal funding in order to implement it throughout the city. The program was devised by citizens and their local beat officers to increase the extent to which the citizenry served as the "eyes and ears" of the police. Each police beat had a volunteer civilian beat captain who was responsible to see that each block within the beat had a block captain. Block captains were, in turn, responsible for organizing the citizenry on their blocks. This cadre of citizens was supposed to provide information to their local patrol officers about suspicious or criminal activity in their neighborhoods.

The loosely knit Beat-Rep groups that operated before LEAA funds were given to the Chicago Police Department may have contributed to the prevention of crime in their neighborhoods, but no documentation was available. However, after the federal aid started flowing, the program became overly politicized and bureaucratized, which resulted in a potentially good idea being "doomed by success." Although a local consulting firm evaluated the effort, no meaningful impact was ever demonstrated.

Anti-Crime Initiatives in Public Housing

Created by the Public Housing Security Demonstration Act of 1978, the Urban Initiatives Anti-Crime Demonstration channeled federal funds directly to 39 public housing authorities ostensibly to fund a variety of local crime prevention initiatives that were to include CPTED-type physical design changes, the involvement and organization of residents, provision of employment opportunities to high-risk youth, and leveraging other public and private funds.

Another division of the Department of Housing and Urban Development (HUD) commissioned the Police Foundation to conduct an evaluation of the program. The study concluded that as a result of various bureaucratic and political problems within HUD (during the last year of the Carter administration), the program never received the amount and/or quality of support required for success. In particular, "the provision of technical assistance to local housing authorities was almost universally inadequate; as a result, programs had to depend upon existing local technical assistance or, in many cases, had to risk implementation without any assistance at all" (Pate et al., 1984). In sum, the evaluators concluded that the program, "by diffusing its attention over a large number of projects, many of which were not experiencing serious problems, and by being incapacitated by management problems, was unable to provide concentrated effective assistance to those projects which most needed it. As a result, few local programs were effective, leading to virtually no measurable impact" (Pate et al., 1984).

Urban Crime Prevention Program

By the early 1980s, the only community anti-crime demonstration program the federal government was sponsoring was the Urban Crime Prevention Program (UCPP), which was a joint ACTION/LEAA initiative started earlier in the Carter administration and was based on a premise similar to the Community Anti-Crime Program—that it was good public policy to provide *direct* funding to community organizations to help plan and implement their own anti-crime strategies in order to "reclaim their neighborhoods" from deterioration and crime (ACTION and LEAA, 1980). The goal of UCPP was significant in that it aimed to stimulate "greater involvement by neighborhood organizations in community crime prevention activities [with] the intent to focus on the social and economic factors directly associated with criminal activity." The UCPP was charged with "[forging] a working partnership among neighborhood groups, criminal justice agencies, and other public/private sector institutions" in ways that were "interrelated rather than separable, and reinforcing rather than conflicting" (ACTION and LEAA, 1980).

Eighty-five community-based programs received $4.5 million in funding to promote crime prevention in their neighborhoods. Unlike other federally funded programs of the time, the grant-recipient organizations received very modest funding—all less than $50,000—to encourage them to develop financial self-sufficiency. As discussed later in this section, one of the UCPP grantees was a Chicago-based group, Citizens Information Service (CIS), which later evolved into Chicago Alliance for Neighborhood Safety (CANS) after help from Ford Foundation funding (see Rosenbaum, Lewis, and Grant, 1985).

The UCPP again demonstrated the overriding importance of providing community organizations with sufficient technical assistance to "help them help themselves" (Cook, 1982). Roehl and Cook (1984), in evaluating UCPP *process,* concluded that the complexity of the crime problem required that planned solutions involve very complicated ameliorative processes. From this perspective, it is likely that nearly all neighborhood groups are ill equipped to take the lead in marshaling an effective strategy to prevent, and thereby reduce, their local crime problems, especially in low-income and deteriorated (i.e., high-crime inner-city) neighborhoods.

Neighborhood Watch

Neighborhood Watch (NW) has been described as "one of the most popular community crime prevention programs in the United States . . . [with] the typical Neighborhood Watch model [having] been accepted and implemented in hundreds of communities across the nation" (Garofalo and McLeod, 1989, p. 326). This program is primarily intended to increase surveillance by residents over the public and private spaces in their neighborhoods. The NW concept is similar to what evolved in Chicago as the Beat-Rep program. Unlike CPTED theory, which advocates changes in the physical environment to enhance "natural surveillance," NW sets about to explicitly organize neighbors to engage in more formalized watching—what Rosenbaum (1987) refers to as *intentional surveillance*—primarily as individuals but also in groups (e.g., civilian patrolling), so as to detect suspicious and/or criminal behavior. (Some critics of NW have suggested that this amounts to no more than neighbors "snooping" on neighbors.) In almost all cases, NW is introduced—"implanted" in Rosenbaum's (1987) terminology—by the local police or sheriff's department, which oftentimes uses it as their flagship community-based crime prevention strategy. In the terms of the crime prevention framework discussed earlier, NW represents secondary crime prevention in the sense that it is *proactive* in advocating constant attention to possible trouble. It also represents tertiary crime prevention in that it is *reactive* in encouraging residents to contact the local law enforcement agency once trouble is spotted.

A national assessment of NW for the National Institute of Justice concluded:

> NW has shown some success in reducing certain kinds of crime, particularly residential burglaries and thefts of property from the immediate vicinity of households. However, the re-

ductions appear to be modest . . . [with] frequent claims of spectacular results . . . based on methodologically weak evidence (see Lurigio and Rosenbaum, 1986). Furthermore, we developed skepticism about the potential for NW having a *sustained* impact on crime because of . . . the difficulties of maintaining involvement and activity in NW programs (Garofalo and McLeod, 1989, p. 335).

Despite these realistic reservations about the NW concept, the evaluators correctly note that the program often has been deployed as "a useful vehicle for the implementation of a variety of other crime prevention . . . activities." An added benefit from NW is its potential to improve police and community relations, if it is implemented wisely.

Others have not been as sanguine about the NW concept. Henig (1984) questioned whether NW might not be used as a guise by middle-class Whites, as part of a neighborhood gentrification process, to keep out "undesirables" (e.g., Blacks and the poor) who have legitimate reasons to be there. Even more compelling is Rosenbaum's extensive critique of the unfounded assumptions implicit in NW's theoretical framework (Rosenbaum, 1988a). In particular, Rosenbaum questioned the assumption that NW meetings of residents will naturally and routinely lead to positive outcomes. For example, there was evidence that such meetings among organized groups of neighbors may exacerbate, rather than reduce, fear of crime and feelings of helplessness against crime (Rosenbaum, Lewis, and Grant, 1985).

Citizens Information Service of Chicago

As noted above, Chicago was a city in which community organizations had received UCPP funding. Following LEAA/ACTION involvement, the Ford Foundation continued to fund nine community organizations associated with Citizens Information Service (CIS). The anti-crime programs of four of these organizations (Northwest Neighborhood Federation, Northeast Austin Organization, Back of the Yards Neighborhood Council, and Edgewater Community Council) were rigorously evaluated with Ford funding (Rosenbaum, Lewis, and Grant, 1985; Rosenbaum, 1986).

Each community organization tried to "organize residents of selected neighborhoods through door-to-door contacts, block meetings, neighborhood meetings, the distribution of educational materials, and related strategies. [Each organization was encouraged to] adopt the block watch [i.e., Neighborhood Watch] model, but the extent to which this strategy was adopted varied considerably across the groups" (Rosenbaum, 1986, p. 110).

Among the most important conclusions of the evaluation were that (1) the organizations were quite successful in making residents aware of opportunities to become involved in the program and, to a lesser extent, in increasing participation levels among residents; (2) no consistent pattern of changes in residents' own crime prevention behaviors was associated with the programs; (3) the programs did not increase social integration in the target neighborhoods; (4) a highly unexpected pattern of increases in personal fear of crime and perceptions of the amount of crime was found; and (5) a similarly unexpected decrease in optimism about one's neighborhood and commitment to remain in the neighborhood was found (Rosenbaum, 1986). In sum, the general NW model that was implemented as part of the continuing CIS community-based anti-crime program successfully attained only a few of its objectives and unexpectedly may have contributed to a worsening of some aspects of residential life in the target neighborhoods.

Crime Stoppers

In the early 1980s, an integrated anti-crime program that innovatively combined the resources of the police, the local news media, and the local business community rapidly expanded in cities and towns throughout the United States, Canada, Britain, and elsewhere (MacAleese and Tily, 1983). The primary purpose of the program was to encourage the citizenry to provide information to the police to help solve especially difficult felony crimes. To implement Crime Stoppers, local private-sector funds are raised to establish a reward pool to pay for "tips" from anonymous informants that lead to convictions (see Bickman et al., 1976). At least one local news media organization must cooperate with the local law enforcement agency to publicize a "crime of the week" for which information is being sought. With television, the crime often is reenacted to dramatize the details of the crime to both increase its appeal to the public and, possibly, aid recall. (This aspect of some programs has been rightly criticized for being overly sensationalistic and adding to citizens' unrealistic fear of crime.)

A national evaluation of Crime Stoppers concluded: "Despite some impressive [police] statistics on felony arrests, convictions, and recovery of property and drugs, the impact of [the program] on community crime levels remains unknown. Furthermore, Crime Stoppers has been criticized by journalists, civil libertarians, and members of the legal profession for offering cash rewards and anonymity to encourage more citizen participation in the criminal justice system" (Rosenbaum, Lurigio, and Lavrakas, 1989, p. 401). Apart from this assessment of its direct effects, Crime Stoppers appears to have the potential for a positive impact on citizens' proclivities to engage in crime prevention, similar to that of the McGruff campaign, by creating favorable public relations (i.e., further legitimizing) for the general concept of citizen participation in crime prevention.

Neighborhood Anti-Crime Self-Help Program

In 1982, the Milton Eisenhower Foundation developed and implemented a self-help anti-crime program in which modest funding (approximately $50,000) was provided to each of ten community organizations in high-crime inner-city neighborhoods to "seed" a long-term "bubble-up" attack on crime and other local problems (Curtis, 1985; Lavrakas and Bennett, 1988; Bennett and Lavrakas, 1989). With several procedural similarities to the federally funded UCPP demonstration, Eisenhower's neighborhood program relied heavily on building non-federal local funding partnerships to support each local demonstration. Extensive technical assistance was provided to the groups—Eisenhower allocated 20 percent of its central program budget for technical assistance—in addition to original data gathered as part of a community needs-assessment study, specifically for use in the planning process. (In fact, unlike any other of the major anti-crime initiatives, local residents were employed and trained to aid these information-gathering activities.) At each site, a local advisory council was established, consisting of the administrators of the local community organization, other key leaders in the community, residents, and representatives from other agencies (e.g., the local police) that were part of the partnership that was formed to reduce crime and improve the quality of life in the neighborhood.

Another significant feature of the program was its two-pronged advocacy for preventing crime, whereby each local group was encouraged (*but not required*) to devise strategic plans that included both primary (root-causes) and secondary (opportunity-reduction) crime prevention initiatives. On average, the demonstration in each site lasted approximately 30 months.

The three-year process and impact evaluation concluded that almost all of the participating site organizations "planned a [community-based] crime prevention program *tailored to their communities,* implemented diverse and numerous strategies during the grant period, generated a moderate level of [citizen] participation, and raised [at least one more] year of funding" (Bennett and Lavrakas, 1989, p. 360). Compared with the experience of other community anti-crime initiatives in "resource-poor" inner-city neighborhoods (see Lavrakas et al., 1980), the Eisenhower neighborhood program generated a relatively high level of citizen participation: more than one-fifth of target-area residents participated in those sites that sponsored community-wide anti-crime activities. Furthermore, the evaluation documented "slight reductions in residents' fear of crime and in concern about community problems in several sites as well as an increase in residents' knowledge of and participation in crime prevention activities. The programs, however, did not seem to achieve the 'ultimate' goals of crime reduction and improved quality of life" (Bennett and Lavrakas, 1989, p. 361).

Rosenbaum (1988b) has noted the relative paucity of documented findings showing meaningful effects on crime associated with even the better-conceptualized and better-funded community-based initiatives. Similarly, Lavrakas and Bennett (1988) suggested that despite the generally well-conceived and modestly well-implemented site-level Eisenhower programming, several reasons may have accounted for the basic lack of any documentable effects on the program's ultimate goals: (1) the magnitude and number of problems in these "enduring" high-crime communities (see Schuerman and Kobrin, 1986); (2) the communities' own very limited indigenous resource base; (3) the necessarily modest funding level; and (4) many difficulties in documenting changes produced by this type of community program.

Community Responses to Drug Abuse

Building in part on the Eisenhower "self-help" model (which itself was based partially on the UCPP model), the U.S. Bureau of Justice Assistance funded a "bubble-up" demonstration program in ten high-crime, drug-plagued communities from 1989 through

1991, including two Chicago communities—South Austin and Logan Square (Rosenbaum, Bennett, et al., 1992). The actual demonstrations were developed jointly by the Chicago-based National Training and Information Center, the National Crime Prevention Coalition, and the respective local community organizations.

The goals of the program were to (1) empower residents to feel more positive about living in their respective neighborhoods; (2) increase resident awareness of local resources; (3) test a variety of anti-drug strategies (e.g., closing drug houses, creating safe school zones); (4) build local action coalitions among a wide range of community, city, and state institutions; and (5) establish a local community task force to further develop and monitor progress in the community-based fight against illegal drugs and crime.

Results from the three-year evaluation (Rosenbaum, Lavrakas, Wilkinson, and Faggiani, 1995; Rosenbaum, 1994) indicated that the local programs showed modest successes along the lines of the Hartford and Portland CPTED programs and the Eisenhower neighborhood program in: (1) further developing local coalitions in the absence of large amounts of federal funding; (2) stimulating citizen awareness of and participation in a variety of anti-drug strategies (e.g., drug-free school zones, drug-abuse prevention education programs, and educational and job-training programs); and (3) improving some quality of life indicators. This major community-based anti-drug initiative reinforced the importance of local efforts receiving a broad range of technical assistance (i.e., not merely crime focused) and being part of a multi-agency anti-drug/crime coalition.

COMMUNITY POLICING INITIATIVES

It is important for the policy-oriented reader to understand that "community policing" is best thought of as a *process*. Community policing is not a specific program but can embrace varied substantive components. The promise this process holds for revolutionizing how we deploy our law enforcement resources within a comprehensive crime prevention effort is what forms its appeal.

What, then, is community policing? In the preface to a compendium of scholarly articles on this "new" approach, Greene and Mastrofski observe that previous reform efforts have been criticized for causing the police to lose their "community context."

According to critics of the legacy of administrative police reform, the police have become "bureaucratic, indifferent to their clientele, organized into a passive and reactive response to community disorder and crime . . . ." The term "community policing" has been used to refer to a wide range of programs and activities; it involves several key conceptual elements, including a broadened conception of the police mission to include an integral role in promoting the common welfare and in becoming proactive in resolving community problems (Greene and Mastrofski, 1988, pp. xi-xii). Drawing from Goldstein (1987), Greene and Mastrofski note that common tactics of community policing may include:

(1) increased police-citizen accessibility; (2) use of problem-oriented approaches to policing; (3) aggressive and/or punitive order maintenance strategies requiring the police to intervene without a specific complaint; (4) increasing contact between the police and community organizations, and supporting the development of community organization in those neighborhoods where it does not exist; (5) strengthening community cohesion, including perceptions of community order and citizen willingness to "retake the streets"; and (6) encouraging and sponsoring community crime prevention activities (Greene and Mastrofski, 1988, p. xii).

To better understand current thinking on developing public policy for policing, it is instructive to review the history of policing in the United States. Kelling and Moore (1988) identify three major eras of American policing. Starting in the mid-1800s and continuing through the early 1900s, the "political era" was marked by close ties between the police, politicians, and politics. The "reform era" of American policing developed as a direct response to the abuses of the political era and continued into the 1960s, when what had come to be regarded as traditional, professional, and appropriate policing was found incapable of meeting the crime-related needs of the times, evidenced by the "violence commissions" established by Presidents Johnson and Nixon. Beginning in the 1970s, and with considerable reluctance, policing began to evolve into the "community era." Presently, this new era of community policing is still in its infancy, with many vested interests within and without law enforcement still resistant to change to a new order.

Most early opinion about changes that were needed within policing to combat the rise of crime took a conservative tact, in that they continued to embrace a view of the police as the principal force through which crime could be *prevented*. For example, a report to the Solicitor General of Canada was entitled *Community-Based Preventive Policing* (Wasson, 1977). The writings of James Q. Wilson, the highly regarded police and criminal justice policy analyst, implicitly suggest that the formal mechanisms for society's reactions to crime and maintenance of order (i.e., police departments) are the principal means through which crime is reduced (Wilson, 1976; Wilson and Kelling, 1982; Wilson and Herrnstein, 1985). In contrast, a new breed of criminal justice policy analysts, not wedded to "traditional thinking," have suggested that many recognized experts on policing (e.g., Wilson and many criminologists) have held far too narrow and restrictive a perspective when considering crime *prevention* public policy (see Roehl and Cook, 1984; Lavrakas, 1985; Currie, 1988; Rosenbaum, 1991). Most of these new viewpoints include the police and the community policing "process" as an integral and necessary part of any comprehensive crime prevention policy. However, the police and community policing are not a *sufficient* condition for success.

Demonstrations in Houston and Newark

In the early 1980s, the Police Foundation was commissioned by the National Institute of Justice to help devise and evaluate community-policing "field tests" in Newark and Houston (Pate, Skogan, Wycoff, and Sherman, 1985; Sherman, 1986; Wycoff, 1988). Several innovative strategies in community-oriented policing were developed jointly by the Police Foundation and its consultants and advisory task force members in each city's respective police departments. For example, a strategy implemented in both cities was the publication of a police-community anti-crime newsletter that included crime prevention educational content and detailed information about all recent incidents of reported felonies in the neighborhood (Lavrakas, 1986). The newsletter experiment found residents to be very favorable toward this new form of information flow from their police, but there were no consistent effects on residents' fear of crime or their crime prevention dispositions.

Another Houston strategy established "storefront police offices" to test whether "the operation of a police community station in a neighborhood could reduce fear of crime and increase citizen's satisfaction with their neighborhood and the police"

(Skogan and Wycoff, 1986, p. 179). Through the local storefront offices, the police initiated well-attended monthly meetings with residents, regular meetings with local school officials to discuss mutual problems, a fingerprinting program for children, a health-prevention program (e.g., free blood-pressure readings), a patrol "ride along" program for representatives of local community organizations, a high-intensity park patrol program, and the publication and distribution of the aforementioned anti-crime newsletter. The evaluation found that this intervention had differential effects on different demographic groups within the community, with Blacks, low-income and less educated individuals, younger adults, and renters having less awareness of, and contact with, the storefront offices. Nonetheless, the program was found to lead to reduced fear and concern about crime among all groups of residents and to greater satisfaction with the police and the neighborhoods.

A "victim recontact" program and a "citizen contact patrol" program was devised and implemented in Houston. In each of these, police officers took the initiative to contact victims and other residents via telephone or door-to-door to offer support and discuss crime-related issues about which residents were concerned (Pate et al., 1986; Wycoff, 1988). Although victim recontact was not found to have any measurable effects, the citizen contact patrol was found to reduce residents' fear and concern about crime and increase satisfaction with the police and the neighborhood.

In another Houston community, police officers from the community services division organized block meetings that were attended by local patrol officers. A neighborhood committee met monthly with the local district captain and jointly developed special anti-crime and order-maintenance projects. This initiative was found to reduce residents' fear and concern about crime and to increase their satisfaction with the police.

In Newark, a "signs of crime" program focused on reducing social and physical disorder/deterioration. This included directed "foot patrols to enforce laws and maintain order on sidewalks and street corners; . . . bus checks to enforce order; enforcement of disorderly conduct laws; road checks for DWI; . . . an intensification of city services and the use of juvenile offenders to conduct clean-up work in the target area" (Wycoff, 1988, p. 108). Surprisingly, the evaluation of the "signs of crime" program found no effects.

In contrast, another area of Newark received a coordinated community policing program that Wycoff (1988) refers to as the "kitchen sink" initiative in that it included a neighborhood police office, a directed police-citizen contact program, the anti-crime newsletters, intensified law enforcement and order maintenance, and a neighborhood clean-up campaign. This comprehensive initiative was found to reduce residents' fear and concern about crime and to increase their satisfaction with the police and the quality of life in their neighborhood.

In addition to the myriad strategies and positive results in the Houston and Newark programs, community-oriented policing can have important benefits for the participating officers. For example, one seasoned veteran of the old style of policing typified the effect of participation on many officers: "I used to think I was a mean and cynical cop; now I realize how effective I can be while still being a considerate human being" (Wycoff, 1988, p. 112).

Madison, Wisconsin

More recently, the Quality Policing Demonstration in Madison, Wisconsin, involved creating a police subdistrict in which the new approach would be implemented and tested. The innovation included community-oriented policing, problem-oriented policing, and employee-oriented management. An evaluation of the program concluded: "After an implementation period of two years, it was determined that: a new, participatory management approach was successfully implemented in the [test area]; [officers'] attitudes towards the department and work improved; and physical decentralization was accomplished. These changes were associated with a reduction in citizens' perceptions that crime was a problem in their neighborhood and an increase in the belief that police were working on problems of importance to people in the neighborhood" (Wycoff and Skogan, 1992, p. 1).

Joliet and Aurora, Illinois

Most recently, a major test of community policing, using the cities of Joliet and Aurora as tests sites, was funded by the State of Illinois. The goals of this program were to "reduce criminal activity thereby improving the quality of neighborhood health, reduce fear of crime, and increase neighborhood confidence" (Rosenbaum, Yeh, and Wilkinson, 1994, p. 1). As part of the demonstration program, several police storefronts were opened, attention was targeted to gangs and drug activity, there was strict enforcement of no-trespass orders and selective use of eviction procedures, and a bicycle patrol of business districts was implemented.

Results from this Neighborhood Oriented Policing and Problem Solving Demonstration indicated that police officers who participated in the test programs perceived their job responsibilities as having broadened and felt an increase in job autonomy. However, several anticipated changes relating to officers' interactions with management failed to occur. Despite this, there was a consistent pattern of increased job satisfaction among the participating officers. Significant positive changes in attitudes toward the community policing concept also resulted.

In terms of community impact, an expected increase of awareness among residents of formal and informal community organizing activities associated with the program did not materialize. Furthermore, no positive changes in citizens' awareness of new police programs in their neighborhoods resulted. Neither was there evidence of positive changes in residents' feelings of efficacy or increased informal social control associated with the program. Although residents' self-protection behaviors showed some increase, no change was found in home protection or neighborhood surveillance behaviors. Finally, there was little evidence that within a year of its start-up date the program had any effect on residents' perceptions of crime, victimization experiences, or fear of crime. An evaluation of the program concluded that "the present results are consistent with previous evaluations in suggesting that it takes longer than expected to plan and implement [community policing] initiatives, and [therefore] it may take substantially longer to realize hypothesized community-level changes" (Rosenbaum, Yeh, and Wilkinson, 1994, p. 16).

Current State of Knowledge on Community Policing

Despite some promising successes, community policing is not a panacea, and it is too soon to form definitive and final conclusions about its true costs and benefits. Bayley (1988, pp. 226-236) identified several *potential* problems with the community policing concept: (1) Public safety might decline if the police lose the will and/or the capacity to maintain order. (2) It may be perceived as presenting a less demanding approach for police, while, at the same time, offering an easy explanation for any lack of progress against local crime. (3) The public may become an "interest group" that the police try to manipulate and control through mere public relations gimmickry. (4) It may increase the power of the police relative to other government agencies creating an unhealthy balance. (5) It may serve to legitimize the "penetration of communities by forceful agents of the government," thereby threatening the actual freedoms the police ostensibly are charged to protect. (6) It "may weaken . . . equal protection and evenhanded enforcement" and thereby weaken the protection of the law for "unpopular persons." (7) It may further polarize *haves* from *have nots* by being relatively difficult to implement and to show successes in underclass neighborhoods. (8) It challenges traditional and accepted internal "standards" for assessing police performance and, as a result, may undermine police professionalism.

All of these potential problems are important to consider in future community policing demonstrations and their evaluations, including the most ambitious implementation program and evaluation study to date—one that began in Chicago in 1993 and is scheduled for citywide implementation by 1996. As Bayley acknowledges, these potential problems "are not yet social fact" (p. 236). However, as with almost all processes and practices, community policing can be perverted and corrupted if it is not carefully implemented and closely monitored. As one who sees its potential for good as far outweighing its potential for abuse and harm, I believe that any realistic public policy for crime prevention is likely to include some form of community policing, as explained later in more detail. I hold this view recognizing the clear inadequacies of traditional approaches and valuing the logic that underlies the community policing process. Nonetheless, it would be prudent for any implementation of community policing to receive regular and rigorous monitoring. This should be done by an objective (neutral) party, and feedback should be made directly to an oversight board empowered to both modify the approach and correct any subversion (purposeful or inadvertent) of the process. I am optimistic that none of Bayley's concerns need come to fruition if careful attention is paid by the department's chief executive and the oversight board.

PROGRAM FAILURE VERSUS THEORY FAILURE

In his compelling critique of the conceptualization of Neighborhood Watch as a plausible crime *prevention* strategy, Rosenbaum (1987) identified the central failing of most community-based programming. This failure is one of *not marshaling potent enough anti-crime programs given the magnitude of the crime problems faced*—a situation that would be regarded in the public health field as "treating the patient with too little medicine." This problem of too small a "dosage" in most anti-crime "treatments" explains, in my own view, why many community-based crime prevention demonstration programs have not shown greater positive effects on the ultimate goals of reducing crime, lessening fear of crime, and improving the quality of life. In public health, a promising new medicine would not be abandoned prematurely because it was not properly or adequately tested. Instead, it would be given *more than adequate testing at different dosage levels* to determine its true potential for aiding the afflicted. Unfortunately, our political leaders, criminal justice policymakers, and practitioners, as well as the public as a whole, have yet to realize (or acknowledge) the magnitude of the effort that must be mounted (i.e., the dosage necessary) to have any realistic chance to begin to reduce the prevalence and severity of our nation's crime problems.

Assessing the community-based anti-crime programming implemented and tested in the United States during the past two decades, I conclude that we have little, if any, true evidence of "theory failure" but considerable examples of "program failure" (see Weiss, 1972). The loosely formulated "theory" of community-based crime prevention has never been adequately tested. That theory includes the following ideas:

- that the police, by themselves, are incapable of preventing crime;
- that traditional policing is inadequate for our present needs, but new community-oriented policing holds much promise;
- that citizens must play a central and organized role in preventing crime;
- that many, if not all, social service agencies (public health, mental health, housing, education, employment, etc.) and other social institutions (the family, churches, the media, etc.) must play important roles in any comprehensive crime prevention program;

- and that, ultimately, all *crime prevention* should be viewed as "community-based."

Many times, what may have been perceived as relatively large-scale, well-funded attempts to test the community crime prevention idea were actually very small in an absolute sense. For example, although the $4 million demonstration of the CPTED program in the 1970s may have appeared very well funded relative to the amount of resources being allocated to other anti-crime demonstration programs, it probably was under-funded in terms of the actual goals it sought to achieve. In sum, we have yet to commit adequate resources to attack the size of the crime problems we face.

SOME PUBLIC POLICY RECOMMENDATIONS

In 1982, I wrote a prescriptive chapter for the Eisenhower Foundation about what I believed was needed to develop successful community-based crime prevention policy for our nation (Lavrakas, 1985). However, I now believe that my perspective at that time was overly optimistic in thinking that the voluntary mobilization of citizens through local community organizations and other indigenous community-based institutions (e.g., churches) working in partnership with their local law enforcement agency might be sufficient to begin to turn the tide against crime, even in our most troubled neighborhoods. I held this perspective through the mid-1980s, fully aware of the difficulties faced in organizing neighborhoods, motivating citizens to engage in proactive primary-level and secondary-level crime prevention, and building effective citizen-police coalitions.

Now, more than a decade later, I retain the strong belief that these three components—citizens *qua* neighborhood residents, indigenous community institutions, and local law enforcement—must form the core of effective crime prevention programming. However, the past decade has demonstrated that the combined capacities of these three bodies are not likely to be enough, especially in "enduring" high-crime and drug-plagued communities (see Schuerman and Kobrin, 1986). Much larger partnerships must be forged that include representatives and resources from many social service agencies and many other public- and private-sector institutions. These include, but are not limited to, the physical and mental health care systems; education, employment, transportation, and housing agencies; the business community; philanthropic foundations; and the media. That is, what is needed is a massive, comprehensive, coordinated effort not unlike the one currently being debated concerning our nation's health care policies.

The crime prevention process must be organized and implemented at the local level. The Office of the Mayor, or its equivalent, should serve as the conduit at the municipal level for state and federal resources and provide the upper-level leadership to start the process in motion and see that it keeps on track. It is the mayor's responsibility to leverage funding from various sources to put the municipality and its programs on a sound financial base. Without solid funding, very little real progress in building effective crime prevention programming will result. (This observation is made with an explicit awareness of the international-, national-, and state-level forces that greatly determine local economic conditions.)

The mayor should speak out strongly and regularly on behalf of the comprehensive crime prevention initiative and should insist that the head of each municipal department hire a full-time, high-level representative, from *existing* budgetary resources, to work entirely on the comprehensive crime prevention initiative. By insisting that existing resources be used, the mayor can signal the importance of this effort and point out the anticipated savings all agencies should experience if any headway were made on local crime problems. For example, transportation should experience less vandalism of public transit vehicles.

Under this process, the mayor would appoint a high-level crime prevention task force, which would include the aforementioned department representatives, to devise and monitor policy and implementation. The task force would be small enough in size to be an actual working body. Therefore, it should consist of persons who are capable of fairly representing large constituencies, such as law enforcement agencies, community organizations, local school systems, housing agencies, and the media. This is not a time for "politics as usual"—political risks must be taken with the hope that eventual success in reducing crime will win the day.

The task force must be given a multiple-year opportunity (at least five and preferably ten years) to show progress. The task force's action plan should start small by devising a few demonstration programs in geographic subareas within the municipality. These programs should be carefully conceptualized, implemented, and monitored. A planning phase, lasting a year or longer, should be used to gather a variety of information (including original data) identifying the nature of the specific problems facing the test areas and the resources that can/should be committed to address the problems. In each test area, a local task force should be appointed, again with broad representation of agencies and institutions. Some form of community-oriented policing would be implemented within a test area, with full support from the chief of police. Local police should play a "pivotal role" in working to mobilize the voluntary potential of the citizenry to engage in crime prevention strategies within their jurisdiction (see Lavrakas, 1985). However, the police should not be given a disproportionately important (i.e., powerful) role in devising the comprehensive crime prevention program that the municipality will implement. Instead, they should be merely one of several voices heard in the planning phase, even though they will be a key action force in the implementation phase.

The implementation phase in the test areas should be given at least two or three years to begin to show success. Formative evaluation to provide regular and reliable (accurate) feedback on progress within a test area to the task forces must be funded. Otherwise, adequate information will be unavailable to make informed decisions about needed modifications in the local action plans. The media should play an important role in disseminating information about the process and progress in the test areas. If successes can be reported, this should help momentum build for widespread implementation of *the process* throughout the municipality. If success is not forthcoming, publicity might help leverage more resolve and resources to mount a more potent anticrime initiative.

Exactly how all this would work out cannot be well predicted, as idiosyncratic forces will operate in every given place and time. It is possible that devising and implementing a truly comprehensive crime prevention initiative is a task of such daunting magnitude that it may not be accomplished until it is too late. However, if we wish to preserve the best parts of our democratic society, we must come to be willing to invest the resources and efforts needed for *preventing* crime, not merely reacting to it and trying to control it.

This chapter has tried to illustrate that a very different mindset is needed if we are to succeed in *preventing* crime and thereby succeed in reducing its prevalence and its impact on society. One may not agree with all the specific criticisms and suggestions I have advanced. However, after studying this topic area for nearly

20 years, and observing what has worked and what has not, I am confident that we will not make any meaningful headway in this realm until we are willing to make the very large-scale commitments called for here.

REFERENCES

ACTION and LEAA (1980). *Urban Crime Prevention Program Guideline Manual*. Washington D.C.: U.S. Government Printing Office.

Angel, Solomon (1969). *Discouraging Crime through City Planning*. Berkeley: University of California Press.

Bayley, David H. (1988). "Community Policing: A Report from the Devil's Advocate." In Jack R. Greene and Steven D. Mastrofski, eds., *Community Policing: Rhetoric or Reality*. New York: Praeger.

Bennett, Susan F., and Paul J. Lavrakas (1989). "Community-Based Crime Prevention: An Assessment of the Eisenhower Foundation's Neighborhood Program," *Crime and Delinquency*, vol. 35, no. 3 (July 1989), pp. 345-364.

Bickman, Leonard, Paul J. Lavrakas, John Edwards, Susan Green, and Nancy North-Walker (1976). *Citizen Crime Reporting Projects: Executive Summary*. Washington, D.C.: U.S. Government Printing Office.

Brantingham, Paul J., and Frederic L. Faust (1976). "A Conceptual Model of Crime Prevention," *Crime and Delinquency*, vol. 22, no. 3 (July 1976), pp. 284-296.

Brown, Roger M. (1978). "The American Vigilante Tradition." In Hugh Davis Graham and Ted Robert Gurr, eds., *Violence in America*. Washington, D.C.: U.S. Government Printing Office.

Clotfelter, Charles T. (1977). "Urban Crime and Household Protective Measures," *Review of Economics and Statistics*, vol. 59, no. 4 (November 1977), pp. 499-503.

Cook, Royer (1982). Personal communication. Reston, Va.: Institute for Social Analysis.

Currie, Elliot (1985). "Crimes of Violence and Public Policy: Changing Directions." In Lynn A. Curtis, ed., *American Violence and Public Policy*. New Haven, Conn.: Yale University Press.

———— (1988). "Two Visions of Community Crime Prevention." In T. Hope and M. Shaw, eds., *Communities and Crime Reduction*. London: HMSO.
Curtis, Lynn A. (1985). "Neighborhood, Family, and Employment: Toward a New Public Policy Against Violence." In Lynn A. Curtis, ed., *American Violence and Public Policy*. New Haven, Conn.: Yale University Press.
———— (1988). "The March of Folly: Crime and the Underclass." In T. Hope and M. Shaw, eds., *Communities and Crime Reduction*. London: HMSO.
Fowler, F. Jack, and Thomas Mangione (1986). "A Three-Pronged Effort to Reduce Crime and Fear of Crime: The Hartford Experiment." In Dennis P. Rosenbaum, ed., *Community Crime Prevention: Does It Work?* Newbury Park, Calif.: Sage.
Garofalo, James, and Maureen McLeod (1989). "The Structure and Operations of Neighborhood Watch Programs in the United States," *Crime and Delinquency*, vol. 35, no. 3 (July 1989), pp. 326-344.
Goldstein, Herman (1987). "Toward Community-Oriented Policing: Potential, Basic Requirements and Threshold Questions," *Crime and Delinquency*, vol. 33, no. 1 (January 1987), pp. 6-30.
Greene, Jack R., and Steven D. Mastrofski (1988). *Community Policing: Rhetoric or Reality*. New York: Praeger.
Henig, Jeffrey (1984). "Citizens Against Crime: An Assessment of the Neighborhood Watch Program in Washington, D.C." Washington, D.C.: Center for Washington Area Studies, George Washington University.
Jacob, Herbert, and Robert Lineberry (1982). *Government Responses to Crime: Executive Summary*. Evanston, Ill.: Center for Urban Affairs and Policy Research, Northwestern University.
Jacobs, Jane (1961). *The Death and Life of Great American Cities*. New York: Vintage.
Jeffrey, C. Ray (1976). "Criminal Behavior and the Physical Environment," *American Behavioral Scientist*, vol. 20 (November-December, 1976), pp. 149-174.
Kaplan, Howard, Ken O'Kane, Paul Lavrakas, and Edward Pesce (1978). "Crime Prevention Through Environmental Design: Final Report on Commercial Demonstration." Arlington, Va.: Westinghouse Electric, National Issues Center.

Kelling, George L., and Mark Moore (1988). "From Political to Reform to Community: The Evolving Strategy of Police." In Jack R. Greene and Steven D. Mastrofski, eds., *Community Policing: Rhetoric or Reality.* New York: Praeger.

Kushmuk, James, and Sherril Whittemore (1981). *Reevaluation of CPTED in Portland.* Washington, D.C.: U.S. Government Printing Office.

Lab, Steven P. (1992). *Crime Prevention: Approaches, Practices, and Evaluations.* Cincinnati: Anderson Publishing.

Lavrakas, Paul J. (1981). "On Households." In Dan A. Lewis, ed., *Reactions to Crime.* Beverly Hills, Calif.: Sage.

_____ (1985). "Citizen Self-Help and Neighborhood Crime Prevention Policy." In Lynn A. Curtis, ed., *American Violence and Public Policy.* New Haven, Conn.: Yale University Press.

_____ (1986). "Evaluating Police-Community Anti-Crime Newsletters." In Dennis P. Rosenbaum, ed., *Community Crime Prevention: Does It Work?* Newbury Park, Calif.: Sage.

_____ (1989). "America's War on Drugs: Guest Essay," *Center for Urban Affairs and Policy Research Newsletter* (Northwestern University), Fall 1989, p. 4.

Lavrakas, Paul J., and Susan Bennett (1988). "Thinking About the Implementation of Citizen and Community Anti-Crime Measures." In T. Hope and M. Shaw, eds., *Communities and Crime Reduction.* London: HMSO.

_____ (1989). *A Process and Impact Evaluation of the 1983-86 Neighborhood Anti-Crime Self-Help Program: Summary Report.* Evanston, Ill.: Center for Urban Affairs and Policy Research, Northwestern University.

Lavrakas, Paul J., and Elicia J. Herz (1982). "Citizen Participation in Neighborhood Crime Prevention," *Criminology*, vol. 20, nos. 3/4 (November 1982), pp. 479-498.

Lavrakas, Paul J., and James W. Kushmuk (1986). "Evaluating Crime Prevention Through Environmental Design: The Portland Commercial Demonstration Project." In Dennis P. Rosenbaum, ed., *Community Crime Prevention: Does It Work?* Newbury Park, Calif.: Sage.

Lavrakas, Paul J., Janice Normoyle, and Jay Wagener (1978). *Evaluation of the Portland Commercial CPTED Demonstration.* Evanston, Ill.: Westinghouse Evaluation Institute.

Lavrakas, Paul J., and Dennis P. Rosenbaum, (1989). *Crime Prevention Beliefs, Policies, and Practices of Chief Law*

Enforcement Executives: Results of a National Survey. Washington D.C.: National Crime Prevention Council.
Lavrakas, Paul J., Wesley G. Skogan, Janice Normoyle, Elicia J. Herz, Greta Salem, and Dan A. Lewis (1980). *Factors Related to Citizen Involvement in Personal, Household and Neighborhood Anti-Crime Measures: Executive Summary.* Washington D.C.: U.S. Government Printing Office.
Lewis, Dan A. (1979). "Design Problems in Public Policy Development: The Case of the Community Anti-Crime Program," *Criminology*, vol. 17, no. 2 (August 1979), pp. 172-183.
Lurigio, Arthur J., and Dennis P. Rosenbaum (1986). "Evaluation Research in Community Crime Prevention: A Critical Look at the Field." In Dennis P. Rosenbaum, ed., *Community Crime Prevention: Does It Work?* Newbury Park, Calif.: Sage.
MacAleese, Greg, and H.C. Tily (1983). *Crime Stoppers Manual.* Albuquerque, N.M.: Crime Stoppers International.
Maltz, Michael D. (1972). *Evaluation of Crime Control Programs.* Washington, D.C.: U.S. Government Printing Office.
McPherson, Marlis, and Glen Silloway (1981). "Planning to Prevent Crime." In Dan A. Lewis, ed., *Reactions to Crime.* Beverly Hills, Calif.: Sage.
Newman, Oscar (1972). *Defensible Space: Crime Prevention Through Urban Design.* New York: Macmillan.
Pate, Anthony M., et al. (1984). *Final Report of the Evaluation of the Urban Initiatives Anti-Crime Demonstration.* Washington, D.C.: U.S. Government Printing Office.
Pate, Anthony M., Wesley G. Skogan, Mary Ann Wycoff, and Lawrence W. Sherman (1985). *Reducing the "Signs of Crime"—the Newark Experience: Executive Summary.* Washington, D.C.: Police Foundation.
_____ (1986). *Reducing Fear of Crime in Houston and Newark: Summary Report.* Washington, D.C.: Police Foundation.
Percy, Steven L. (1979). "Citizen Coproduction of Community Safety." In Ralph Baker and Fred A. Meyer, Jr., eds., *Evaluating Alternative Law Enforcement Policies.* Lexington, Mass.: Lexington Books.
Roehl, Janice A., and Royer F. Cook (1984). *Evaluation of the Urban Crime Prevention Program: Executive Summary.* Washington, D.C.: U.S. Government Printing Office.

Rosenbaum, Dennis P. (1986). "The Problem of Crime Control." In Dennis P. Rosenbaum, ed., *Community Crime Prevention: Does It Work?* Newbury Park, Calif.: Sage.

―――― (1987). "The Theory and Research Behind Neighborhood Watch: Is It a Sound Fear and Crime Reduction Strategy?" *Crime and Delinquency*, vol. 33, no. 1 (January 1987), pp. 103-134.

―――― (1988a). "A Critical Eye on Neighborhood Watch: Does It Reduce Crime and Fear?" In T. Hope and M. Shaw, eds., *Communities and Crime Reduction*. London: HMSO.

―――― (1988b). "Community Crime Prevention: A Review and Synthesis of the Literature," *Justice Quarterly*, vol. 5, no. 3, pp. 323-395.

―――― (1991). "The Pursuit of Justice in the United States: A Policy Lesson in the War on Crime and Drugs?" *Canadian Police College Journal*, vol. 15, no. 4, pp. 239-255.

―――― (1994). "Community Responses to Drug Abuse: A Program Evaluation," *National Institute of Justice: Research in Brief*, April 1, 1994.

Rosenbaum, Dennis P., Susan F. Bennett, Betsy D. Lindsay, Deanna L. Wilkinson, Brenda Davis, Chet Taranowski, and Paul J. Lavrakas (1992). *The Community Responses to Drug Abuse National Demonstration Program Evaluation: Executive Summary*. Chicago: Center for Research in Law and Justice, University of Illinois at Chicago.

Rosenbaum, Dennis P., Paul J. Lavrakas, Deanna Wilkinson, and Donald Faggiani (1995). *Estimating the Effects of Community Responses to Drugs: Final Impact Evaluation Report*. Chicago: Center for Research in Law and Justice, University of Illinois at Chicago.

Rosenbaum, Dennis P., Dan A. Lewis, and Jane A. Grant (1985). *The Impact of Community Crime Prevention Programs in Chicago: Can Neighborhood Organizations Make a Difference?* Evanston, Ill.: Center for Urban Affairs and Policy Research, Northwestern University.

Rosenbaum, Dennis P., Arthur J. Lurigio, and Paul J. Lavrakas (1989). "Enhancing Citizen Participation and Solving Serious Crime: A National Evaluation of Crime Stoppers Programs," *Crime and Delinquency*, vol. 35, no. 3 (July 1989), pp. 401-420.

Rosenbaum, Dennis P., Sandy Yeh, and Deanna L. Wilkinson (1994). *Community Policing in Joliet: Impact on Police Per-*

sonnel and Community Residents. Chicago: Center for Research in Law and Justice, University of Illinois at Chicago.

Schuerman, Leo, and Solomon Kobrin (1986). "Community Careers in Crime." In Albert J. Reiss, Jr., and Michael Tonry, eds., *Communities and Crime*. Chicago: University of Chicago Press.

Sherman, Lawrence W. (1986). "Policing Communities: What Works?" In Albert J. Reiss, Jr., and Michael Tonry, eds., *Communities and Crime*. Chicago: University of Chicago Press.

Silberman, Charles E. (1978). *Criminal Violence, Criminal Justice*. New York: Random House.

Skogan, Wesley G., and Mary Ann Wycoff (1986). "Storefront Police Offices: The Houston Field Test." In Dennis P. Rosenbaum, ed., *Community Crime Prevention: Does It Work?* Newbury Park, Calif.: Sage.

Tien, James M., Thomas A. Reppetto, and Lewis F. Hanes (1976). *Elements of CPTED*. Arlington, Va.: Westinghouse Electric, National Issues Center.

Washnis, George (1976). *Citizen Involvement in Crime Prevention*. Lexington, Mass.: Lexington Books.

Wasson, D.K. (1977). *Community-Based Preventive Policing: A Review*. Toronto: Solicitor General of Canada.

Weiss, Carol (1972). *Evaluation Research*. Englewood Cliffs, N.J.: Prentice-Hall.

Wilson, James Q. (1976). *Thinking About Crime*. New York: Basic Books.

Wilson, James Q., and Richard J. Herrnstein (1985). *Crime and Human Nature*. New York: Simon and Schuster.

Wilson, James Q., and George L. Kelling (1982). "Broken Windows: The Police and Neighborhood Safety," *Atlantic Monthly*, March 1982, pp. 29-38.

Wycoff, Mary Ann (1988). "The Benefits of Community Policing: Evidence and Conjecture." In Jack R. Greene and Steven D. Mastrofski, eds., *Community Policing: Rhetoric or Reality*. New York: Praeger.

Wycoff, Mary Ann, and Wesley G. Skogan (1992). *Quality Policing in Madison—An Evaluation of Its Implementation and Impact: Draft Final Executive Summary*. Washington, D.C.: Police Foundation.

COMMENTS

Karen N. Hoover

The chapter by Paul Lavrakas begins with a quotation from Dan Rather on the *CBS Evening News:* "It's the job of the police to protect us from crime and to make us safe in our neighborhoods." We should not be surprised at Rather's statement. The media appeals to the most common denominator, and many segments of the community would probably agree with him. While there may have been changes in public policy in the fight against crime, many still hold on to traditional attitudes and beliefs that the police are primarily responsible for public safety. We, as a nation, are confronted with several generations who have grown up with this belief. There are many who contend that public safety is an entitlement for paying taxes and that safe neighborhoods should require no more effort from the citizenry than signing a check, whether it be for taxes or additional private security. This dichotomy points out how much education needs to be done if a philosophical change in public policy is going to become public practice.

Dan Rather aside, many of us living in an urban environment have come to recognize that our current system of maintaining public safety has failed. On a daily basis, we are bombarded by the media pointing out how the very fiber of our neighborhoods is threatened by drugs and gangs. Even more threatening to many is the increase in violence. Drive-by shootings gone astray emphasize the vulnerability of the innocent. It is also interesting to note the increase in crime being experienced by our brothers and sisters in suburbia who fled, seeking sanctuary from the threat of the city.

Lavrakas offers a model for evaluating the implementation of citizen and community crime prevention strategies by comparing these strategies with primary, secondary, and tertiary prevention strategies in public health. What is missing from this discussion is an examination of how communities actually work. Any discussion of the implementation of community-based strategies that neglects this factor perpetuates the shortcomings of many of the community-based strategies of the past—that the community as an entity was the "recipient" of these strategies without being included as an equal working partner.

Obviously, primary prevention is the most desirable and potentially effective long-term strategy. Most communities develop secondary and tertiary prevention strategies first, in reaction to having been victimized. Primary prevention tends to follow only after the community feels it has a handle on the acute crisis or threat. Also, faced with the issues of massive unemployment, deteriorating educational systems, and dwindling financial resources for states and municipalities, individuals and communities often feel powerless to deal with the "root causes" of crime. Finally, communities have come to rely on governments to deal with these issues.

Primary prevention is not only community-regarding but also pragmatic. In order for the individual and the community to make more of a commitment at this level, they must be encouraged to recognize this. The community can have an impact if the individual makes a commitment to take responsibility for dealing with "root causes" at the neighborhood level.

Lavrakas provides us with a well-documented review of government-funded and foundation-funded crime prevention strategies that, for the most part, appear to have fallen short of anticipated outcomes. While there appears to have been a number of these programs developed with the intent of fostering community-based crime prevention, in reality a very small percentage of the population has been part of these experiments, much less benefited from them. Communities are smart. Despite a dearth of assistance, many communities have risen to the challenge and, stumbling along, have developed strategies for dealing with crime prevention in their own neighborhoods.

Individuals and communities are frequently well versed in secondary and tertiary prevention strategies. Communities are "target-hardening" themselves, with or without the benefits of organized programs. They have initiated programs to restrict pay-phone use in order to limit criminal activity on the public way. They are taking aggressive actions to eliminate problem landlords, problem buildings, and problem tenants. They participate in "good guy loitering," spending many hours sitting in their parks and on high-drug-trafficking corners to deter illegal activities. Many of these efforts have gone unnoticed and have not been evaluated.

It is interesting to note that many secondary strategies, while attempting to limit the probabilities of being a victim, also limit the freedom of the individual. This discussion is not one that often finds its way into the public forum. At some point, there needs to be an evaluation on the benefits of target-hardening versus the personal limitations imposed on the "potential victims."

If the community is to take ownership of crime prevention strategies, it has to be included at all levels in the development of these strategies. It is obvious from Lavrakas's summary that it has not been. In actuality, many of the new policing models cited by Lavrakas have been developed primarily by police departments, without consultation or input from the community. These "pseudo" community policing efforts have found themselves in the position of having to backtrack and develop their own community partners. Should this not be the role of the community? If the community is included at the start, it can do what the community does best—develop its own resources.

While I agree with Lavrakas that the community, police, and other public- and private-sector agencies are the essential partners in crime prevention, he has minimized the roadblocks to achieving this ideal. The communities I am familiar with have found that the police play a significantly less critical role than anticipated. In keeping in line with Lavrakas's "public health" model, communities have found that they needed to develop holistic "care plans" for crime prevention. These care plans require calling on a myriad of resources, the police being but one of many. In the course of this process, the community has been confronted by a host of inefficient and apathetic agencies and institutions including court systems, city agencies, and business interests.

Community policing offers the possibility of more effective partnerships between the community and the police. But unless other public-sector agencies and private institutions are decentralized, brought on board, and held accountable—get with the program, so to speak—all we will have is effective community-police partnerships that will be undermined by the bureaucracy that exists in most cities today. One role the community will have to take is insisting that its governmental agencies and its institutions get on the bandwagon. This is not a role the police can fill.

Moreover, if the community is going to successfully establish broad-based strategies in crime prevention, it must move beyond the focus on gangs and drugs. For example, the fact that domestic violence is the second highest cause of death in many communities is rarely addressed by community-based prevention programs on any level.

Lavrakas refers to the concern regarding the potential for abuse in these new community-based strategies. The potential for abuse is inherent in any system. I agree that new strategies for community crime prevention, which include community policing, offer a minimal potential for abuse when weighed against the potential for increasing the safety and public welfare of the community as a whole. Community-based strategies have a better chance of maintaining a system of checks and balances as well as accountability when the community is involved from the beginning. Society will have to trust that there is far less potential for abuse from the community and its neighborhood members than there is from politicians and quasi-military organizations.

In the conclusion of his chapter, Lavrakas reminds us that almost all crime prevention can be regarded as "community based." I would extend this thought to include the premise that all components of the community have a responsibility to dedicate some resources to community-based crime prevention strategies. More and more responsibility has fallen to the individual community member to take a proactive role in prevention, not only because this policy is cost-effective but because it holds the promise of being more successful than the current system. The community must have access to the resources it requires to ensure the success of this initiative. Not only is it critical that the community receive cooperation from all its institutions, it is imperative that the community, particularly at the micro level, be provided with the technical resources it needs to become an effective partner. The *community* must be at the heart of any community-based strategy. The role of the community should no longer be minimized.

THE CRIMINAL JUSTICE SYSTEM: UNFAIR AND INEFFECTIVE

Randolph N. Stone*

Following the acquittal of the police officers who beat Rodney King and the subsequent rebellion in Los Angeles in 1992, several surveys revealed the gaping chasm separating Black and White perceptions of the criminal justice system. The results, though disheartening, were not unexpected. One survey found that 81 percent of Blacks saw the criminal justice system as racially biased; only 36 percent of Whites agreed (*USA Today*, 1992). Another survey revealed that nine out of ten Blacks believed that Blacks and other minorities did not receive equal treatment from the criminal justice system; among White respondents, fewer than 50 percent agreed (*Washington Post*, 1992). Several years earlier, a national poll prepared for the NAACP Legal Defense and Educational Fund found nearly identical results (NAACP, 1989). Black confidence and White confidence in the criminal justice system are as different as the two colors.

Over 30 years ago, President John F. Kennedy launched a plan to finance the exploration of the solar system. More recently, President George Bush initiated a plan and spared no expense to expel Iraqi forces from Kuwait. Today, the crisis in the criminal justice system demands an equally committed effort and strategy. Critical to success is the restoration of confidence in and respect for the criminal justice system. The strategy must focus on crime prevention, not on crime control; on getting smart and being effective, not on getting tough; and on the essential nexus between social justice and criminal justice.

Policies and practices aimed at reducing crime—arrest, prosecution, and incarceration—have instead given rise to a crisis in America's criminal justice system. While failing to reduce crime rates or create safety in the inner city, these uncoordinated policies are threatening to bankrupt the capacity of the legal system to provide justice. This chapter examines elements of the criminal

---

* The author acknowledges the significant contributions of Michael G. Cartier, second-year student, University of Chicago Law School, and the valuable assistance of Adrian White, administrative assistant, Mandel Legal Aid Clinic.

justice crisis from the perspective of Cook County and Chicago, suggesting strategies for reform within and beyond the criminal justice system.

COOK COUNTY: A CRIMINAL JUSTICE MICROCOSM

Cook County covers an area of 958 square miles and has a population of 5.1 million, including 2.8 million in the city of Chicago. Twenty-five percent of county residents are Black, and 14 percent are Hispanic. The Cook County County Jail houses almost 9,000 prisoners, 80 percent of whom are minorities, mainly from concentrated pockets of urban blight on the south and west sides of Chicago (John Howard Association, 1992). Like most other detainees and defendants in the United States, those in Cook County enter a criminal justice system characterized by inconsistent policies and internal contradictions. The problems here are the problems of a nation: arrest and prosecution policies appear and often are biased and discriminatory; courts struggle under excessive caseloads and resort to assembly-line justice; jails are overcrowded and unsafe.

Public officials in Illinois, in Cook County, and nationwide often turn to arrest, jail, and prison as answers to the problems of crime, poverty, and despair. The transfer of juveniles to adult court, mandatory sentencing schemes, and increased reliance on incarceration are three common responses to demands for tougher criminal laws. As an example, in Illinois, a 15-year-old first-time offender charged with selling a controlled substance within 1,000 feet of public housing is treated as an adult.[1] In contrast, a 15-year-old first-time offender charged with selling a controlled substance from or near his home in the suburbs is treated as a juvenile. Counseling, drug treatment, and targeted programs are made available to the juvenile suburbanite, while the inner-city youth most in need of social services enters the resource-starved adult criminal justice system. Given that over 90 percent of the Chicago Housing Authority's tenants are African-American, the unequal treatment of juvenile offenders is even more flagrant.

The disparity in treatment becomes more striking if these young offenders are arrested a second time. The suburbanite, arrested for selling drugs in his home, continues to participate in the juvenile court system. The inner-city youth, arrested for selling drugs within 1,000 feet of his home in a public housing proj-

---

[1] *Illinois Compiled Statutes,* 705 ILCS 405/5-4 (7)(a) (1992).

ect, once again enters the adult criminal justice system but this time faces mandatory incarceration. Mandatory minimum sentencing provides a simplistic response to a complex problem. In Illinois, a repeat offender convicted of selling one to fifteen grams of cocaine or crack receives a minimum sentence of four years.[2] The law prohibits sentencing the offender to a period of probation, a term of periodic imprisonment, or conditional discharge. Mandatory incarceration ignores the particular circumstances of the individual and contributes heavily to prison overcrowding and its attendant unsafe conditions.

When entering the Cook County criminal justice system, indigent defendants, unable to retain private counsel, face an uphill battle. The state's attorney has twice the budget and almost twice the personnel of the public defender, the office with responsibility for representing the poor. While some of this disparity may be attributable to the state's attorney's civil cases, the public defender's office annually strains to provide adequate legal services to over 200,000 individuals who are unable to afford private counsel.

Once arrested, Cook County citizens face even more deprivation and degradation. Cook County Jail, despite several recent additions, remains severely overcrowded. In March 1992, the City of Chicago cited Cook County for 32 fire code violations for failing to provide functioning heat and smoke detectors in almost half of the jail (*Chicago Tribune*, 1992a, 1992b). In June 1992, an average of over 2,000 inmates slept on mattresses on floors, and a prison-monitoring group strongly criticized the county jail's hospital facilities (John Howard Association, 1992, p. 92).

Significant minority frustration with the criminal justice system is aggravated by the perception that Whites are responsible for making arrests, prosecuting offenders, defending the accused, and dispensing justice. As of 1992, Blacks accounted for 40 percent of Chicago's population but only 25 percent of its police force. The employment picture for African-Americans who wish to join the police force has improved only marginally in recent years despite the presence of a court-ordered affirmative action plan (BJS, 1994, p. 53). Meaningful minority participation in Cook County's legal profession and judiciary is also marginal.

The criminal justice crisis in Cook County typifies the crisis that confronts virtually every other urban jurisdiction in America today. The problems of poverty, unemployment, and failing pub-

---

[2] *Illinois Compiled Statutes*, 720 ILCS 570/401, 730 ILCS 5/5-8-1 (1992).

lic education evidence themselves in urban crime. The system turns a blind eye to the root causes of the disease, instead seeking to alleviate its symptoms by applying short-term solutions. Legislators skew resource allocation toward conviction and incarceration, while imprisonment and its inhumane conditions offer little hope for rehabilitation and recovery. A recent report on the organization and administration of justice in Cook County noted:

> Unfortunately, we found a "nonsystem." Conflicts between agencies continue unresolved, and juveniles are lost through the "cracks" as they are shifted among agencies. The major agencies—such as police, prosecution and the courts—act in isolation. Antagonism, rather than harmony, too often characterizes agency relationships. The system, in short, has no core actors. And it has no central cooperative purpose nor direction (Manikas et al., 1990, p. vii).

The failure of the criminal justice system to respond effectively to those most affected by and involved in the system perpetuates the cycle of injustice.

ARREST: THE WEAPON OF CHOICE IN THE WAR ON DRUGS

At the federal level, every administration since that of Richard Nixon has chosen to fight the "war on drugs" by dedicating additional resources to arrest and interdiction. Always, we are on the brink of success. When will we succeed? As interdiction and arrest efforts focused on marijuana, users turned to cocaine. As efforts focused on cocaine, users turned to crack. As efforts focus on crack, users turn to heroin. There is little direct evidence that the efforts to control the problem of drug use by increasing arrests and interdiction have been or can be effective.

The federal drug control budget in 1981 totaled about $1.5 billion. Arrest, interdiction, prosecution, and incarceration efforts accounted for 57 percent of the budget authority. Drug abuse prevention and treatment totaled 36 percent. By 1991, budget authority for drug control had increased to $10.5 billion. Resources dedicated to arrest, interdiction, prosecution, and incarceration accounted for more than two-thirds of the total; the money dedicated to drug abuse prevention and treatment totaled only 28 percent (BJS, 1991, pp. 16-17; 1994, pp. 19-20). This pattern has been echoed throughout the United States: a focus on arrest, prosecution, and incarceration at the expense of prevention and treatment.

Drug-related arrests accounted for 27 percent of criminal cases filed in U.S. District Court in 1992 (BJS, 1994, p. 499). Most drug arrests are prosecuted at the local court level, where drug prosecutions have also increased dramatically. Between 1980 and 1990, the number of drug arrests doubled, producing a nationwide flood of defendants into overcrowded and ill-equipped local courts and jails (ABA, 1991, p. 11; BJS, 1994, p. 419). The nationwide arrest rate for drug-abuse violations in 1992 was 431 per 100,000 inhabitants; in the city of Chicago, the arrest rate exceeded 1,150. In fact, drug arrests in Chicago are so pervasive that the city's 1980 drug abuse arrest rate of 508 per 100,000 inhabitants exceeded the nationwide arrest rate for 1992 (BJS, 1991, p. 453; 1994, p. 420). Not only have drug arrests been on the rise, but these offenses constitute an ever-increasing percentage of all offenses charged. Almost 30 percent of those in Cook County jail in 1992 were charged with drug possession or delivery (BJS, 1994, p. 459; *Chicago Tribune*, 1992c).

State, county, and city officials, like their counterparts at the national level, continue to stress arrest as a solution to drug abuse and crime. Nonetheless, aggressive arrest and interdiction policies have failed to prevent the drug abuse and crime that are manifestations of a greater problem—the economic, educational, and spiritual poverty in those communities most ravaged by crime. Funding for prevention and treatment is essential; equally important are viable opportunities for education, training, and employment. Early childhood intervention programs such as Head Start must be funded. Day care and community activity centers must be built. Job training and community health centers services must be provided. The preventive medicine of intervention and empowerment must be dispensed to treat the disease afflicting the inner city.

COURTS, PROSECUTION, AND DEFENSE

While officials continue to promote law-and-order solutions to social and economic problems, numerous additional roadblocks confront those who enter the criminal justice system. Public defenders struggle with ever increasing caseloads to provide effective legal advice and services to indigent defendants. Judges fret about case disposition rates, paying little heed to the quality of justice they dispense. Prosecutorial discretion produces criminal charges and subsequent trials that are tainted by racial and class prejudice. Such misguided practices and policies aggravate the already significant frustrations of minorities and the poor.

Indigent Defense: An Empty Promise

In 1902, the famed attorney Clarence Darrow, addressing the inmates of Cook County jail, observed:

> If the community had provided a system of doing justice, the poorest person in this room would have as good of a lawyer as the richest, would he not? . . . . If the courts were organized to promote justice, the people would elect somebody to defend all these criminals, somebody as smart as the prosecutor—and give him as many detectives and as many assistants to help, and pay as much money to defend you as to prosecute you (Darrow, 1975, pp. 34-35).

The Cook County Public Defender's Office, established in 1930, provides representation to over 95 percent of the indigent criminal defendants in the county, representing over 200,000 clients a year. The office is responsible for providing representation in death penalty, other felony, misdemeanor, juvenile (delinquency and abuse/neglect), paternity, appellate, post-conviction, and mental health cases.

Until recently, the chief public defender was appointed by the chief judge of the Circuit Court of Cook County. Pursuant to an amendment to the state statute, the public defender is now appointed by the president of the Cook County Board with the advice and consent of the other board commissioners. In addition, the office now presents its budget directly to the county board as opposed to being part of the judicial budget. This change in the appointment and budget process was the result of criticism relating to a perceived lack of independence of the public defender's office from the judiciary.

Despite an increased emphasis on training and supervision in the public defender's office, the quality of services provided in some areas is questionable due to the exceedingly high caseloads that attorneys are required to handle. For example, in the juvenile division, it is not uncommon for individual attorneys to have active and pending caseloads of over 400 clients. Similarly, in the felony trial division, lawyers may be responsible for more than 100 pending cases. The office has a murder task force of about 25 lawyers, each handling over 20 pending murder cases at any given time, and often a third of these cases involve eligibility for the death penalty. In the misdemeanor courtrooms, lawyers may be responsible for 25-35 clients a day. There are no caseload standards; instead, public defenders are responsible for virtually all of the indigent cases in their respective courtrooms.

The office operates primarily under a "horizontal" or zone representation system. This means that lawyers are assigned to courtrooms first and clients second. Therefore, an individual client may be represented by a number of different public defenders before the case is resolved. After arrest, for example, the client appears in bond court represented by the public defender assigned to that courtroom; thereafter, his case is assigned for preliminary hearing or arraignment, where he is represented by the defender assigned to that court. When the case is assigned to a trial court, a different public defender receives the case. If the case is transferred, the lawyer does not follow the case; instead, the lawyer assigned to the receiving courtroom represents the accused. In addition to the obvious impact on attorney/client rapport, the quality of representation suffers as the responsibility for case preparation and planning is diffused, valuable time for investigation is lost, and gaps in legal representation leave the client without the assistance of counsel at critical stages of the case. The office does provide "vertical" representation in murder cases, at least to the extent that the same lawyer who represents the client at the preliminary hearing normally follows the case to conclusion. Furthermore, efforts are being addressed to expand vertical representation in other areas of the office. However, the judiciary is resistant, preferring the status quo; some judges have expressed concerns that vertical representation may negatively impact on the disposition rate and the efficiency of processing cases.

Recent initiatives by the management and union (staff attorneys are unionized) have resulted in relatively comparable salary and benefit levels between the defender and local prosecutor's office. However, the Cook County State's Attorney has almost twice the budget and over 60 percent more personnel than the public defender. Despite repeated requests, the level of non-attorney support staff (investigators, clerical staff, social workers) and other non-personnel accounts in the public defender's office remain insufficient.

As noted earlier, the Cook County Public Defender's Office represents almost all the indigent defendants in the criminal courts. Rarely are private counsel appointed, except in the most egregious instances of conflict among multiple defendants in the same case. The judiciary and the County Board created a multiple defendant division within the public defender's office to avoid private appointments in cases of more than one defendant. (There are problems with both the concept and implementation of this initiative that extend beyond the scope of this chapter). There is no professionally administered system of private counsel appointments because public defenders are perceived as less expensive. While in the short-term this view may appear to be cost-effective, in the long-term, the effect on the quality of justice, individual and community respect for the criminal justice system, and potential civil litigation related to ineffective assistance of counsel may undermine any perceived short-term cost saving.

Although private counsel is rarely appointed, some private lawyers involve themselves in the criminal justice system through *pro bono* efforts. These lawyers make themselves available to the chief judge of the criminal division, who, on occasion, will appoint them to a limited number of cases. While it is admirable that private lawyers involve themselves in the representation of the indigent, their limited involvement has little or no impact on the crushing caseloads of the assistant public defenders. Moreover, some commentators suggest that since the state has the responsibility for providing competent and effective counsel to the accused, this responsibility should not be abrogated by *pro bono* participation.

As more and more indigent defendants enter the criminal justice system, those who are constitutionally required to defend them are unable to provide effective service. In 1978, about 13,000 felony cases were filed in Cook County; by 1990, the number had tripled to more than 39,000 felony filings (ICJIA, 1990, p. 98; 1991, p. 190). Public defenders represented almost 70 percent of those defendants. On a nationwide basis, 7.4 percent of justice system expenditures in 1990 were dedicated to prosecution and legal service, while only 2.3 percent was dedicated to indigent defense services (BJS, 1994, p. 2). In Illinois, the more than $2.6 billion spent in 1990 to operate the criminal justice system was allocated as follows: 54 percent for police protection, 27 percent for corrections, 11 percent for courts, 5.4 percent for prosecution, and 1.4 percent for public defense. Three times as much personnel was dedicated to prosecution as was dedicated to public defenders (BJS, 1994, pp. 5, 33).

Given that 70 to 90 percent of those arrested in the "war on drugs" require the services of a public defender, the pressure on those who provide services to the indigent defendants continues to grow (Murphy, 1991). Little is done, however, at the national, state, or local level to alleviate the burden. State after state has faced major crises in the delivery of services to the indigent accused. A judge in Louisiana struck down as unconstitutional the state's system for securing and compensating lawyers for poor defendants. Defendants awaiting trial in Fulton County, Georgia, often languish for months before even meeting with an attorney (*Atlanta Journal and Constitution*, 1991). In an attempt to balance its budget, San Francisco laid off ten public defenders (*L.A. Daily Journal*, 1992).

The situation is as bad at the federal level. In June 1992, the Administrative Office of the U.S. Courts notified lawyers compensated under the Criminal Justice Act for representing indigent defendants that funding for the fiscal year had been exhausted. Although the director of the Administrative Office "apologized for any hardship the suspension of payments had on those providing services to the poor," the plight of the accused forced to rely on uncompensated counsel to protect their right to a fair trial was not addressed. Funding for the indigent defense program was restored, but other accounts were frozen, including one for substance abuse referrals (*National Law Journal*, 1992).

As the poor and minorities wait in local jails for inadequate or nonexistent legal representation, we must ask whether the right to legal representation is an empty promise. In *Gideon v. Wainwright*, the U.S. Supreme Court found a constitutionally mandated entitlement to legal representation. Today, "Gideon's trumpet" is increasingly muted; effective and competent legal representation for the poor and minorities is too often a case of form over substance. A lack of confidence in and respect for the criminal justice system is the logical consequence of a system that regularly denies access to justice to the most needy people.

The Criminal Courts: Assembly-Line Justice

While quality legal representation is often denied to the indigent accused, the judiciary, struggling under excessive caseloads, often measures its success by case-disposition rates, meaning the number of cases resolved in a given period of time. Justice is too often treated as a byproduct of an efficient court system rather than as the *goal* of the system. The integrity of the criminal justice system is sacrificed at the altar of judicial efficiency and case disposition rates.

Judicial conferences focus on how to run a court system more efficiently rather than on how to administer justice more fairly. In enumerating the accomplishments of one appeals court circuit, the chief judge noted that despite a shortage of judges, the case disposition rate was only slightly below that of the previous year. Fewer judges handled almost the same total number of cases, and

71 percent more criminal cases, in the same amount of time. However, the quality of the justice dispensed was not discussed (Wald, 1991).

In 1989, Cook County created a night narcotics court as a "temporary" solution to relieve the backlog of drug cases, despite concerns about assembly line justice. In its first year, five judges aimed to hear 5,000 cases. In 1991, this temporary solution had expanded to eight courts and had disposed of almost *13,000 felony cases*, many in less than one hour (*Chicago Tribune*, 1992d). Drug arrests have overwhelmed the now apparently permanent night court, and some cases have been transferred back to the regular day courts. Unfortunately, judges and prosecutors focus on the *number* of cases processed, while failing to address quality-of-justice issues such as the virtual certainty of re-arrest and recidivism, given the lack of attention to drug treatment and other rehabilitative programs.

Prosecution: An Abuse of Discretion

The Cook County State's Attorney, who is elected every four years, has wide discretion to establish policies for screening charges, investigating and preparing cases, filing formal charges in court, coordinating the roles of victims and witnesses, negotiating pleas, administering pretrial and trial procedures, and making sentencing recommendations. Although the majority of its staff and resources are devoted to prosecuting criminal cases at trial and on appeal, the office has significant civil responsibilities as well, including advising county government, representing county officials, collecting debts, and enforcing housing and nursing home standards.

At the earliest stage in the criminal process, the felony review unit examines the cases against those accused. Five percent of those arrested are diverted to agencies such as the Illinois Department of Mental Health and Developmental Disabilities. Another 22 percent of the cases are dropped prior to any court proceedings. Of the remaining 73 percent, 18 percent are dismissed after some processing in the court system. Only 3 percent go to trial, resulting in two convictions for every acquittal. Defendants plead guilty in 53 percent of felony cases (ICJIA, 1990, p. 130).

Prosecutors have virtually unlimited discretion in decisions to file charges and prosecute cases. In a review article on racism in the criminal justice process, three areas in particular were examined: the initial assessment of the severity of the offense, the decision concerning what specific charges to file, and the decision whether to seek the death penalty in homicide cases (*Harvard Law Review*, 1988, pp. 1525-1532). Prosecution at the maximum possible level is more likely if the victim is White (Meyers and Hagan, 1979, pp. 441-447). In Los Angeles, Whites were statistically more likely to have charges against them dropped than were African-Americans or Hispanics (Spohn, Gruhl, and Welch, 1987). Selective upgrading of charges occurs in cases involving a Black defendant and/or a White victim, and a selective downgrading of charges occurs when there is a White defendant and/or a Black victim (Bowers and Pierce, 1980, pp. 612-614). Following the decision whether to charge, prosecutors' decisions on the level of crime with which to charge the defendant also reflect strong undercurrents of racism. Once the decision to prosecute has been made, Black defendants involved in cases with White victims are more likely to be charged with the more serious level of offense (LaFree, 1980; Bowers, Pierce, and McDevitt, 1984, pp. 244-46). Another study found that the race of the victim played a crucial role in the decision whether to seek the death penalty (Baldus, Pulaski, and Woodworth, 1983, pp. 709-710; Paternoster, 1984). Prosecutors are statistically more likely to seek the death penalty in those cases involving White victims than in those involving Black victims.

Aggressive arrest and inflexible prosecution polices have produced yet another major disparity—the race-tinged use of the plea bargain. As more and more defendants enter the criminal justice system and as courts become clogged with cases, over 95 percent of prosecuted cases end with a guilty plea. The result of the plea, however, varies widely, depending on the race of the defendant. The *San Jose Mercury News* analyzed over 650,000 criminal cases that were prosecuted between 1981 and 1990. After the prosecutors decided to charge a defendant, a significantly higher proportion of White adults arrested on felony charges were later convicted of misdemeanors. Moreover, a higher proportion of Whites had the charges reduced or dismissed. The study concluded that at virtually every stage of pre-trial negotiation, Whites were more successful than non-Whites (*San Jose Mercury News*, 1991).

Undercurrents of racism also taint laws that, on their face, may seem racially neutral. Pursuant to a statute passed by the Minnesota legislature, possession of crack cocaine carried a more severe penalty than possession of powdered cocaine. Over 95 percent of those arrested for possession of crack were Black, while almost 80 percent of those arrested for possession of powdered cocaine were White. Ultimately, the Minnesota Supreme Court invalidated the statute as violating the equal protection guarantee of the state constitution.[3]

In many jurisdictions, a drug-using expectant mother has a better chance of being reported, prosecuted, or incarcerated than receiving treatment. Since the outbreak of the crack epidemic, prosecutors and judges, concerned about the effect of crack use on a pregnant woman's fetus, have often threatened drug-addicted women with incarceration for the duration of their pregnancies. This threat of incarceration has no significant deterrent effect on the behavior of pregnant, substance-dependent women, and prisons are ill-equipped to handle the medical, social, and psychological effects of detoxification combined with pregnancy (Barry, 1991, p. 24).

Beyond being shortsighted and ineffective, this misguided policy has a disproportionate impact on poor African-American women who typically use public hospitals, where the risk of government detection of drug use is much higher (Roberts, 1991). While there exists little difference between the rate of substance abuse by pregnant women along either racial or economic lines, Black women are ten times more likely to be reported to authorities (Chasnoff, Landress, and Barrett, 1990). This law enforcement focus on crack use by African-American women in the inner city is in stark contrast to the availability of health and treatment facilities available to affluent White women whose use of harmful drugs is just as prevalent. Without adequate prenatal care or drug abuse treatment, inner-city Black women are more likely to have children who will become part of the cycle of poverty and despair. Jailing women, in the absence of adequate prenatal, health care, drug treatment, and prevention programs, is counterproductive in both human and economic costs.

JUVENILE INJUSTICE

Almost 100 years ago, Cook County established the first juvenile court system in the United States. Its humane vision and unique approach served as a model for similar efforts throughout the country. Today, however, its vision is blurred, and its goals are unfocused. The juvenile court merely processes children, rarely pausing to assess individual needs (Kotlowitz, 1991). The system's intended beneficiaries, the children of Cook County, have become its inadvertent victims.

---

[3] *State v. Russell*, 477 N.W. 2d 886 (Minn. 1991).

Cook County's delinquency division and its abuse and neglect division share overcrowded facilities on the city's near southwest side. Every day the poorly lit hallways and sparsely furnished waiting rooms teem with mothers and grandmothers, children and infants, waiting for their names to be shouted by court personnel indicating the time for their day (or, in this case, minutes) in court. In 1991, each juvenile delinquency courtroom handled between 1,100 and 1,700 new cases. Contrast this with the criminal courts, where each courtroom handled around 210 new cases. One juvenile court judge estimated that he made 1,700 decisions per month. Assuming 22 eight-hour working days per month, the judge issued 10 decisions per hour, or one every 6 minutes (*Chicago Sun-Times*, 1992a, p. 1).

Much of the overcrowding results from the failure to effectively screen out those cases in which a finding of delinquency is unlikely. In 1991, prosecutors declined to prosecute only 3 percent of those cases referred to them by the police, down from a 16 percent screening rate in 1985. Of the remaining cases, 64 percent were dropped after an initial hearing, and 33 percent either were sentenced to state prison or a term of probation or were assigned to another social services agency such as the state Department of Mental Health and Developmental Disabilities (*Chicago Sun-Times*, 1992a, p. 19).

The number of mandatory transfers from juvenile to adult criminal court in Cook County has grown exponentially. In 1984, the State automatically transferred 145 juvenile offenders to criminal court. In 1991, that number exceeded 500, and there were so many drug-related mandatory transfers of juveniles that the state's attorney stopped counting (*Chicago Sun-Times*, 1992c, p. 20).

The state legislature has increasingly reduced the juvenile court's discretion by expanding the number of offenses that must automatically be transferred to criminal court. Many first-time juvenile offenders find themselves being tried as adults. The already strained resources of the criminal justice system, struggling to process its adult caseload, is ill-equipped to meet the special needs of children. Transfers to criminal court place children beyond the reach of the limited, but vital, social service programs for juveniles. Moreover, the transferred juvenile offender will carry the stigma of an adult criminal record, further restricting limited opportunities for a legitimate and productive future.

Racial bias manifests itself in juvenile justice as well. For example, in 1991, when reviewing minor crimes from Chicago's mostly White north side, juvenile court personnel chose not to prosecute 38 percent of the cases. The comparable figure for cases from Chicago's heavily African-American west and south sides was only 17 percent. In other words, it appears that a substantially greater percentage of children of color are being prosecuted for minor offenses, while White children charged with the same types of crimes are being diverted from the system. Not surprisingly, the racial makeup at the Juvenile Detention Center reflects many of the same disparities found in County Jail: 77 percent African-American, 15 percent White, 8 percent Hispanic (*Chicago Sun-Times*, 1992b, p. 12).

INCARCERATION: INJUSTICE AGGRAVATED

Arrest and prosecution policies, fraught with undercurrents of racism, serve as the foundation for discriminatory incarceration policies. For those imprisoned, facilities are grossly overcrowded, with resources in pathetically short supply. Mandatory minimum sentencing and the failure to develop sufficient intermediate sanctions aggravate the problems of an overcrowded corrections system.

Rates of Incarceration

A comparison of incarceration rates in the United States and other countries is revealing. The incarceration rate in the United States is second in the world, with 519 citizens per 100,000 population in the prison system. The incarceration rate has increased by 22 percent since 1989 and is generally five to eight times the rate of most industrialized nations. Russia leads the world with 558 per 100,000 inhabitants. More dramatic still is the comparison with Western European countries. The United Kingdom has an incarceration rate of 93 per 100,000; France, 84; and the Netherlands, 49. There are also striking differences in the incarceration rates for Black and White men. The United States imprisons Black males at a rate four times as high as in South Africa: 3,822 per 100,000 as compared with 851 per 100,000 (Mauer, 1994, pp. 1-7). A racial breakdown of the U.S. inmate population indicates that African-Americans are incarcerated at a rate six times that of Whites. In light of these figures, it is no surprise that African-Americans' distrust of the criminal justice system is so high.

Broken down even further, these statistics are even more disturbing. The Sentencing Project found that for African-American males between the ages of 20 and 29, almost one in four is involved in the criminal justice system. Compare this with one in 16 White males and one in 10 Hispanic males in the same age group. In our urban centers, the situation is grim. For example, on any given day in the District of Columbia, 42 percent of young Black men (ages 18 to 35) were involved in the criminal justice system in some way—parole, probation, bond, imprisonment. An estimated 70 percent of Black males in the District of Columbia are arrested before the age of 35, and 85 percent will be arrested sometime during their lives (Miller, 1992). In Chicago, it has been estimated that 29 percent of all Black males between the ages of 20 to 29 were admitted to the Cook County Jail in 1989 (Cook County Corrections, 1991, pp. 2-15).

These trends in criminal justice reverberate far beyond the immediate loss of freedom for young Black men. The repercussions are particularly grave in the African-American community. While most White men at this age are developing skills, raising families, and starting careers, a significant number of Black men are developing criminal records, raising bail, and starting sentences. Furthermore, large numbers of African-American men live with the stigma of an arrest and/or conviction record that restricts the availability of employment opportunities.

Sentencing Practices

Patterns of discrimination also manifest themselves in sentencing decisions. Statistically significant and racially correlated differences exist in both the length of court-imposed sentence and the length of sentence served. A study by the Rand Corporation found that Michigan courts imposed statistically significant longer sentences on Blacks than on Whites. In Texas, African-Americans and Hispanics served statistically significant longer sentences than did Whites. The correlation of race with length of sentence and length of time served confirms the suspicion that racial and class bias infects even this stage of the criminal justice system (Petersilia, 1983).

The federal courts and a number of other states have established guidelines for sentencing with the hope of eliminating disparity and racial bias from sentencing decisions. Although the results are subject to debate, any success will be all but illusory unless bias at the arrest and prosecution stages can be eradicated (see Heaney, 1991). The success of guidelines systems are questionable. Michael Tonry, among others, has criticized the U.S. Sentencing Guidelines as a "punitive and mechanical set of sentencing standards that remove most meaningful discretion from sentencing judges, that crowd our prisons, waste our money, impose enormous amounts of unnecessary suffering, and diminish the life chances of individual offenders . . ." (Tonry, 1990). Tonry recognizes the essential nexus between criminal justice and social justice, arguing that sentencing, particularly in the context of non-violent crime, should be used to enhance, or at least not diminish, the offender's "life chances."

Overreliance on the traditional punishment of incarceration must be also addressed. Forty-six states have mandatory minimum sentences that place an increasing burden on an already overcrowded prison system. In 1991, two-thirds of the inmates in Illinois's 23 prisons were convicted of offenses for which they could not receive probation (*Chicago Tribune*, 1991a). In 1980, the average length of prison sentences for drug offenses in U.S. District Courts was 47 months; in 1991, that average reached more than 85 months (BJS, 1991, p. 481; 1994, p. 495).

Several aspects of mandatory sentencing are particularly noteworthy. First, such a myopic policy often reflects the politically expedient idea of how best to deal with those convicted of committing a crime. It ignores more effective and less costly strategies such as offender rehabilitation and crime prevention via intensive intervention. Second, such a policy shifts discretion from the judge to the prosecutor and precludes meaningful judicial consideration of individual and particular circumstances of the crime and characteristics of the individual. Discretion is shifted to prosecutors, who are now in the position to charge or not to charge an offense that carries a mandatory sentence; the judge must sentence the defendant to a minimum period of incarceration, regardless of the particular circumstances of the crime or the individual.

Mandatory sentences also serve as a catalyst for prison overcrowding. In 1990, federal and state prison systems were operating, on average, at 22 percent above design capacity (BJS, 1994, p. 610). At the end of 1992, the state prison population in Illinois was nearly 32,000, which was 52 percent above the system's design capacity and 29 percent higher than its rated capacity (Illinois Task Force, 1993, p. 19).[4] These overcrowded conditions disproportionately affect African-Americans and other minorities. In 1991, Black inmates accounted for 63 percent of the adult prison population in Illinois (BJS, 1994, p. 606).

---

[4] Rated capacity refers to the prison population level considered to be acceptable on the basis of administrative judgments and sound correctional practices (Illinois Task Force, 1993, p. 19).

Cook County Jail

The Cook County Department of Corrections, more commonly known as the Cook County Jail, is a massive complex of buildings adjacent to the criminal courts building. The jail houses inmates in one of eight divisions, segregating them on the basis of gender, level of dangerousness, and special needs. For example, one division houses only women, while another houses inmates who need regular medical attention.

In 1982, the County signed a federal court-ordered consent decree to improve conditions, reduce overcrowding, and provide each inmate with a bed in a cell. Finding that the jail's administration had violated that agreement in 1983, the court ordered officials to reach the population limit by releasing inmates with less serious offenses. In 1989, the court fined the county $1,000 per day for every day that the jail population exceeded its allowable limit. Fines totaled over $200,000 before the court discontinued the fine order in December 1989. The overcrowding persisted, however. In 1988, the daily average overflow population was 139 prisoners; in 1992, the overflow reached 2,508 (John Howard Association, 1992, p. 18). Despite recent additions that raised the jail's capacity to about 7,900 beds, there was still an average daily overflow of 1,456 inmates in 1994 (John Howard Association, 1995).

Overcrowded jails, by their very nature, are dangerous. Large numbers of desperate persons, housed in cramped conditions, with limited outlets for frustrations or resources for rehabilitation, can wreak havoc on a system grounded on order and control. Beyond being overcrowded, such facilities are often unsafe and unhealthy. Cook County Jail can offer little in terms of job training, substance abuse programs, and remedial education classes when a facility designed for 7,900 holds 9,000 or more detainees. If Cook County (or any jurisdiction) hopes to gain control of its jail overcrowding problem, it must provide rehabilitation, treatment, and training programs that offer the chance to break the cycle of poverty and the attendant circumstances that contribute to crime.

Recent initiatives involving intermediate sanctions are a product of the pressure of overcrowding. In 1991, the Cook County Sheriff reacted to a severe overcrowding crisis in the women's unit by developing an overnight release plan. Women with families were released overnight, returning every morning to attend classes for general equivalency degrees and parenting skills, as well as drug treatment and counseling programs (*Chicago Tribune*, 1991b, p. 20). This effective, efficient, and innovative program was born of necessity, and the sheriff has developed a comparable day reporting program for men.

In 1991, the Cook County State's Attorney and the U.S. Attorney for Northern Illinois called for the construction of more jails as a means to combatting Chicago's alarming homicide rate. "The police are doing a good job, the prosecutors are doing a good job, the judges are doing a good job. But there's not enough jail space" (UPI, 1991). There will never be enough jail or prison space, however, so long as policies of arrest and incarceration are politically expedient but practically ineffective solutions.

CRIME AND THE COMMUNITY: CREATIVE SOLUTIONS TO CHRONIC PROBLEMS

Politicians and the general public tend to view law enforcement and criminal justice as the first and only line of defense in the war on crime. Unfortunately, it is a Maginot line, an ineffective and inappropriate strategy overrun by the very problems it was designed to prevent. Aggressive arrest policies and "get tough" but ineffective prosecution policies, utilized in conjunction with prison construction programs, are not a panacea for either reducing, preventing, or controlling crime.

There are other, less costly, more humane, and more effective methods to reduce or eliminate the problems that lead to a rising incidence of crime. The abysmal failure of elected and appointed officials to endorse and promote realistic plans for restructuring the criminal justice system means that leadership must come from the community. Those most affected by crime and the criminal justice system must demand, articulate, and push for the implementation of reforms that will produce the results that the present system has failed to achieve. Below are four suggested areas of focus to reduce crime and restore justice to the criminal justice system.

Crime Prevention Strategies

Long-range and short-term strategies to prevent crime must be developed at the national, state, county, and community levels. Effective law enforcement policy is a necessity, but without comprehensive planning—involving the criminal justice system, public schools, the private bar, the business community, public health professionals, the media, community organizations, and other institutions—crime will not be reduced. In the absence of national leadership, each local community must create a crime prevention plan and assist in the creation and placement of community treatment and corrections facilities. In addition to those elements discussed below, a comprehensive strategy should include gun control, reducing televised and film violence, childhood training in dispute resolution and violence prevention, and drug education. Moreover, economic revitalization of the inner city, involving job training and corporate responsibility, is central.

One encouraging development in police forces around the country, from small cities such as Elgin, Illinois, to large cities such as New York, has been the initiation of community policing programs (*Washington Times*, 1992, p. A6; *Newsday*, 1992, p. 19). Instituting community policing is one of the main goals of a recent reorganization of the Chicago Police Department. Typical community policing efforts range from opening storefront police offices in crime-plagued neighborhoods, to patrolling on foot in high-density communities, to providing housing for police officers and their families in areas where a more permanent police presence is required. These efforts have one goal in common: preventing crime by forging greater mutual respect and cooperation between the police and the community.

Intermediate Sanctions

The concept of expanding the range of sanctions for criminal behavior, both to reduce our costly reliance on incarceration and to fashion more appropriate punishments, is not a novel idea. Such sanctions include intensive probation, community-based alcohol, drug treatment, and mental health programs, house arrest and electronic monitoring, community service orders, day reporting centers, intermittent imprisonment, forfeiture, restitution, fines, and fees for services. The use of intermediate sanctions "can serve the community, the victim, and the criminal better and more economically than the prison terms they supplant" (Morris and Tonry, 1990, p. 8). The General Accounting Office found that at a time when the federal prison system was operating at 150 percent of capacity, the system had a 27 percent vacancy rate in halfway house beds (*Chicago Tribune*, 1991c, p. 10). It costs almost $18,000 per year to keep an inmate in prison, $11,600 to provide work release privileges, $2,300 to provide intensive supervision, and $569 to provide regular probation (Pranis, 1989).

Some may fear that this approach will result in more "criminals" in the community. However, the United States is already second in the *world* in its rate of incarceration, with no meaningful reduction in crime. We cannot afford, in economic or human costs, to incarcerate our way out of the problems of crime. Those whom we lock up eventually come out, often more "criminal" and more violent. Our precious jail and prison space should be reserved for those who must be confined. Other offenders should be more effectively monitored, punished, and provided with opportunities to rehabilitate themselves in the community.

Adequate and Balanced Funding

The crisis in state and county budgets, coupled with the substantial growth in workload, are major contributors to the crisis in the criminal justice system. Further, poor planning and deliberately unbalanced investment resulting in the disproportionate spending on police and corrections has weakened the ability of the courts to function. Within the courts, the delivery of legal defense services to the indigent is severely compromised. Although all elements of the criminal justice system are inadequately funded, increased budgets must be carefully planned and coordinated. Significant increases in law enforcement and prosecutorial spending significantly affects the workloads of the courts, public defenders and correctional facilities. Strategies for securing adequate and balanced funding include legislative advocacy, litigation (particularly in securing resources for indigent defense), funding formulas designed to measure the effect of one component of the system on other institutions, justice system impact statements (describing legislation's impact on all components of the justice system), and public information campaigns (ABA, 1992).

Minimizing Racial Bias

This chapter has described only some of the injustices of the criminal justice system: Underfunded representation discriminates against the poor, typically minority, defendant. Prosecution assessment and charging policies discriminate against minority victims and defendants. Legislators write laws that have a disparate impact on the poor and minorities. And the judicial system, preoccupied with efficiency and disposition rates, diminishes the integrity of the criminal justice system.

Several state court systems have studied the problem of racial bias and suggest some of the following remedies: increasing the number of minority judges, prosecutors, and defense attorneys; promoting cross-cultural training; funding pilot programs designed to reduce the high incarceration rate of African-American males;

monitoring prosecutorial charging and plea-bargaining discretion; providing adequate funding and resources for indigent defense services; re-examining bail, sentencing, and jury-selection policies; and reviewing crime legislation for disparate impact on minorities (ABA, 1988).

Reducing crime and creating a fair and effective criminal justice system are monumental tasks. However, a rational discussion devoid of political rhetoric, involving key players in the system, as well as those communities and institutions concerned with and affected by the problems of crime, can produce positive change. Local community organizations and individuals must pressure our government and business leadership to develop and implement creative solutions.

REFERENCES

ABA (1988). *Criminal Justice in Crisis.* Washington, D.C.: American Bar Association.
_____ (1991). *Crime, Drugs, and Criminal Justice.* Chicago: American Bar Association.
_____ (1992). *Funding the Justice System: A Call to Action.* Report by the American Bar Association Special Committee on Funding the Justice System. Chicago: American Bar Association.
Atlanta Journal and Constitution (1991). January 6, 1991.
Baldus, David, Charles Pulaski, and George Woodworth (1983). "Comparative Review of Death Sentences: An Empirical Study of the Georgia Experience," *Journal of Criminal Law and Criminology*, vol. 74, no. 661 (1983), pp. 709-710.
Barry, Ellen M. (1991). "Pregnant, Addicted and Sentenced," *Criminal Justice*, vol. 5, no. 4 (Winter 1991), pp. 23-27.
BJS (1991). *Sourcebook of Criminal Justice Statistics—1990.* Washington, D.C.: Bureau of Justice Statistics, U.S. Department of Justice.
_____ (1994). *Sourcebook of Criminal Justice Statistics—1993.* Washington, D.C.: Bureau of Justice Statistics, U.S. Department of Justice.
Bowers, William, and Glenn Pierce (1980). "Arbitrariness and Discrimination Under Post-Furman Capital Statutes," *Crime and Delinquency*, vol. 26, no. 4 (October 1980), pp. 563-635.

Bowers, William, Glenn Pierce, and John McDevitt (1984). *Legal Homicide*. Boston: Northeastern University Press.
Chasnoff, Ira, Harvey Landress, and Mark Barrett (1990). "The Prevalence of Illicit-Drug or Alcohol Use During Pregnancy and Discrepancies in Mandatory Reporting in Pinellas County, Florida," *New England Journal of Medicine*, vol. 322, no. 17 (1990), pp. 1202-1206.
Chicago Sun-Times (1992a). March 22, 1992.
——— (1992b). March 23, 1992.
——— (1992c). March 27, 1992.
Chicago Tribune (1991a). February 10, 1991.
——— (1991b). November 21, 1991.
——— (1991c). December 30, 1991.
——— (1992a). March 6, 1992.
——— (1992b). March 13, 1992.
——— (1992c). May 29, 1992.
——— (1992d). July 21, 1992.
Cook County Corrections (1991). "Long-Range Master Plan."
Darrow, Clarence S. (1975). *Crime and Criminals: An Address Delivered to the Prisoners in Cook County Jail*. Chicago: Charles H. Kerr Publishing Company.
Harvard Law Review (1988). "Developments in the Law: Race and the Criminal Process," *Harvard Law Review*, vol. 101, no. 7 (May 1988), pp. 1475-1641.
Heaney, Gerald (1991). "Reality of Guidelines Sentencing," *American Criminal Law Review*, vol. 28, no. 2 (Fall 1991), pp. 161-232.
ICJIA (1989). *Trends and Issues 89: Criminal and Juvenile Justice in Illinois*. Chicago: Illinois Criminal Justice Information Authority.
——— (1990). *Trends and Issues 90: Criminal and Juvenile Justice in Illinois*. Chicago: Illinois Criminal Justice Information Authority.
——— (1991). *Trends and Issues 1991: Education and Criminal Justice in Illinois*. Chicago: Illinois Criminal Justice Information Authority.
Illinois Task Force (1993). *Final Report*. Chicago: Illinois Task Force on Crime and Corrections, March 1993.
Jaynes, Gerald, and Robin Williams, eds. (1989). *A Common Destiny: Blacks and American Society*. Washington, D.C.: National Academy Press.
John Howard Association (1991). "Jail Conditions and Compliance with the Consent Decree Relating to the Cook County

Department of Corrections." Court Monitoring Report. Chicago: John Howard Association, October 25, 1991.
───── (1992). "Jail Conditions and Compliance with the Consent Decree Relating to the Cook County Department of Corrections." Court Monitoring Report. Chicago: John Howard Association, May 22, 1992.
───── (1995). "Conditions at the Cook County Department of Corrections and Compliance with the Consent Decree." Supplement to the Court Monitoring Report of February 1, 1995. Chicago: John Howard Association, March 23, 1995.
Kotlowitz, Alex (1991). *There Are No Children Here*. New York: Doubleday.
LaFree, Gary (1980). "The Effect of Sexual Stratification by Race on Official Reactions to Rape," *American Sociological Review*, vol. 45, no. 5 (October 1980), pp. 842-854.
L.A. Daily Journal (1992). February 19, 1992.
Manikas, Peter, John P. Heinz, Mindy S. Trossman, and Jack C. Doppelt (1990). *Criminal Justice Policymaking: Boundaries and Borderlands: Final Report of the Criminal Justice Project*. Chicago: Criminal Justice Project of Cook County; Evanston, Ill.: Center for Urban Affairs and Policy Research, Northwestern University.
Mauer, Marc (1990). *Young Black Men and the Criminal Justice System: A Growing National Problem*. Washington, D.C.: The Sentencing Project.
───── (1994). *Americans Behind Bars: The International Use of Incarceration, 1992-1993*. Washington, D.C.: The Sentencing Project.
Miller, Jerome (1992). "Hobbling a Generation: Young African-American Males in Washington, D.C.'s Criminal Justice System." Alexandria, Va.: National Center on Institutions and Alternatives.
Morris, Norval, and Michael Tonry (1990). *Between Prison and Probation*. New York: Oxford University Press.
Murphy, Timothy R. (1991). "Indigent Defense and the U.S. War on Drugs," *Criminal Justice*, Fall 1991, pp. 14-20.
Myers, Martha and John Hagan (1979). "Private and Public Trouble: Prosecutors and The Allocation of Court Resources," *Social Problems*, vol. 16 (April 1979), pp. 441-447.
NAACP (1989). *The Unfinished Agenda on Race in America*. New York: NAACP Legal Defense and Educational Fund, Inc., January 1989.
Newsday (1992). July 29, 1992.

Paternoster, Raymond (1984). "Prosecutorial Discretion in Requesting the Death Penalty: A Case of Victim Based Racial Discrimination," *Law and Society Review*, vol. 18, no. 3 (Summer 1984), pp. 437-478.

Petersilia, Joan (1983). *Racial Disparities in the Criminal Justice System*. Prepared for the National Institute of Corrections, U.S. Department of Justice. Santa Monica, Calif.: Rand.

Pranis, Kay (1989). "Options in Criminal Corrections: A Study of Costs and Opportunities in Delaware, Minnesota." Citizens Council on Crime and Justice, 1989.

Roberts, Dorothy (1991). "Punishing Drug Addicts Who Have Babies: Women of Color, Equality and the Right of Privacy," *Harvard Law Review*, vol. 104, no. 7 (May 1991), pp. 1419-1482.

San Jose Mercury News (1981). December 8, 1991.

Spohn, Cassia, John Gruhl, and Susan Welch (1987). "The Impact of the Ethnicity and Gender of Defendants on the Decision to Reject or Dismiss Felony Charges," *Criminology*, vol. 25, no. 1 (February 1987), pp. 175-191.

Stone, Randolph N. (1991). "Crisis in the Criminal Justice System," *Harvard BlackLetter Journal* (Harvard Law School), vol. 8 (Spring 1991), pp. 33-39.

Tonry, Michael (1990). "Criminal Justice and Social Welfare." Minneapolis: University of Minnesota Law School, April 3, 1991.

UPI (1991). September 5, 1991.

USA Today (1992). May 13, 1992.

Wald, Patricia M. (1991). Welcome and Opening Remarks by the Honorable Patricia M. Wald, Chief Judge, U.S. Court of Appeals. Proceedings of the Fifty-First Judicial Conference of the District of Columbia Circuit, Hershey, Pennsylvania, May 21, 1990, *Federal Rules Decisions*, vol. 134 (1991), pp. 324-328.

Washington Post (1992). May 3, 1992.

Washington Times (1992). April 28, 1992.

COMMENTS

Frances Kahn Zemans

Randolph Stone, with clarity and considerable passion, articulates many of the ills that beset the criminal justice system in Cook County and in many American cities. Having served as the Cook County Public Defender, he certainly knows from personal experience the frustrations of many of the system's participants and is attuned to the racism that pervades that system. Although I regret and deplore that racism, I cannot feign surprise. Because the criminal justice system is the context in which society's authority is most visibly played out, it should not be surprising that society's prejudices and power relationships are amply represented and arguably exaggerated in such a context. Having said that, there is no question that if justice is to prevail, racism within criminal justice must be addressed directly and forcefully. Yet even if racism were reduced in the criminal justice system (there have been efforts to do so, some of them somewhat successful), we would still be faced with a system that is overwhelmed and is viewed by the public with increasing skepticism.

Stone offers a number of suggestions, including a "crime prevention strategy," "intermediate punishments," "adequate and balanced funding," and "minimizing racial bias." These are good ideas that are worth pursuing. I fear, however, that with the possible exception of adequate funding, they basically amount to tinkering that fails to address "the essential nexus between social justice and criminal justice" noted by Stone in the introduction to his chapter. When that nexus is discussed in justice system circles, it is generally an acknowledgment of powerlessness as articulated by those within the system who, like Stone, express frustration over policy and funding decisions driven by political rhetoric.

While I find such political rhetoric abhorrent and dysfunctional, we cannot find it all that surprising in a democracy where many citizens live in fear. The reality is that the public wants protection and looks to the criminal justice system to provide it. For example, Stone seems to lament the increase in mandatory transfers from juvenile to adult criminal court. But we now have "children" who carry AK-47's and commit murder and rape—people are afraid. And while Stone focuses on the racial disparities among criminal defendants, minorities are also overrepresented among the victims. Thus, reports indicate that the residents of Chicago's Cabrini-Green public housing project welcomed the police sweeps after three young children were killed within a few months of each other doing nothing more offensive than walking to school!

Criminal justice personnel surely cannot solve the problems of poverty, homelessness, disintegrated families, joblessness, and drug and alcohol abuse that so directly relate to criminal behavior. However, we can ask whether there is anything that can be done within the criminal justice system besides dismissals, plea bargains, acquittals, and convictions.

Some have begun to suggest that the answer is yes, and some have even begun to act on it. Like the changes that have been developing in civil justice, the approach I am suggesting raises implicit questions about the validity of the purely adjudicatory model. It even goes so far as to question whether a criminal defense attorney, public or private, necessarily does the client a favor by achieving a verdict of not guilty if that verdict is only part of a revolving door by which the defendant returns to the same conditions that led to the original crime, only to return again to the criminal justice system in short order for repeat behavior. Legalistic advocacy of that sort appears to some as socially and personally destructive for those who could have been better helped by some other kind of intervention.

For example, Attorney General Janet Reno, who was previously prosecutor for Dade County, Florida, has suggested a "carrot and stick" approach for drug offenders, which combines real treatment with a serious and enforced threat of incarceration followed by long-term drug testing (Reno, 1990). She particularly suggests focusing on doing more for those who, given the right direction and opportunities, will not be repeat offenders. The criminal justice system cannot change the world. However, it does have control over individual defendants that could be exercised in a different fashion. While this has been done by individual judges, it is being suggested in some quarters that more systematic implementation would be very beneficial.

A variation on this has been suggested in the report of the Massachusetts Commission on the Future of the Courts (1992). Recognizing the limitations of pure adjudication even for criminal justice, the commission proposes a statewide network of "comprehensive justice centers," bringing a variety of agencies under a single roof. These would include, for example, on-site emergency services such as crisis counseling and psychological evaluations, complemented by "efficient referral to off-site providers." While individual judges have frequently intervened to order necessary evaluation and treatment, the Massachusetts model goes much further by institutionalizing such alternatives.

It may be that such approaches are not appropriate to all who are accused of what has been labeled criminal behavior. We already make distinctions in law and practice between repeat offenders and first offenders and between more and less serious offenders. But these models suggest that we may need to divide the pie somewhat differently and that failure to do so will result in greater burdens on both the criminal justice system and society at large.

One way to implement what may appear to some (although surely not to all) as somewhat radical modifications in the criminal justice system would be to focus on juveniles. A recent report on prisoners in the state of Maryland indicates that the overwhelming proportion of incarcerated adults had juvenile records. We cannot estimate whether some would have landed elsewhere had they been firmly guided in ways suggested by the Reno and Massachusetts models. And we will not know if we never experiment.

These models significantly diverge from the traditional rights-oriented adjudicatory approach that is firmly grounded in our constitutional history. We need not, indeed should not, diminish these time-honored protections that have served us well. But neither should we be irrevocably wedded to patterns of behavior that may not always serve the purposes for which they were intended. For we need to recognize that as society changes so must our mechanisms of justice if we are to achieve a just result.

REFERENCES

Massachusetts Commission on the Future of the Courts (1992). *Reinventing Justice 2022: Report of the Chief Justice's Commission on the Future of the Courts*. Boston.

Reno, Janet (1990). Speech to the 1989-90 Second Annual Issues Conference, Florida House of Representatives. Tallahassee, February 6, 1990.

THE FUTURE OF CORRECTIONS: PROBATION

Patrick D. McAnany

Corrections is most commonly thought of as the system dealing with offenders after they leave the courtroom. However, the most commonly imposed sanction is probation, which is administered largely from the courtroom. Policymakers and researchers have paid far less attention to probation than to prisons. In an era of high incarceration rates, this appears to be attention well paid, but the use of incarceration is coming up against a fiscal wall. This will require the public to explore other correctional programs. Probation is the main alternative.

Probation today is a good deal different from what it was 20 years ago. With its central feature of community release, the public image of probation suffers because it appears to be lenient, offender-oriented, and risky to community safety. However, probation has undergone several changes that have transformed it into a more clearly punitive sanction that is based on the offense and offers intensive supervision for community protection. These transformations have not come about easily and reflect a struggle for probation to find its place in the general sentencing reform that took place between 1970 and 1985.

There remain several problems, however. First, the conflict between a desert-based approach to sentencing and a crime-control approach remains unresolved. Probation, as one of the main sentences, embodies this conflict. Second, intermediate sanctions, which have been fashioned for probation to fill the gap between prison and community release generally, have not been fully integrated into sentencing reform. Part of this is a lack of resources to support enhanced probation programs. But the integration has faltered as well because of the lack of a common device to allocate different types of sanctions—that is, how to equate time on probation with time in prison. Finally, probation differs from prison because it requires cooperation among several officials—judge, probation officer, and prosecutor—as well as cooperation by the offender. Little has been done to test the effectiveness of such a complicated set of relationships.

This chapter begins by examining the data on corrections and noting that current data point clearly away from use of incarceration at current rates. Next, it will look at the jurisprudence underlying sentencing reform and examine the meaning of the current "just deserts" philosophy. The third section will place probation within the context of the reform to determine how it has—and has not—been transformed. The fourth section is a discussion of issues remaining for probation, such as resources, the role of judges, and the need for a better articulated system of intermediate sanctions. The chapter closes with some recommendations for policy action.

SOME REFLECTIONS ON CORRECTIONAL DATA

The American criminal justice system is notably fragmented. Any basic text will start with the notion that jurisdictionally the system is divided into at least three levels of authority: federal, state, and local. It will also note the separation of powers that subdivides these levels. For corrections, a boundary-ladened criminal justice system has its special problems. The power to commit persons to the system, as well as the power to release, frequently lies across boundaries of authority. The central example is the power of a (county) judge to sentence offenders to state correctional institutions without consent of state officials.

This fragmentation makes data collection and utilization problematic. The Illinois Criminal Justice Information Authority has noted this every year in its *Trends and Issues* volumes, where it summarizes data on police, courts, and corrections. Not only are the data aggregated, preventing case-tracking, but use of terms changes from agency to agency. Beyond basic head count, much criminal justice data, both state and national, are unreliable.

Probation is a case in point. There have never been adequate national data on probation despite early attempts by the National Probation Association. The explanation given has been the nature of probation itself. Each state had created a unique set of community release conditions. Many probation agencies were local, rather than state, operations and did not systematically collect information. Only recently has a national data collection been attempted through federal funding to the National Association of Criminal Justice Planners (Cuniff and Bergsmann, 1990). As yet, we have only limited comparative data across jurisdictions.

Having said this, we do have a very firm basis for making at least one judgment about corrections: the secure institutions (prisons and jails) are terribly overcrowded. At the end of 1993, the head count in federal and state prisons stood at 948,881, an overall annual increase of 7.4 percent from 1992 (BJS, 1994). While states differed in overcrowding (e.g., North Dakota at 85% of rated capacity vs. California at 183%), every state and the federal system were at or above their capacity to house prisoners (BJS, 1992). Rated capacity is the bed level currently judged by professional standards to be acceptable. One can note, however, without excessive cynicism, that this standard has served only to increase capacity, never to decrease it. This latter point illustrates the historical diversity among states as to population size, capacity, and rates of imprisonment. North Dakota held 492 prisoners and had a rate of imprisonment of 49 per 100,000, as compared with California, which held 101,808 and had a rate of 120 (BJS, 1992; Cahalan, 1986). What causes these variations is subject to much debate, and little satisfactory evidence has been mounted to both explain and address the scale of imprisonment issue (Zimring and Hawkins, 1991). How large a system can society tolerate and afford?

Illinois is no exception to these dismal figures. It held nearly 35,000 prisoners at the end of 1993, an increase of 9 percent over the previous year (Illinois Department of Corrections, 1994). At the same time it was at 122 percent of even its rated capacity (BJS, 1992). The Illinois Task Force on Crime and Corrections issued a report in March 1993 that indicated that the state would reach its capacity ceiling by July 1994 (Illinois Task Force, 1993, p. 4). Illinois has been unusual, however, in its herculean efforts to keep up with the flood-tide of incarceration since 1980 (see Table 1). It has built and opened 15 new prisons and four work camps and has plans to finish two more prisons and a converted high school facility of 500 beds, plus a super-maximum prison for incorrigible offenders. These earlier efforts, according to the Task Force, kept up with prison population growth until the late 1980s. What happened then was a surge in admission of drug offenders, the first fruits of the war on drugs (Illinois Task Force, 1993). "Drug offenders are the fastest growing population of inmates being admitted by the courts [in Illinois]. Drug offenders currently make up more than one-quarter of all prison admissions and about 18 percent of the prison population" (ICJIA, 1993, p. 5).

TABLE 1: Illinois Adult Felony Probation Caseload and Adult Prison Population (as of December 31 of each year)

	Probation	Prison	Ratio (Probation:Prison)	Total (Probation + Prison)	Pct. in Prison
1980	30,377	12,539	2.42:1	42,916	29.2%
1981	32,793	13,917	2.36:1	46,710	29.8
1982	31,413	13,895	2.26:1	45,308	30.7
1983	29,786	15,432	1.93:1	45,218	34.1
1984	25,574	16,854	1.52:1	42,428	39.7
1985	26,039	18,279	1.42:1	44,318	41.2
1986	29,499	19,456	1.52:1	48,955	39.7
1987	30,835	19,850	1.55:1	50,685	39.2
1988	31,139	21,081	1.48:1	52,220	40.4
1989	35,064	22,576	1.55:1	57,640	39.2
1990	38,943	26,369	1.48:1	65,312	40.4
1991	41,214	29,115	1.42:1	70,329	41.4
1992	45,492	31,640	1.44:1	77,132	41.0
1993	41,794	34,495	1.21:1	76,289	45.2

Sources: Administrative Office of the Illinois Courts, Probation Division, *Probation Statistics* (various years); Illinois Criminal Justice Information Authority, *Trends and Issues 89*; Illinois Department of Corrections, *Human Services Plan* (1990, 1993).

This surge, which adds a higher pitch to an already steep trend line, has given pause to those who felt building more prisons was the answer. Illinois's fiscal condition has given urgency to answering the question, "What do we do with offenders?" As the state Task Force indicates, "[T]here will be *no* physical space left in which to house any additional offenders. As a practical matter, this means that by the end of FY96 there will be more than *4,000* sentenced offenders whom the Department of Corrections will not be able to incarcerate" (Illinois Task Force, 1993, p. 22; emphasis in original).

Beyond increasing capacity by building more prisons and doubling up inmates in cells, both of which Illinois pursued vigorously in the 1980s, there are the "alternatives" to incarceration.

Traditionally, probation has served that role. I will discuss the development of probation later in this chapter. Here, I want to present some data on the use of probation during the rise in prison populations since 1980.

Nationally, there were more than 2.6 million adults on probation in 1990. That represents more than three probationers for every prisoner in that year. Another way to put it is that about 70 percent of all sentenced offenders are placed on probation. Of course, that accounts for misdemeanants and other minor offenders who cannot—or would not—be imprisoned. The growth of probation over the five-year period of 1985-90 was 36 percent as compared with 53 percent growth for prisons (BJS, 1991). In Illinois, there was a 25 percent growth in adult probation cases in the four years between 1988 and 1991. However, *felony probation* caseloads increased at a faster rate of 32 percent for the same period (AOIC, 1994). For these same four years, the number of adults in Illinois prisons grew by 38 percent. From 1980 to 1993, the felony probation caseload increased 38 percent, while the state's prison population grew 175 percent (see Table 1).

This growth trend for prisons needs to be reassessed. Not only are there fiscal costs to be examined, but the long-term implications for community protection in terms of recidivism need to be looked at as well. Do we sacrifice long-term protection in later careers of persons we incarcerated, as opposed to persons we retain in the community at short-term risk? This would be true if incarceration increases the risk of reoffending at a higher rate, or at a more serious level, than community release, whatever the initial fiscal costs.

To get a more complete picture of prisons versus probation, it would help to add figures from parole. Parole is the community release portion of a sentence of incarceration. Thus, to accurately compare probation as an alternative, parole population needs to be added to prison figures. Nationwide in 1990, there were 457,000 people on parole, plus 773,000 in prisons, for a total of more than 1.2 million under the prison/parole regimen, compared with 2.6 million on probation. The ratio then is about two-thirds on probation and one-third in the prison/parole system.

While head count figures may offer some grounds for comparison, the reader needs to keep in mind certain factual differences. Probation terms are considerably shorter than prison and parole terms combined. The turnover for probation is higher, and more individuals pass through probation. Further, probation failures may contribute to the prison population. Each year a significant percentage of prison admissions are based on violation of probation. Prison figures also may be fed by parole failures. Zimring and Hawkins note that advances in drug-testing technology added considerably to California's prison population, as parolees were found to have "dirty urine" and were revoked from parole (1991, p. 174). This flow of cases to the prisons, as the catch basin of the system, illustrates the inability of prison administrators to control their own populations. Officials outside of the system, judges or parole board members, control the spigot.

A final point about corrections data would be to note the overall number of persons under penal sanction in the United States. Table 2 illustrates the numbers, percentage of total population, and the rate of growth over a period of five years for those serving (or paying off) penal sanctions. The absolute number of 4.35 million individuals under penal sanction in 1990 is strking. The 2.4 percent of the total adult population that this figure represents is even more shocking. But the rate of growth of offenders under correctional sanction in relation to population is a figure that underscores the issues raised by Zimring and Hawkins's discussion of the scale of imprisonment. How large is large enough for our overall correctional enterprise?

These data have not contained a highly salient factor: race. They have not done so because that issue reflects a complex set of factors that cannot be covered here. But it would be wrong to omit all reference to race, as American culture is often dominated by it. Recent research on parole suggests that community release of prisoners reflects a changing correctional paradigm. Whereas earlier models reflected a disciplinary and then a clinical role for parole agents, today's agent pursues a management approach (Simon, 1993). For minorities, this management approach is built on the fact that their communities do not have the social resources to offer any real support. The system offers certain containment elements, such as drug testing and surveillance, but very little social support. The fact that one in four young Black males in the United States between the ages of 17 and 29 is under some sort of penal control suggests the racial dimension reflected in the overcrowding phenomenon discussed above (Mauer, 1990). While the rest of the chapter passes over these sobering facts without further mention, this says nothing of their salience for corrections.

TABLE 2: Correctional Population in the United States, 1985-1990

	Correctional Population	As Pct. of Adult Population
1985	3,011,000	1.7%
1986	3,240,000	1.8
1987	3,460,000	1.9
1988	3,713,000	2.0
1989	4,055,000	2.2
1990	4,350,000	2.4
Pct. change 1985-90	44%	

Source: Bureau of Justice Statistics, *Bulletin: Probation and Parole 1990* (November 1991).

CORRECTIONAL GROWTH AND PHILOSOPHICAL CHANGE

The growth of imprisonment rates began from a low point in 1974. At approximately the same time, the American sentencing system was undergoing a period of scrutiny and change. The system then in place had evolved over a period of 50 years. It was called "indeterminate sentencing," in which the prison term was set at an indeterminate range from a minimum to a maximum period, such as 10-to-20 years. The judge imposed the initial sentence, and the parole board reviewed the sentence once the minimum was served to determine whether the prisoner should be released. There were other elements that affected the outcome, such as "good time" given or taken away by prison administrators. Thus, the basic structure was highly discretionary in nature.

Underlying this indeterminate sentencing system was the rehabilitation philosophy then prevailing in corrections. Among the traditional goals of corrections—retribution, deterrence, incapacitation, and rehabilitation—the orientation of the time was clearly rehabilitational. This philosophy posited that the primary purpose of corrections was to identify the problem that gave rise to criminal behavior by the offender and to treat the problem. While many admitted that the ideal had rarely been achieved, few were willing to forsake the rehabilitation model for more punitive outcomes attached to other goals (Gerber and McAnany, 1967). But as critics later pointed out, the rehabilitation ideal itself produced massive suffering in the name of benevolence (Fogel, 1975; Allen, 1964).

Sentencing, as opposed to corrections, always served other goals. The American Law Institute's *Model Penal Code* (1962) retained a rehabilitation orientation in its sentencing but required sentences to be determined initially by deterrence. That meant that the prison term was set by the court to protect the community, based on the seriousness of the offense and the likelihood of other crimes being committed by the offender or other potential offenders. Naturally, there was a broad range of sentences that could be imposed under such a discretionary approach, though the code created a graduated level of severity of sentence based on the perceived seriousness of the crime.

Incapacitation was accepted as a secondary goal in sentencing. When offenders were dangerous and could not otherwise be rehabilitated, they might be sentenced to an extended term to physically restrain them from further offending. Clearly, the indeterminate system could be easily adjusted to serve this purpose, as suggested by the National Council on Crime and Delinquency's Model Sentencing Act (NCCD, 1963).

Retribution was broadly rejected as a goal of either sentencing or corrections (Gerber and McAnany, 1967). Such a goal was served by imposing sentences on guilty offenders because they deserved them. Most critics of the 1950s and 1960s considered such an approach as little more than fulfilling a primitive desire for revenge by society against the offender (e.g., Packer, 1968).

Both the indeterminate structure and its underlying philosophy were subject to severe attack in the early 1970s. In essence, the critics perceived a great deal of disparity and injustice in this highly discretionary system. Both judges and parole boards had very little by way of objective standards to guide their decisions. Whether these decisions were made on the basis of race or class, as suggested by some, or were merely capricious, they produced very different sentences for persons who had been guilty of the same offense (American Friends Service Committee, 1971; Fogel, 1975; Von Hirsch, 1976).

The critics quickly identified rehabilitation as the culprit ideology. There was no agreed scientific basis for judgments of rehabilitation. Further, where rehabilitation programs had been tried and carefully evaluated, there was little or no difference in recidivism rates between treated and non-treated inmates (Lipton, Martinson, and Wilks, 1975). The same was true for measurements of future dangerousness. There was little evidence to substantiate the predictability of future offending (Von Hirsch, 1976). The use of deterrence as a measure of punishment was also discounted because it, too, depended a great deal on the personal judgment of the judge or parole board member on what future offenses might be committed.

This led to a reexamination of retribution. While some still felt desert was nothing more than a mask for revenge, others found in it a moral basis for justice (Von Hirsch, 1976). However one came down on this philosophical issue, retribution or just deserts had the advantage of offering an objective sentencing measure. Each offense deserved a punishment that was proportioned to its seriousness and the culpability of the offender. A judge could determine objectively what had been done to the victim and the rough level of the defendant's culpability. Sentencing could eliminate most discretion by adopting a retributive sentencing framework.

Out of this professional debate came sentencing reform, which did three things. First, it changed the philosophy of sentencing from rehabilitation to punishment. Second, it created a realignment of offenses into categories of seriousness to serve proportionality in sentences. Third, it put the focus on the court rather than on the parole board because each sentence was to be determined in advance by the nature of the offense, not by what the offender might do in the future. While not all states adopted the most stringently determinate structure (sentencing guidelines), most accepted the underlying retributive or just-deserts philosophy and the notion of proportionality (Shane-DuBow, Brown, and Olsen, 1985).

Because these sentencing reforms accompanied rising rates of imprisonment, many were inclined to see a causal relationship between sentencing reform and overcrowding. Desert-based sentencing created a punitive atmosphere in the court room, which drove up imprisonment rates (Cullen and Gilbert, 1982). Others saw a more general shift in the attitude of the public toward punitiveness (Pillsbury, 1989). This could account independently for the rise in imprisonment rates, because prosecutors and judges, despite some restraint from determinate sentencing reform, could still select more severe sentences. However, Scheingold's research questions the assumption of rising punitiveness in the general public, at least in its effect on the political process (Scheingold, 1991).

Illinois was a state that adopted an early version of determinate sentencing. In its 1978 legislation, Illinois changed its system by eliminating discretionary parole release and substituting a "flat" sentence that had to be served before the offender was released to serve a parole term in the community. It left the court free, however, to select from a very broad range of prison terms as compared with other determinate sentencing reforms.

Sentencing guidelines were the structural reform most closely approximating true proportionality and minimal discretion. Under this system, the sentence was determined by the seriousness of the offense and the past record of the offender. Very narrow ranges of choice were given to the judge under a matrix of possible levels of seriousness and numbers of past convictions. Other culpability factors could be added to the system to further distinguish among offenders. Minnesota was the first—and most often evaluated—among a handful of states to adopt this system. The federal courts followed in 1987 (Von Hirsch et al., 1987).

In all of these reform efforts, one of the most commonly imposed sentences—probation—was left almost unnoticed. This may have been based on the perception that probation was not punishment. It may also have been because the probation profession had resisted the change in correctional philosophy from rehabilitation to retribution.

PROBATION AS PUNISHMENT

As the most commonly imposed sentence, probation affects a significant portion of the correctional population. As prison rates went up, probation managed to grow as well. However, as illustrated by the Illinois figures in Table 1, probation has lost ground to prisons. This may have been because the community was growing more punitive in its attitude toward criminals. It may have been a structural outcome of sentencing reform. One sentencing reform common to almost every state during this period was the elimination of probation as a sentencing option for most serious offenses (Shane-DuBow, Brown, and Olsen, 1985). Further, sentencing guidelines created a structured system in which the choice between incarceration and probation was clearly demarcated by a line that divided prison and community release. Depending where the line was drawn based on seriousness and prior record, the structure favored either prison or community release. The federal guidelines set the level for imprisonment very low and thus guaranteed the decreased use of probation (Freed, 1992).

Part of the problem, however, lay with probation itself. As sentencing reform went forward, probation was left out of the debate. Probation professionals simply did not have the public visibility of prison administrators. When probation did become a matter of public discussion, judges often were considered the primary spokespersons. Further, probation had always considered itself rehabilitationist in approach. It was not interested in a debate where rehabilitation was attacked and rejected.

There was a central legal feature to probation that made it poorly suited for inclusion in sentencing reform. In most jurisdictions, probation was not a sentence but a conditional status that involved the postponement of a binding legal sentence (McAnany, 1975). It was imposed to avoid the harshness of prison and thus served leniency purposes. It was also based on the notion that certain offenders were more amenable to rehabilitation and less of a threat to the community. The judge had discretion to select probation instead of prison and impose any conditions thought conducive to these goals. Until 1972, the judge also had discretion to revoke probation without a hearing (*Morrisey v. Brewer*, 1972).

As sentencing reform moved forward, probation's anomalous situation as the most widely imposed sentence almost untouched by reform structures became apparent. Some criminal justice experts began to question whether probation could accommodate the requirements of "just deserts" (McAnany, Thomson, and Fogel, 1984). The lively discussion around these issues forced probation to recognize that, however benevolent its philosophy, it was serving basic penal purposes as a sentence. This new approach enhanced the public image of probation as public protection and not mere leniency (Harris, 1984).

Despite this effort to harden the image of probation, it still lacked authentic credentials as effective punishment. In 1985, the Rand Corporation contributed an important study that alerted probation to its exposure in this area. Using a California sample of serious felony probationers, Petersilia and associates found that they had recidivated at a rate of 65 percent over a period of forty months, often committing further serious felonies (Petersilia et al.,

1985). Later researchers have contested these outcomes as not generalizable to other jurisdictions (e.g., Whitehead, 1991). Nonetheless, the findings underlined the fact that while prison guarantees total protection of the community during sentence, probation can offer only probabilities of success.

These doubts about the risks of probation for the public led to the creation of probation programs with enhanced protective features, most frequently called "intensive supervision probation" (ISP). Initially in Georgia, then in New Jersey and Massachusetts, ISPs were established (Byrne, Lurigio, and Baird, 1989). The logic driving these programs was conflicted. On the one hand, they were a response to the retributive approach of sentencing reform—probation was punitive in nature. On the other hand, they were intended to alleviate prison crowding by encouraging judges to impose probation instead of incarceration. Because that meant release of more serious offenders into the community, surveillance became more pervasive to assure acceptable levels of risk. As in other areas of sentencing reform, the conflict between a philosophy of just deserts and crime control remains essentially unaddressed.

POLICY ISSUES FOR THE 1990s: PROBATION AS INTERMEDIATE SANCTION

There are four sets of issues surrounding the creation of intermediate sanctions that could move corrections away from expanding use of incarceration. (1) There needs to be a better understanding of how to reconcile the competing goals of desert and crime control. (2) A better integration of intermediate sanctions into current sentencing reforms needs to be undertaken. (3) The issue of resources is critical for effective intermediate sanctions. (4) The pivotal role of the judge needs to be reassessed.

Competing Goals

It may sound like a philosophical discussion of little practical import to ask how a desert-based system can accommodate incapacitation goals. But it has real-world implications, especially for probation. The sentencing reforms of the past 15 years made clear that our most objective criterion was the seriousness of the offense. Allowing this criterion to be adjusted for future dangerousness appeared incompatible with proportionality and justice (Von Hirsch, 1985; Robinson, 1987). On the other hand, disallowing any consideration of future offending went against consistent research that showed that judges and parole board members used this factor in assessing release decisions (Gottfredson and Gottfredson, 1988). The practical compromise was struck by allowing past convictions, which reflected some desert factors, to be used as a surrogate measure for dangerousness (Von Hirsch, 1985; Von Hirsch, Knapp, and Tonry, 1987).

There remains a dispute about the range of sentence adjustment allowed by a just-deserts philosophy. Some argue that proportionality is a broad concept that allows for considerable flexibility within the norm of unfairness. We ask the question of whether a particular sentence is *unfair* regarding the offense, making way for some adjustment in favor of dangerousness (Morris, 1976). Others oppose this idea and suggest that proportionality requires positively fair sentences within much narrower ranges (Von Hirsch, 1985). This dispute may be raised in especially direct ways in determining whether the sentence should be prison or probation. Two offenders with identical current and past offense histories may present quite different patterns of dangerousness. Selecting probation for one and prison for the other may make eminent common and correctional sense. But allowing this may very well distort the principles of just-deserts fairness that grounds sentencing reform. Until a carefully articulated policy can be worked out, the clash of values will continue to afflict the system on a daily basis.

Integrating Intermediate Sanctions into Current Sentencing

The second issue is the integration of intermediate sanctions into current sentencing. One approach is simply to add more restrictive community release programs to the mix of alternatives, thus increasing the range of choices offered to judges. Illinois now has an ISP operating in 18 of 102 counties, as well as some home confinement and electronic monitoring (Grundell, 1994). But community release sentences, unlike a great number of mandated prison sentences, remain largely discretionary with judges. This means that there is little statutory pressure directing judges toward probation and a good deal of pressure, both in law and public opinion, toward prisons.

An optimal system would be one in which all sanctions were governed by a common penal measure across different types, with each offense and each past conviction narrowly determinative of outcome (Morris and Tonry, 1990). In such a system, punishment for minor offenses would rely solely on some type of probation and fines; for the most serious felonies, prisons and jails would be used; and for a middle set of offenses, either would be used. All sanctions would be measured by a common unit of punishment across different types of sentence. That such a system has not yet been substantially attempted is partially attributable to the difficulty in giving some common weight to prison time and other sanctions. How many dollars of fine are worth a day of incarceration? When the U.S. Supreme Court faced such an issue, it sidestepped it, acknowledging the difficulties (*Bearden v. Georgia*, 1983).

For Illinois, the most practical step would be to re-examine its list of non-probationable offenses and create a more flexible, yet disciplined, approach to selecting probation as a sentence. This approach has been endorsed recently by the state's Task for Crime and Corrections (Illinois Task Force, 1993, pp. 97-98). The state needs to adopt a form of guidelines where consideration of middle-range sanctions would find a place. It already recognizes that probation is a sentence, and it already has a crude proportionality for probation sentences. What remains is a step toward a more explicit recognition of proportionality that includes all sentencing options.

Resources

The third issue is resources. If intermediate sanctions are to be employed, judges must have confidence that there are sufficient resources to ensure compliance with court orders. Cost savings have been the staple of intermediate sanctions support. There is evidence of large cost savings when enhanced community-release sanctions are used as a substitute for prisons (Byrne, Lurigio, and Baird, 1989). However, most ISPs have served very small numbers of potential offenders. Illinois, for example, has had ISP in place since 1986, but as of December 31, 1993, only 1,052 adult offenders were on such programs (Grundel, 1994). This contrasts with 35,000 in prisons as of the same date, despite the per-offender cost differential of $17,000 for prisons and $4,000 for intensive supervision (Grundel, 1994). The fact that intensive programs operate in only 18 counties, despite the overcrowded condition of the prison system in Illinois, illustrates the peripheral nature of intermediate sanctions in the present corrections system.

The other side of the resource issue is net-widening. Critics of intermediate sanctions point out that ISPs, created to reduce prison populations, often are filled with offenders who would have been assigned to regular probation anyway, thus widening the net of social control intended for more serious offenders. Overcoming the waste of resources reflected in net widening will be difficult. Even in highly structured programs, the temptation to place "better" cases on ISP is considerable (Byrne, Lurigio, and Baird, 1989).

The Role of Judges

The final set of issues involves the administration of intermediate sanctions. If one assumes that all of the above issues are resolved favorably for the use of intermediate sanctions, how judges participate in the administration of them is critical. Unlike a prison sentence administered by a distant warden, community-release sanctions are the continuing business of the judges imposing them.

The problem of enforcement is critical to intermediate sanctions. Unlike incarceration, which is largely a passive sanction (it is executed by mere presence within prison), community release sanctions require a large degree of cooperation. The probationer is expected to avoid certain behaviors and perform others. The system ultimately depends on the implicit threat of incarceration if the probationer refuses to cooperate. Very little research has been devoted to the revocation process (McAnany and Thomson, 1982). The ISPs have almost all included a series of graduated penalties to increase the threat of ultimate revocation. These have been administered by probation departments in cooperation with courts. Rigorous evaluation of these disciplinary efforts has yet to be done, though some researchers have found that technical violations of probation short of new criminal offenses are not themselves indicative of further new offending (Byrne, Lurigio, and Baird, 1989; Petersilia and Turner, 1991).

The role of probation officers in an intermediate system is only now being assessed. There is no reason to believe that probation officers will not take their community protection role seriously, but they should not assume strict enforcement roles delegated to police (Conrad, 1984). Rehabilitation of the offender may be the natural inclination of probation officers, but they can adjust to a desert system where punishment and just outcome are uppermost, and probably already share many values found in it (Thomson, 1984). There is evidence, too, that community protection against recidivism in ISPs may derive as much from treatment factors as from surveillance factors (Byrne and Kelly, 1989; Petersilia and Turner, 1991).

For many practical reasons, the use of ISPs will increase over the next decade, both in Illinois and elsewhere. Much of this will have to do with costs of imprisonment. Thus, the cooperation between judges and probation officers will be intensified. If more offenders are diverted from prison to the community, greater risks are inevitable. The way risks are shared between probation and court has to do with the process of initial assessment. The probation officer provides a profile of the offender in the pre-sentencing investigation report. Currently probation utilizes some version of a risk-assessment instrument that can be validated over time for the locale (Baird, 1981; Glaser, 1987). While there is no guarantee of accuracy in individual cases, these instruments still offer some assurance to both judge and probation officer that idiosyncratic factors are moderated (Gottfredson and Gottfredson, 1988). The judge under ISPs is more likely to have a choice of conditions of probation rather than a choice of prison. Thus, the judge will have to depend more heavily on the pre-sentence report and the probation officer in order to tailor the conditions to fit offenders and their circumstances.

The central problem in ISPs is the need to take risks. This risk-taking is, indeed, a cooperative venture among the judge, probation officer, prosecutor, and community. A clearly articulated program that states its goals and objectives, as well as remedial steps of enforcement, has the best chance of making cooperation successful. The role of judges remains central because it is they who have final authority to both impose and revoke the sentence.

RECOMMENDATIONS

The Illinois Task Force on Crime and Corrections made a series of recommendations in its final report. Its posture was clear: Illinois can no longer build its way out of prison overcrowding. The report proposed a reduction of recidivism that would reduce the flow of repeat offenders to the system, particularly the prisons. It would accomplish this by means of improving treatment opportunities for incarcerated and paroled offenders. The following recommendations build on those of the Task Force but reflect the community-release side of corrections, which was substantially excluded by the mandate of the Task Force.

(1) *Create a guidelines commission to reassess sentencing in Illinois:* Illinois underwent two sentencing reforms during the 1970s. Unfortunately, each came at the wrong time. The Illinois Code of Corrections (1973) came just prior to the reform efforts for indeterminate sentencing. The Class X and Determinate Sentencing Act of 1978 came too soon to take advantage of sentencing guidelines. Illinois has gone halfway in each reform and left a great deal of discretion with judges and almost none with prison administrators. It is time to reassess sentencing outcomes in light of a more rational system.

(2) *Establish a task force on sentencing and corrections to create a database for policy:* Despite an excellent start with the Illinois Criminal Justice Information Authority's *Trends and Issues*, Illinois lacks an adequate database for correctional policy. Court data, vital to assessing community release and other correctional outcomes, are often slow in coming and not easily integrated across different judicial districts. The ideal would be an offender-based transactions system, in which each offense is associated with a specific offender or offenders (ICJIA, 1989). Whether the Information Authority or another entity would best serve in this role needs to be discussed.

(3) *Focus policy research on correctional issues, especially community release:* As noted in many places, current research on probation is quite insufficient (Petersilia et al., 1985; Gottfredson, Finckenauer, and Rauh, 1977). We are much more able to pinpoint the problems of prisons and jails than we are those of community release. While some evaluation has been done on current intermediate sanction programs, much remains to be done (Morris and Tonry, 1990). Little has been done in Illinois. An evaluation of its ISP was undertaken but then dropped for lack of state funding (Thomson, 1987). This shows little commitment to the obvious impending policy shift that Illinois now faces, from prisons to some form of community release.

(4) *Create a task force of judges and probation officers for policy and training development:* Despite the fact that judges and probation officers interact every day in court, there has been very little common development. As community release takes a more prominent role in Illinois correctional decisions, judges and proba-

tion officers must share policy discussions and develop joint training sessions. The Administrative Office of the Illinois Courts appears to be the natural locus for such efforts. It could coordinate these efforts across the several circuit courts involved.

The skeptical will note that resources are not included in this list of immediate steps to be taken to bolster the community release options for Illinois. This partly reflects a sober estimation of what needs to precede the major structural change in sentencing and corrections in the state. It also assumes that the legislature will act on the recommendations of the Task Force on Crime and Corrections, which include increased funding for the community release option (Illinois Task Force, 1994, pp. 51-60). There is need for policy to precede expenditure. There is need for data to precede policy. I think the recommendations create a basis on which funding will follow wise policy, based on information now only partially available.

REFERENCES

Allen, Francis A. (1964). *The Borderland of Criminal Justice*. Chicago: University of Chicago Press.
American Friends Service Committee (1971). *Struggle for Justice: A Report on Crime and Punishment in America*. New York: Hill and Wang.
American Law Institute (1962). *Model Penal Code*. Philadelphia: American Law Institute.
AOIC (1994). *1993 Probation Statistics*. Springfield: Probation Division, Administrative Office of the Illinois Courts.
Baird, Christopher S. (1981). "Probation and Parole Classification: The Wisconsin Model," *Corrections Today*, vol. 43, no. 3 (May-June 1981), pp. 36-41.
Bearden v. Georgia (1983). 461 U.S. 660 (1983).
BJS (1991). *Bulletin: Probation and Parole 1990*. Washington, D.C.: Bureau of Justice Statistics, U.S. Department of Justice.
──── (1992). *Bulletin: Prisoners in 1991*. Washington, D.C.: Bureau of Justice Statistics, U.S. Department of Justice.
──── (1994). *Bulletin: Prisoners in 1992*. Washington, D.C.: Bureau of Justice Statistics, U.S. Department of Justice.
Byrne, James M., Arthur J. Lurigio, and Christopher Baird (1989). "The Effectiveness of the New Intensive Supervision Programs," *Research in Corrections*, vol. 2 (1989), pp. 1-48.

Cahalan, Margaret (1986). *Historical Corrections Statistics in the United States, 1850-1984.* Washington, D.C.: Bureau of Justice Statistics.

Conrad, John P. (1984). "The Redefinition of Probation: Drastic Proposals to Solve an Urgent Problem." In Patrick D. McAnany, Doug Thomson, and David Fogel, eds. *Probation and Justice: Reconsideration of Mission.* Cambridge, Mass.: Oelgeschlager, Gunn & Hain.

Cullen, Francis T., and Karen E. Gilbert (1982). *Reaffirming Rehabilitation.* Cincinnati: Anderson.

Cuniff, Mark A., and Ilene R. Bergsmann (1990). *Managing Felons in the Community.* Washington, D.C.: National Association of Criminal Justice Planners.

Fogel, David (1975). *We Are the Living Proof.* Cincinnati, Ohio: Anderson.

Freed, Daniel J. (1992). "Federal Sentencing in the Wake of Guidelines: Unacceptable Limits on the Discretion of Sentencers," *Yale Law Journal,* vol. 101 (June 1992), pp. 1681-1754.

Gerber, Rudolph J., and Patrick D. McAnany (1967). "Punishment: Current Survey of Philosophy and Law," *St. Louis University Law Journal,* vol. 11, no. 4 (Summer 1967), pp. 491-535.

_____ eds. (1971). *Contemporary Punishment: Views, Explanations, and Justifications.* Notre Dame, Ind.: Notre Dame University Press.

Glaser, Daniel (1987). "Classification for Risk." In Don M. Gottfredson and Michael Tonry, eds., *Prediction and Classification: Criminal Justice Decision Making. Crime and Justice: A Review of Research,* vol. 9. Chicago: University of Chicago Press.

Gottfredson, Don M., James O. Finckenauer, and Carl Rauh (1977). *Probation on Trial.* Newark, N.J.: School of Criminal Justice, Rutgers University.

Gottfredson, Don M. (1987). "Prediction and Classification in Criminal Justice Decision Making." In Don M. Gottfredson and Michael Tonry, eds., *Prediction and Classification: Criminal Justice Decision Making. Crime and Justice: A Review of Research,* Vol. 9. Chicago: University of Chicago Press.

Gottfredson, Don M., and Michael R. Gottfredson (1988). *Decision-Making in Criminal Justice.* 2nd ed. New York: Plenum.

Grundel, James R. (1994). *1993 Probation Statistics*. Springfield: Administrative Office of the Illinois Courts.

Harris, M. Kay (1984). "Rethinking Probation in the Context of the Justice Model." In Patrick D. McAnany, Doug Thomson, and David Fogel, eds., *Probation and Justice: Reconsideration of Mission*. Cambridge, Mass.: Oelgeschlager, Gunn, and Hain.

ICJIA (1989). *Trends and Issues 89*. Chicago: Illinois Criminal Justice Information Authority.

_____ (1993). "Full House: Not a Winning Hand," *The Compiler* (Illinois Criminal Justice Information Authority), Winter 1993, pp. 4-5.

Illinois Task Force (1993). *Final Report*. Chicago: Illinois Task Force on Crime and Corrections, March 1993.

Lipton, Douglas, Robert Martinson, and Judith Wilks (1975). *The Effectiveness of Correctional Treatment: A Review and an Agenda for Research*. New York: Praeger.

Mauer, Marc (1990). *Young Black Men and the Criminal Justice System: A Growing National Problem*. Washington, D.C.: The Sentencing Project.

McAnany, Patrick D. (1975). "Recommendations for Improving an Ailing Probation System." In Rudolph J. Gerber, ed., *Contemporary Issues in Criminal Justice*. Port Washington, N.Y.: Kennikat Press.

_____ (1984). "Mission and Justice: Clarifying Probation's Legal Context." In Patrick D. McAnany, Doug Thomson, and David Fogel, eds. *Probation and Justice: Reconsideration of Mission*. Cambridge, Mass.: Oelgeschlager, Gunn, and Hain.

McAnany, Patrick D., Frank S. Merritt, and Edward Tromanhauser (1976). "Illinois Reconsiders 'Flat Time': An Analysis of the Impact of the Justice Model," *Chicago-Kent Law Review*, vol. 52, no. 3, pp. 621-662.

McAnany, Patrick D., and Doug Thomson (1982). *Developing Equitable Probation Revocation Practices: Preliminary Report*. Chicago: Center for Research in Law and Justice, University of Illinois at Chicago.

McAnany, Patrick D., Doug Thomson, and David Fogel, eds. (1984). *Probation and Justice: Reconsideration of Mission*. Cambridge, Mass.: Oelgeschlager, Gunn, and Hain.

Morris, Norval (1976). "Punishment, Desert, and Rehabilitation." In *Equal Justice Under Law: U.S. Department of Justice*

Bicentennial Lecture Series. Washington, D.C.: U.S. Government Printing Office.

Morris, Norval, and Michael Tonry (1990). *Between Prison and Probation: Intermediate Punishments in a Rational Sentencing System.* New York: Oxford University Press.

Morrisey v. Brewer (1972). 408 U.S. 471 (1972).

NCCD (1963). *Model Sentencing Act.* New York: National Council on Crime and Delinquency.

Packer, Herbert (1968). *The Limits of the Criminal Sanction.* Palo Alto, Calif.: Stanford University Press.

Petersilia, Joan, and Susan Turner (1985). *Guidelines-Based Justice: The Implications for Racial Minorities.* Santa Monica, Calif.: RAND Corporation.

_____ (1991). "An Evaluation of Intensive Probation in California," *Journal of Criminal Law and Criminology*, vol. 82, no. 3 (Fall 1991), pp. 610-658.

Petersilia, Joan, Susan Turner, James Kahan, and Joyce Peterson (1985). *Granting Felons Probation: Public Risks and Alternatives.* Santa Monica, Calif.: RAND Corporation.

Pillsbury, Samuel H. (1989). "Understanding Penal Reform: The Dynamic of Change," *Journal of Criminal Law and Criminology*, vol. 80, no. 3 (Fall 1989), pp. 726-780.

Robinson, Paul H. (1987). "Hybrid Principles for the Distribution of Criminal Sanctions," *Northwestern University Law Review*, vol. 82, no. 1 (Fall 1987), pp. 19-42.

Scheingold, Stuart A. (1991). *The Politics of Street Crime.* Philadelphia: Temple University Press.

Shane-DuBow, Sandra, Alice Brown, and Erik Olsen (1985). *Sentencing Reform in the United States.* Washington, D.C.: National Institute of Justice.

Simon, Jonathan (1993). *Poor Discipline: Parole and the Social Control of the Underclass, 1890-1990.* Chicago: University of Chicago Press.

Thomson, Doug (1984). "Prospects for Justice Model Probation." In Patrick D. McAnany, Doug Thomson, and David Fogel, eds. *Probation and Justice: Reconsideration of Mission.* Cambridge, Mass.: Oelgeschlager, Gunn, and Hain.

_____ (1987). "The Changing Face of Probation in the USA." In John K. Harding, ed., *Probation in the Community.* London: Tavistock.

Von Hirsh, Andrew (1976). *Doing Justice: The Choice of Punishments.* New York: Hill & Wang.

_____ (1985). *Past or Future Crimes: Deservedness and Dangerousness in Sentencing Criminals.* New Brunswick, N.J.: Rutgers University Press.

Von Hirsch, Andrew, Kay A. Knapp, and Michael Tonry (1987). *The Sentencing Commission and Its Guidelines.* Boston: Northeastern University Press.

Whitehead, John (1991). "The Effectiveness of Felony Probation: Results from an Eastern State," *Justice Quarterly*, vol, 8, no. 4 (December 1991), pp. 525-543.

Zimring, Franklin E., and Gordon Hawkins (1991). *The Scale of Imprisonment.* Chicago: University of Chicago Press.

COMMENTS

Norval Morris

Patrick McAnany's central idea is that community-based corrections will become the focus of attention in the next decade and that, at present, the consequences of such a shift are insufficiently understood. There is no doubt that he is right about this. He makes a compelling demonstration that imprisonment has grown disproportionately in relation to other punishments over the past two decades and that the resources are lacking for a continuation of this unwise trend.

McAnany sees prison as an "out of sight, out of mind" punishment of the convicted offender, requiring little or no community cooperation. He contrasts this situation with that of "probation," under which rubric he groups all community-based, nonincarcerative punishments. Community release, he suggests, requires cooperation among judges, probation officers, prosecutors, and offenders, as well as the community. This idea merits discussion, but I find myself thinking about how to minimize and work around the very likely general *community rejection* of those on probation (as McAnany defines it), that is, how to make community-based punishments work absent community cooperation.

A judge cannot, of course, guarantee that the offender placed on community release will not re-offend. Indeed, the only guarantee that could be offered is that a substantial number of those sentenced by the judge to community-based punishments will indeed re-offend. This is not a likelihood; it is a statistical certainty. The same is true, of course, of those sent to prison, but not while they are in prison, unless one cares to count crimes committed in prison. In my view, community-based punishments are, if properly selected, *more* community-protective than incarcerative punishments; but the statistical demonstration of this is not at present possible, though the data incline in that direction. But even if it is so, the community will not lightly agree. Immediate threats are more real than distant threats, and certainly more real than distant threats that might not ever impinge on a particular community.

REFLECTIONS ON CORRECTIONAL DATA

McAnany demonstrates that the growth of imprisonment has clearly outpaced the growth of probation; he further notes that probation failures may contribute to the prison population. Though he is certainly correct in his overall assessment, he underestimates the problem of revocations of probation and parole conditions. In several states, more people go to prison on revocation of the conditions of their community-based punishments than go directly from the courts on conviction of a crime. Much of this surge of numbers is attributable to unwise revocations because of one instance of "dirty" urine in a drug test; but there remains the larger problem of how to handle breaches of the conditions of community-based sanctions without further flooding the prisons.

It is unfair to criticize an author for what he has *not* written about; but the way in which race intersects with all the problems examined by McAnany merits attention. The grossly excessive use of imprisonment over the past two decades, including a doubling of prison and jail populations over the last decade, itself a period of broadly stable crime rates, is revealed as an instance of gross racial discrimination when the figures on imprisonment by race are unpacked. Again, much of this is attributable to the socially disruptive, mindlessly conducted "war on drugs"—but not all of it.

CORRECTIONAL GROWTH AND PHILOSOPHICAL CHANGE

McAnany precisely delineates the movement away from rehabilitative and deterrent purposes in punishment to retributive and desert-defined punishments, and he correctly suggests that this was an important cause of the shift to the dominance of incarcerative over community-based punishments. My only comment would be to stress the contribution made to this more punitive trend by misguided public opinion and populist political opportunism. It came to be thought in the mid-1970s that judges were excessively lenient in their punishments, that legislators should be presumed to have the capacity to define mandatory minimum punishments, and that a "war on crime" made sense. Political campaigns were won on that weird platform.

PROBATION AS PUNISHMENT

In this section of his chapter, McAnany demonstrates the need to blend all community-based punishments into an integrated and principled sentencing system. My only comment is little more than a quibble: This needs to be done not only because a better balance between incarcerative and non-incarcerative punishments should result, but, more important, because it is the only way to achieve a just and principled system of punishments for crime.

PROBATION AS INTERMEDIATE SANCTION

Here McAnany isolates the central issues in developing intermediate sanctions between prison and probation, stressing the need for more adequate resources and more critical research. He demonstrates that, so far, such punishments have been insufficiently deployed and inadequately studied. Whether one can reasonably expect more community cooperation in these processes is, however, debatable.

RECOMMENDATIONS

McAnany's policy recommendations include a sentencing guidelines system to integrate intermediate sanctions into law, a task force on sentencing and corrections that would generate data for policy and research utilization, policy research focusing on community release, and policy discussions and training sessions involving both judges and probation officers. The details of these recommendations merit critical discussion, but not their broad thrust, since McAnany offers a sensible plan for reform. It is, however, depressing to confront these proposals at a time when the budget of the Illinois Criminal Justice Information Authority, an agency doing excellent work for the state and addressing the tasks involved in meeting McAnany's recommendations, has been severely cut. Restoration of these cuts, which will have to take place sooner or later, will cost a great deal more than the cuts will save.

DRUGS AND VIOLENCE: MYTH AND REALITY

Paul J. Goldstein

There is surprisingly little systematically collected data that elaborate on the drugs/violence nexus and provide necessary empirical support for creation of informed and effective social policies that might enhance community safety. In delineating five priority areas for research and intervention to prevent homicide, the Centers for Disease Control listed, as number three, "improved understanding of the role of alcohol, drugs and drug trafficking in homicide" (Centers for Disease Control, 1990, p. 872). The intent in writing this chapter is to contribute to such improved understanding.

The initial motivations for beginning the series of research projects that form the basis of this chapter arose in 1978, in East Harlem, New York City. I was employed as project director of a study of the economic behavior of street opiate users. The project operated a series of ethnographic field stations in East Harlem. Over 200 male and female opiate users participated in a five-week series of in-depth ethnographic interviews. In addition to formal interviews, research staff engaged in continuous fieldwork activities. A total of five years (1978-1982) was devoted to this study.[1]

The East Harlem study was not designed to address issues of violence, but violence was a ubiquitous phenomenon in the East Harlem drug scene. Interviewees frequently arrived at the field station bloody and bandaged from wounds. A number of interviewees failed to complete the study because they had been severely injured or killed. A staff member was robbed at gunpoint at one of our field sites.

Most of the violence that we observed was connected to the drug business. For example, a young man (code name "Top")

---

[1] Substantive findings and a more complete description of methods have been published previously. See Johnson et al., 1985; Goldstein, 1979, 1981.

kept running afoul of drug dealers for whom he worked. His transgressions usually involved what was known on the streets as "messing up the money." Top would be given drugs to sell by a dealer and would be expected to return after his workday with a specific sum of money and/or any unsold drugs. All too frequently, Top would return with insufficient money. Or he would not return at all. On one occasion, Top was severely beaten and thrown into the East River. Another time he was stripped naked, a tube was inserted in his rectum, and raw alcohol was pumped into him.

Top was a frequent victim of violence. He generally brought this victimization on himself. His own drug use had gotten out of control, and he was constantly bilking people whom he knew would be willing and able to hurt him. Top lacked the capacity to defend himself and usually tried to talk his way out of threatening situations with outlandish stories that nobody believed. His only effective defense, which he employed on several occasions, was to become a police informant so that the police would arrest the person who was after him.

The continuous pattern of violence in Top's life was hardly unique. Another of our research subjects was a male in his mid-thirties (code name "Modigliani"). Modigliani was tall and lean, with angular features. He had an amiable disposition and was quite articulate and candid about his behavior. Both Modigliani and his wife were in our study sample. They would usually arrive for their interviews together and frequently brought their young son with them. The boy was about ten years old. He seemed hyperactive and would annoy everybody in the field station. On one occasion, he was running about with a pencil in his mouth. Staff members were concerned that the boy might fall and hurt himself. When they told him to stop running and to take the pencil out of his mouth, the boy grinned and grasped the pencil as if it were a hypodermic needle. He then mimicked giving himself a "shot" in the arm.

Modigliani was a "lieutenant" in a drug-dealing operation. This role combines the functions of a middle manager and a foreman. A lieutenant is a middle man between a "big dealer" and the street pushers. He recruits the street pushers and is responsible for keeping them in line. He receives the drugs from the big dealer, distributes the drugs to the pushers, collects the money from the pushers after they have sold the drugs, and returns the money to the big dealer. The street pushers seldom know who the big dealer is or where he lives. Most important, they are not supposed to know where drugs may be stored or where money is kept.[2]

One day Modigliani arrived at the field station looking pale and shaken. We asked him what was wrong. He told us the following story. He had been rather lax in overseeing his street pushers. A number of them were "messing up the money." The big dealer (in this case, the "big dealer" was actually three brothers) had become increasingly annoyed at the loss of money. They had warned Modigliani on several occasions, but he had not resolved the situation. This particular morning the three brothers picked up Modigliani in their car and drove around until they found the most egregious offender among the pushers. The three brothers jumped out of the car and beat the pusher with metal pipes until he was unconscious. Then they positioned his body so that the torso was on the sidewalk and the legs were in the street. They got back in the car and drove the vehicle over his legs. They told Modigliani afterwards that the same punishment would be meted out to him if he did not perform his duties properly.

A short time after the completion of our East Harlem study, Modigliani was killed. He had been sitting on an apartment house stoop with some of his buddies. It was a warm summer afternoon. They were drinking cheap wine, probably "Night Train Express," which was the local favorite. A teenage boy walked by carrying a large radio that was blasting out the music of the day. Modigliani, perhaps emboldened by the spirits that he had been consuming, decided to take the radio away from the boy. He left the stoop and confronted the boy in the street. The boy refused to give up his radio. A struggle ensued. The boy pulled a knife and stabbed Modigliani. He bled to death in the street.

The tragedy and senselessness of Modigliani's death was compounded for all of us because of our acquaintance with his wife and son. Modigliani's son certainly was growing up in a difficult situation. He had been born to poor parents who lived in a violent, ghettoized area of New York City. Both of his parents were convicted criminals and heroin users. The previously described event where the boy had pretended that a pencil was a hypodermic needle suggested that his parents had injected drugs in his presence. And now his father had died violently in the gutter.

---

[2] It should be noted that while the drug-dealing organizational structure described above was common in New York City, other drug-dealing operations may be organized in a different fashion.

Another child that we encountered on the East Harlem study was Jose, an adorable and charming little hustler. Jose was about five years old when we first made his acquaintance. He lived above one of our field stations, and we got to know him quite well the first summer that we were on his block. He and his friends would cool off by playing in his bathtub. They would let the water overflow until it was gushing through our ceiling. Somehow, in the process of our going upstairs to complain, Jose became a "member" of our research team.

He would come down to our field station and offer to sweep up for a quarter. He would be waiting most mornings when I drove up, and he would offer to guard my car for a quarter. When I left in the evening, little Jose would be waiting with tales of the "bad men" who had tried to steal the car during the day, and how he had fought with them and made them run away. Jose would act out these stories, doing a little dance in which he would show off his fearsome karate moves. Of course, Jose would receive another quarter for his valiant efforts.

We knew Jose for about two years. He begged for and received rides in the car that he had so bravely defended from the "bad men." We frequently chatted about many things. I had a daughter about the same age as Jose, and he was very interested in hearing stories about her. He would occasionally send her a little present, for example, a tiny plastic cat.

Jose was a sensitive and communicative child. Yet, his conversations were filled with images of violence. When asked how things were going, he would inevitably reply with a tale of violence. He would tell us about the gunshots on the street the night before. He would tell us about the husband who had beaten his wife. He would tell us about the man who had jumped or been pushed from a rooftop and had been impaled on a fence. All of these stories were told with graphic detail. Were any of the stories true? Perhaps some of them were. What was clear, however, was that much of Jose's ideation concerned violence. His knowledge of the sorts of violence that adults inflict on one another seemed far in excess of what should be known by such a little boy. His presentation of this knowledge, though rich in gory detail, was usually delivered in a matter-of-fact tone that implied that he "knew" that this was the way things were in the world.

Jose is now in his late teens. Modigliani's son is now in his twenties. What sort of young men have they become? Are they currently enmeshed in a life of violence? Are they still alive today? What has become of Top? These questions and the stories and experiences that precipitated them are drawn from personal contacts with just a small number of individuals. However, they are illustrative of a much larger social problem. The phenomenon of violence has profound public health and criminological significance. The relationships between drugs and violence has especially profound implications for community safety.

BACKGROUND DATA ON DRUGS AND VIOLENCE

In the early 1980s, sensitized by the East Harlem experience, I began examining existing data sources for information and insights on the drugs/violence nexus. I was surprised at how few theories and data there were. There were no standardized definitions or empirical indicators of drug-related violence. No national databases in the criminal justice or the health care systems routinely specified the relationship between drugs and violence. Certainly, there were no comparable data that allowed the assessment of trends in drug-related violence over time and/or between localities.

It is important to note that there is considerable confusion about incidence and trends in violent crime in general as reflected in official criminal justice statistics. The two principal data sources here are the Uniform Crime Reports (UCR) and the National Crime Victimization Survey (NCVS). These two sources tend to present very different pictures of violent crime.

The Uniform Crime Reports program was begun in 1930. Administered by the Federal Bureau of Investigation (FBI), it is a data collection effort involving voluntary submissions of statistical data on selected crimes and police activity from most city, county, and state law enforcement agencies in the United States. About 16,000 agencies participate. Generally, data are submitted by the local law enforcement agencies to a single state agency that puts together a complete state submission to the FBI. The UCR collects data on numbers of violent crimes and property crimes that are known to the police, as well as the numbers of arrests for all crimes.

The National Crime Victimization Survey began in 1973, administered by the Bureau of Justice Statistics. One of the major reasons for the initiation of NCVS was dissatisfaction and criticism with the UCR. The most obvious limitation of the UCR police statistics was that the police cannot report crimes that do not come to their attention. Crime victims, however, can describe what happened to themselves, whether or not they reported the crime to the police. The NCVS is a survey of the occupants of a representative sample of housing units in the United States. For 1990, about 95,000 persons, ages 12 or older, living in about 47,000 housing units were interviewed. The NCVS collects information about both violent crimes (rape, robbery, and assault) and property crimes (larceny, burglary, and motor vehicle theft). Because this is a victim survey, no data are collected on homicides. Once the sample data are collected, statistical procedures are employed to make projections to the population as a whole. The NCVS also asks crime victims whether they reported crimes to the police, as well as their reasons for reporting or not reporting the crime.

In general, UCR data indicate that violent crime has been increasing substantially and consistently over the past 20 years. The NCVS data indicate that violent crime has not been increasing, that it has remained very stable or, in some cases, has actually declined since the survey was initiated in 1973. However, NCVS data suggest a higher incidence of violence than appears in the UCR.

A brief look at just one crime should serve to illustrate this confusion. According to the UCR, there were about 421,000 aggravated assaults in 1973—a rate of about 201 per 100,000 population. By 1990, the UCR reported 1,054,860 aggravated assaults—a rate of about 424 per 100,000 population. According to these UCR statistics, both the number and the rate of aggravated assaults had more than doubled between 1973 and 1990.

The NCVS projected about 1,650,000 aggravated assaults in 1973 (about four times as many as UCR). However, by 1990, this had fallen to about 1,600,000 (still more than 50% greater than UCR). The NCVS rate of aggravated assault per 1,000 population had fallen from about 10.1 in 1973 to about 7.9 in 1990.[3]

The UCR presents a picture of aggravated assault that indicates the situation is getting much worse. NCVS data indicate that aggravated assaults are more widespread than suggested by UCR, but that the situation is getting better. There are a variety

---

[3] It is a continuing source of annoyance that UCR computes its rates per 100,000 population, whereas NCVS computes its rates per 1,000 population over the age of 12.

of factors that may be influencing these discrepant trends in UCR and NCVS data.

UCR is strongly influenced by the willingness of citizens to report crimes. Increasing rates of violent crime may reflect, in part, an increased tendency for citizens to report their victimization. Effective police-community relations programs, including "neighborhood watch" programs, hotlines, and the like, may encourage citizens to report crimes. Generally, citizens are more likely to report a crime if they have confidence in the police and believe that something will be done. Citizens may be afraid to report crimes because of fear of retribution, and they must trust that the police will protect them in such cases. Generally, the more serious a crime is, the more likely it is to be reported. Also, if some sort of insurance claim is to be filed, a police report may be required. According to the NCVS, the most common reason given by crime victims for not reporting a violent crime to the police is that it was a private or personal matter. Thus, violence that takes place in the home, including spouse/partner abuse, child abuse, elder abuse, and sexual violence, is probably the most underreported form of violence.

NCVS data are also influenced by a variety of factors. Respondents may be too embarrassed to reveal certain victimizations to an interviewer. The survey's focus on households as a sampling unit eliminates homeless and institutionalized persons who are at great risk of violent victimization. Persons may report "trivial" violence to an interviewer in their living room that they would not bother reporting to the police. Because the NCVS is conducted in respondents' homes, incidents of family violence may be underreported because other family members (e.g., spouses or children) may be present in the house during the interviews. Since NCVS interviews are only conducted twice a year, there may be problems concerning people's ability to recall past events with accuracy. Further, NCVS rate estimates are based on population over the age of 12, and because the U.S. population is aging, the decline in *rates* of violent crime reported by NCVS may be a function of the growth in the proportion of the population over the age of 12.

Given the confusing and contradictory nature of our two principal sources of data on aggravated assault, as well as other violent crimes such as rape and robbery, it is not surprising that we have so little information about incidence and trends of drug-related violence. UCR and NCVS, which cannot even agree on how much violent crime there is, or whether violent crime is increasing or decreasing, collect no useful information on the drug-relatedness of violence. For example, victims interviewed for the NCVS may not be knowledgeable about the motivation of offenders for committing acts of violence or may not be able to assess accurately the pharmacological state of offenders. It would be difficult for a person who is mugged on a Chicago street to know whether his or her attacker had ingested drugs prior to the mugging, was in a state of withdrawal from drugs, or was doing the mugging in order to obtain cash for a drug purchase. Respondents who may have precipitated their own violent victimization through antecedent drug activities—for example, inebriation or drug dealing—may not admit this to the NCVS interviewer. This issue is especially problematic because the interviews, as noted before, are conducted in the home, and other family members may be within earshot.

Data collected and maintained for operational purposes by the national health care community are no more useful for the study of the drugs/violence nexus (American Hospital Association, 1989). There are national databases that annually provide a record of "vital statistics" on the mortality and morbidity of the American population or on "work injuries and illnesses" of American workers (U.S. Department of Commerce, 1988, pp. 301, 303). But these surveys do not give attention to the drug-relatedness of those events, nor can they identify those that are related to violence. There are no valid and reliable sources in either the health care or the criminal justice systems that can be used to examine trends over time within a specific locality such as Chicago or validly compare Chicago to other cities with regard to incidence and trends in drug-related violence.

While politicians and the media are generally quite voluble about the terrifying "threat" of drug-related violence and how it is "destroying the fabric of our society," it is usually impossible to discover what they mean when they refer to "drug-related violence." They seldom define the term. It is usually unclear whether alcohol is included as a drug in these assertions. Politicians tend not to make distinctions between drug use and drug trafficking, and they seldom specify the source of their alleged "data." My own explorations through the various national data sets described above led me to doubt whether any valid and reliable data actually existed.

Law enforcement officials from different cities are frequently quoted as claiming that 20 percent, or 80 percent, or whatever percent, of violence in their jurisdictions is drug-related. They do not define what they mean by drug-related violence, nor do they specify how they determine the proportion of violence that was drug-related. Did they utilize forensic toxicologies conducted by medical examiners? Did they utilize investigative reports of detectives? When there was variation between cities—for example, one city claiming that 20 percent of its violence was drug-related and another city claiming that 80 percent of its violence was drug-related—were there real differences in the nature and amount of drug-related violence between the two cities? Or were they just defining drug-related violence differently? Or counting it differently? It is usually impossible to tell.

Unsupported assumptions or claims about drugs and their relationship to criminal violence have served as the basis for the development of federal and state drug policies and community action. Both government and the media have promoted these unsupported claims with little or no question. If it turns out that these assertions are incorrect, then the policies and community actions based on them are flawed.

It is important that our understanding of the relationship between drugs and criminal violence be based on valid and reliable data and organized in a coherent conceptual framework. One of the major problems in this regard is the lack of a consensually agreed-on definition of "drug-related violence." Because of these problems, and because the first step toward producing the necessary data is to come to an agreement on what we mean by "drug-related violence," I formulated my own definition. Based on the five-year field experience in East Harlem, the definition takes the form of a tripartite conceptual framework.

TRIPARTITE CONCEPTUAL FRAMEWORK

The relationship between drugs and violence may be understood in three different ways: psychopharmacologically, economic-compulsively, or systemically. The *psychopharmacological* model suggests that some individuals, as a result of ingesting specific substances, may become excitable and/or irrational and may act out in a violent fashion. Psychopharmacological violence may also result from the irritability associated with withdrawal syndromes or "crashes" from particular substances. Psychopharmacological violence may involve substance use by either victims or perpetrators of violent events. In other words, substance use may contribute to a person behaving violently, or it may alter a person's behavior in such a manner as to bring about that person's violent victimization. An example of the latter phenomenon is the loud-mouthed inebriate who pesters other tavern patrons until somebody punches him in the nose. Finally, some persons may ingest substances deliberatively in order to reduce nervousness or boost courage and thereby facilitate the commission of previously intended violent crimes.

The *economic-compulsive* model suggests that some persons feel compelled to engage in criminal activity in order to finance costly drug use. Sometimes these economic crimes are inherently violent, as in the case of robbery, and sometimes the violence results from an unintended or extraneous factor in the social context in which the crime is perpetrated. Such factors include the perpetrator's nervousness, the victim's reaction, the presence or absence of weapons carried by either victim or perpetrator, the intercession of bystanders, and so on.

The *systemic* model refers to the normally aggressive patterns of interaction within systems of drug distribution. Most systemic violence arises from the conditions of doing business in a black market. Examples of systemic violence include territorial disputes between rival dealers, assaults and homicides committed within particular drug-dealing operations in order to enforce normative codes, robberies of drug dealers, elimination of informers, punishment for selling adulterated or bogus drugs, and assaults to collect drug-related debts.

Not all drug-related violence can be classified neatly in a single dimension of the tripartite conceptual framework. *Multidimensional* violent events are those that contain two or all three dimensions in sufficiently equal weights so that it is impossible to say that one dimension was more responsible for the violence than any other.

After having formulated this framework, I designed a series of studies to validate it and to elaborate on it. All of the empirical research findings that are reported below come from research done in New York City. Is this research relevant to the experiences of other large cities such as Chicago? I believe that it is, in two very important ways. First, I believe that the methods employed in New York can be easily transposed to Chicago. These methods, as described below, include field studies among drug users and distributors, surveys of existing police records, and special studies done in conjunction with the police. Replication of the New York studies in Chicago could provide important comparative information.

Second, the substantive nature of drugs/violence relationships do not appear to be substantially different in Chicago from what they were in New York. Persons get drunk in both cities and get involved in violence. Persons sell illicit drugs and fight to defend their turf or their product in both cities. Innocent citizens get caught in the crossfire in both cities. In fact, because the "crack" cocaine epidemic began in New York far earlier (late 1984 or early 1985) than in Chicago, there may be much that can be learned in Chicago from the New York experience.

The major difference between Chicago and New York seems to be the existence of a well-organized and complex gang structure in Chicago. The Chicago Police Department estimates that there are over 100 street gangs now operating in city. About 40 are considered large, active, and well established. These major gangs are estimated to have a total membership exceeding 30,000. While New York has a variety of criminal groups that have organized for the purpose of drug distribution, these organizations lack the traditions, roots, and broader "turf" orientations of the Chicago gangs.

EMPIRICAL STUDIES ON DRUGS AND VIOLENCE

Two field studies, funded by the National Institute on Drug Abuse, were conducted on the lower east side of New York City between 1984 and 1987. The first involved 152 male drug users and distributors; the other involved 133 female drug users and distributors. In these "street studies," a field research site was established in an area known for its high levels of drug activity. Male and female drug users and distributors were interviewed on a weekly basis. Our primary focus was on patterns of drug use and sale, patterns of criminality, and involvement in violence, either as a perpetrator or a victim. Our field site became a hangout for drug users. We went with research subjects to their homes, to shelters for the homeless, to shooting galleries, and to other places where they congregated to use or to sell drugs. Both studies were designed to validate and to elaborate on the tripartite conceptual framework.

Two other studies, focusing specifically on homicide, were funded by the National Institute of Justice. The first homicide study was designed to assess the usefulness of existing police records for determining the relationship between drug use/trafficking and homicide. Data were collected in 1986 from existing police records for all homicides (a total of 1,768) committed in New York State in 1984. Due in part to their high volume of cases, New York City data proved to be less detailed and less focused on drug issues than data collected from the rest of the state. For this reason, data analysis could be based only on the 309 non-New York City homicides.

In both the New York City and non-New York City data sets, even in those homicide cases where a classification of drug-relatedness could be made, police departments frequently had not recorded important information about the specifics of the drug involvement. Generally, information about drug-relatedness was recorded only when detectives thought it useful for an ongoing investigation. In cases where there was "scuttlebutt" about drug involvement in a homicide, but it was not perceived as directly relevant to the investigation, it would not be recorded. Narcotics detectives sometimes did not share information with homicide detectives. If a perpetrator was apprehended with the proverbial "smoking gun" in hand, there was little need for detailed investigation, and information about drug use or trafficking was frequently not recorded in the file. Law enforcement officials suggested that detailed data about the drug-relatedness of homicides could only be obtained if the data were collected routinely during the time of active case investigation.

This suggestion was implemented for the second study. Data were collected during ongoing police investigations of all homicides committed in four homicide "zones" of New York City between March 1 and October 31, 1988. These zones were selected to represent the socio-economic diversity of the city. Detectives in these zones recorded information pertaining to drug-relatedness that would *not* have been recorded normally. During the study period, 414 homicide events occurred in the four selected areas. These homicide events involved 434 victims, about 23 percent of the 1,896 homicides committed in New York City in 1988. Over 490 perpetrators were involved in these cases.

Data are now available from these four studies that enable us to examine the nature and scope of drug-related violence and to compare homicidal violence to other forms of violence. Such data are essential to a valid understanding of the impact of the drugs/violence nexus at the community level, especially as it pertains to issues such as family violence, drug trafficking, and determination of risk factors for violent victimization.

FINDINGS

Research findings from the two street studies and the two homicide studies have been presented in far more detail and depth in other publications.[4] The following summary of key findings should prove most useful, however. About half of all violence in all four studies was drug-related. This included 48 percent of the violent activity by male drug users and distributors; 39 percent of the violent activity by female drug users and distributors; 42 percent of the 309 non-New York City homicides that occurred in 1984; and 53 percent of the New York City homicides that occurred in 1988. A conservative definition of drug-relatedness was employed in all of these studies. Sufficient evidence was required to clearly classify a case according to the tripartite framework. If such evidence was lacking, the case was not included in the drug-related category. For example, a young woman who was known to the police as a drug addict and prostitute was found stabbed to death in her residence, which was known to be a "shooting gallery." The case was never solved. The police speculated that the homicide might have been drug-related. But it also might have been the work of a "crazy trick." This case was not categorized as drug-related.

Findings from the Street Studies

(1) Relatively high proportions of violence engaged in by male and female drug users and distributors were unrelated to drug use or trafficking. Specifically, 43 percent of the male violence and 60 percent of the female violence was not drug-related.

(2) About 55 percent of the male drug users and distributors and 59 percent of the female drug users and distributors reported some violent activity during the eight-week study period.

(3) Psychopharmacological and systemic violence were the most common forms of drug-related violence reported by both male and female users and distributors. Economic compulsive violence was rare. Specifically, men reported that 18 percent of their violent actions were psychopharmacological in nature, 17 percent were systemic, 5 percent were economic-compulsive,

---

[4] See, e.g., Goldstein, 1992; Goldstein, Brownstein, and Ryan, 1989.

and 4 percent were multi-dimensional. Women reported that 15 percent of their violent actions were psychopharmacological, 9 percent were systemic, 2 percent were economic-compulsive, and 6 percent were multidimensional. A small proportion of both male and female violence was deemed to be drug-related but could not be classified within the tripartite conceptual framework.

(4) Alcohol was the substance most likely to be associated with psychopharmacological violence for both men (in 70% of the cases) and women (in 78% of the cases). Cocaine was involved in psychopharmacological violence in only 3 percent of the male cases and 15 percent of the female cases. The substances most likely to be associated with systemic violence were heroin for men (in 33% of the cases) and cocaine for women (in 69% of the cases).

(5) Frequency and volume of cocaine use were both related to involvement in violence, but the nature of this involvement was quite different for men and women. Among men, higher frequency and volume of cocaine use were associated with being a *perpetrator* of violence. Among women, higher frequency and volume of cocaine use were associated with being a *victim* of violence.

(6) Males reported that most of their violent encounters occurred with strangers or acquaintances. Females reported that most of their violent encounters occurred with spouses or lovers.

(7) Much of the violence reported by males occurred in the context of robberies or other economic crimes. However, this violence was seldom reported as drug-related economic-compulsive violence. These men might have been drug users, and they might have spent a portion of the proceeds from their robberies on drugs. However, these men usually claimed that they were *not* primarily motivated to commit these robberies as a result of a compelling need to obtain drugs. Much of the violence reported by females involved non-drug-related disputes.

Findings from the Homicide Studies

(1) The two most common types of drug-related homicides in these samples were psychopharmacological and systemic. Very few drug-related homicides were economic-compulsive; that is, very few were motivated by the compulsive need of a drug user to get money for drugs. In the 1988 New York City sample,

39 percent of all homicides and 74 percent of drug-related homicides were classified as systemic.

(2) In the 1988 New York City sample, only 31 homicides (8% of all homicides and 14% of the drug-related homicides) were classified as psychopharmacological. Psychopharmacological homicides were most often alcohol-related (68% of the time). Only 29 percent of the psychopharmacological homicides involved the use of cocaine, and in about half of those cases, the cocaine had been ingested in combination with alcohol.

(3) Systemic cases were most often related to cocaine (predominantly crack). In New York City in 1988, 93 percent of the systemic homicides involved cocaine.

(4) Other drugs, including heroin, were rarely involved in either the 1984 or 1988 homicides.

(5) Only about 5 percent of the homicides studied in 1988 were alcohol-related. Previous research has indicated that domestic homicides are frequently alcohol-related (see, e.g., Browne 1987; Hewitt 1988). A very low proportion of the 1988 homicides were family-related. Only 17 of the 414 homicides involved spouses; nine involved lovers. Taken together, these domestic homicides accounted for only 6 percent of the study total. There were nearly eight times as many drug-related systemic homicides as there were domestic homicides.

Implications of the Empirical Studies

These findings provide empirical evidence suggesting that certain common assumptions about homicide are incorrect or exaggerated. For example, it is commonly believed that an important threat to public safety by drug users is their violent predatory acts to obtain money for drugs. The above data indicate that very few homicide victims were killed by drug users in the context of committing property crimes to get money for drugs. This does not mean that drug users do not commit property crimes when they are in need of money for drugs; it means only that they do not often kill others in such a context. Previous research has indicated that drug users typically try to avoid violent predatory offenses and that their use of drugs is often financed by working in a variety of roles in the illicit drug business (Goldstein, 1981; Johnson et al., 1985). Violence is most likely to arise in the context of the illicit drug marketplace and to involve others who are similarly engaged.

Another common assumption is that the public safety is endangered by persons who are "crazed killers" as a result of the use of illicit substances. The above data indicate that various forms of violence, including homicide, do occur as a result of perpetrator and/or victim inebriation. But generally these cases involve people under the influence of alcohol, a legally obtainable substance.

For many years, it was a truism in the criminological literature that the primary social context of homicidal violence was domestic altercations. Clearly, the nature of homicide has changed. The primary social context of homicidal violence in the United States today is the illicit drug marketplace. It is also commonly believed that heroin users and dealers are responsible for a great number of murders. The above data indicate that, during the study periods in the mid-to-late 1980s, in New York City and New York State, heroin played a very small role in homicide. The drugs most commonly related to homicide in New York at this time were cocaine (including crack) and alcohol. Cocaine homicides were most often systemic, that is, associated with drug trafficking. Alcohol-related homicides were most often psychopharmacological.

Findings from the two homicide studies clearly indicate that existing police records are inadequate for the purpose of documenting complex drug/crime/violence relationships. The primary function of the police is to maintain public order and to arrest violators of the law; police organize their data collection systems to support these functions. Such data collection systems, while of use to the police, may not always serve the interests of researchers and policy planners. However, data presented above clearly demonstrate that researchers can work with an enlightened police department, modify data collection procedures in a fashion that does not interfere with the law enforcement function, and produce data of use to police, prosecutors, and policymakers (see Brownstein and Goldstein, 1990).

CONCLUSIONS

Clearly, the notion of "crazed dope-fiends" or "crack-heads" robbing and killing innocent citizens because of the need to obtain money to buy drugs is an inadequate explanation of the association between drugs and violence. Examination of trends in the national homicide rate over the past several decades indicates a substantial peak from 1979 to 1981, the years of Cocaine War I. Crack had not yet appeared on the scene, and the illicit market being contested involved powdered cocaine. At that time, Miami was the murder capital of the United States. Those who have forgotten how those years were depicted are advised to watch *Miami Vice* reruns.

The national homicide rate then declined in the early and mid-1980s. Especially dramatic decreases occurred in Miami. (Cocaine War I was over!) In the mid-to-late 1980s the homicide rate began to climb again, heralding the arrival of crack and Cocaine War II. New York City and Washington, D.C., replaced Miami as the nation's murder capitals. Crack, a new form of an old drug, was easily manufactured and attracted a large number of small entrepreneurs.

The New York experience suggests that in the early stages of the crack market, a steadily increasing number of new users provided distributors with sufficient business. Rates of violence at this stage of market development were low. As the market matured, and the number of users began to stabilize, competition among distributors for "market share" grew. Organized gangs tried to consolidate turf and bring isolated dealers under their control. For example, some gangs tried to create a monopoly by forcing small dealers to buy raw products from them exclusively and eliminated those dealers who refused. Other gangs required independent dealers to pay a "tax" or "franchise fee" for the right to sell drugs in gang-claimed territory. Sometimes individual gang members would attempt to sell crack for their personal profit in territory claimed by their gang. Such activities have provoked violent responses from gangs in both New York and Chicago.

Intensified law enforcement efforts and honest zeal by anti-drug reformers have probably contributed to increased levels of violence. Law enforcement practices such as street sweeps, neighborhood saturation, and buy-bust operations can lead to increased violence in a number of ways. Removing dealers from their established territory by arresting them creates a vacuum that other dealers may fight to fill. By the time these hostilities have ended, convicted dealers may have returned from prison and attempted to reassert their authority, resulting in a new wave of violence. Removing dealers from their established territory by scaring them off usually leads to their moving into other dealers' territories, also with violent consequences.

Recent trends in drug use in the United States seem to indicate a decline in the use of most substances by casual and middle-class users but little change in volume and frequency of use by "hard-core" substance users. The imposition of mandatory minimum sentences, together with extraordinarily high rates of incarceration for drug-related offenses, does not appear to have substantially reduced problems of substance use. Nor have they led to increased feelings of safety in communities.

There is a clear need to expand research and service activities in order to provide the most effective treatment and prevention programs. Drug treatment on demand must be available for substance users wishing to terminate their involvement with drugs. Programs such as Treatment Alternatives for Special Clients (TASC) in Chicago should be supported and expanded. TASC provides outreach into the courts and recommendations to judges about referring eligible arrestees into drug treatment rather than incarceration. Although drug treatment has been shown to be far more effective than incarceration in reducing criminality, punitive legislation involving the imposition of mandatory minimum sentences has narrowed the pool of arrestees eligible for TASC or other diversionary programs. Further, the lack of treatment capacity has resulted in long waits for arrestees who might benefit from treatment.

Some arrestees, especially those who are deemed too violent, may be ineligibile for diversion into treatment. To accomodate the needs of these individuals, there should also be an expansion of prison-based drug treatment. Research findings on outcomes for coerced treatment are not completely clear. However, they do seem to indicate that those coerced into treatment do at least as well as those who enter treatment voluntarily.

Expansion of drug prevention programs would also appear to be a good idea. Drug prevention programs function most effectively in the context of community-wide efforts. Messages to reduce drug abuse appear to be heard most clearly when they are supported in schools, in churches, in the media, and at home. A program in any one of these milieus is not likely to be as effective as one occurring in all of the milieus simultaneously. However, the present state of knowledge as to what works best with regard to drug prevention is still fairly primitive. There are critical needs for more valid and reliable scientific evaluations of drug prevention efforts, especially those that are community-based.

Legalization of drugs is likely to eliminate drug-related systemic violence, just as repeal of prohibition eliminated alcohol-related systemic violence. Although alcohol is now the major contributor to psychopharmacological violence, other drugs have different psychopharmacological effects. It is beyond the scope of this chapter to evaluate what is known about each sort of drug—for example, barbiturates, cannabis, hallucinogens—and to speculate as to whether legalization of each would likely contribute to the incidence of psychopharmacological violence. In general, I believe that legalization of drugs would substantially decrease violence-related mortality and morbidity. However, it would also probably increase the incidence of accidental injuries, such as those resulting from motor vehicle crashes, falls, and the like. If such is the case, then drug-related injuries would be addressed as a public health issue rather than a criminal justice issue. Such an approach might yield far greater benefits to society than our current policies do.

Ultimately, only one "solution" to problems of drugs and violence is likely to have any truly meaningful impact. I believe that some drug use will always be part of our society. This should be considered acceptable. Individuals can be educated about benefits and detriments of different sorts of drug use and encouraged to engage in "good relationships" with drugs that do not result in harm to themselves or their communities. Under conditions of full inclusion in society—for example, in regard to educational and employment opportunities—and assuming the lack of pre-existing mental disorders, most people would be able to engage in non-harmful, and probably minimal, use of substances. For those individuals (e.g., alcoholics) who are unable to maintain a "good relationship" with drugs, treatment would be required.

"Bad relationships" with drugs are likely to arise in social conditions characterized by poverty, racism, unequal access to educational resources, and class inequalites, or in those individuals with pre-existing mental disorders. In such situations, drug use is more likely to result in social and individual harm, including violence. As long as our society is more willing to punish individuals than to ameliorate social injustices, more willing to spend millions on treating symptoms of problems rather than addressing the root problems themselves, we will suffer from unacceptable levels of destructive drug use and violence.

REFERENCES

American Hospital Association (1989). *State and Metropolitan Hospital Associations Inventory of Health Care Data Bases*. Chicago: American Hospital Association.

Browne, Angela (1987). *When Battered Women Kill*. New York: Free Press.

Brownstein, Henry H., and Paul J. Goldstein (1990). "Research and the Development of Public Policy: The Case of Drugs and Violent Crime," *Journal of Applied Sociology*, vol. 7 (1990), pp. 77-92.

Centers for Disease Control (1990). "Homicide Among Young Black Males—United States, 1978-1987," *Morbidity and Mortality Weekly Report*, vol. 39, no. 48 (December 7, 1990), pp. 869-873.

Goldstein, Paul J. (1979). "Ethnoeconomical Approach to the Relationship Between Crime and Drug Use: Preliminary Findings." In Louis S. Harris, ed., *Problems of Drug Dependence 1979*. Rockville, Md.: National Institute on Drug Abuse.

―――― (1981). "Getting Over: Economic Alternatives to Predatory Crime Among Street Drug Users." In James A. Inciardi, ed., *The Drugs-Crime Connection*. Beverly Hills, Calif.: Sage Publications.

―――― (1989). "Drugs and Violent Crime." In Neil A. Weiner and Marvin E. Wolfgang, eds., *Pathways to Criminal Violence*. Beverly Hills, Calif.: Sage Publications.

Goldstein, Paul J., Henry H. Brownstein, and Patrick J. Ryan (1992). "Drug Related Homicide in New York: 1984 and 1988," *Crime and Delinquency*, vol. 38, no. 4 (October 1992), pp. 459-476.

Hewitt, John D. (1988). "The Victim-Offender Relationship in Convicted Homicide Cases: 1960-1984," *Journal of Criminal Justice*, vol. 16 (1988), pp. 25-33.

Johnson, Bruce D., Paul J. Goldstein, Edward Preble, James Schmeidler, Douglas S. Lipton, Barry Spunt, and Thomas Miller (1985). *Taking Care of Business: The Economics of Crime by Heroin Abusers*. Lexington, Mass.: Lexington Books.

U.S. Department of Commerce (1988). *Inventory of U.S. Health Care Data Bases, 1976-1987*. Rockville, Md.: National Technical Information Service.

YOUTH GANGS: PROBLEM AND POLICY

Irving A. Spergel

This chapter proposes that gangs—or more specifically, youth gangs or street gangs—have become a serious social problem in America and other societies largely because of major social and economic changes as indicated by social disorganization, especially population movements, and the concentration of poverty in certain communities. The gang problem in the United States has also become the basis for a major "growth industry" because we largely do not understand the problem and are not prepared to prevent or control its development and because the problem, as it continues to exist and expand, serves the interests of particular organizations and political entrepreneurs. Furthermore, policymakers often are unable or do not want to test alternative approaches to determine what really works. In essence, the gang problem comprises two parts: the violence, crime, and community concern that gangs create, and the inadequate response of federal, state, and local policies at various stages of the development of the problem.

I would like to address the youth gang problem in terms of three sets of questions: (1) What is the history, contemporary scope, and seriousness of the problem? (2) What causes the problem, and what are the key models for understanding it? (3) What approaches promise success, especially in reducing the problem? Before proceeding, however, it is important to provide some definition of key terms used in the discussion.

The term "gang" generally refers to a group or collectivity of persons with a common identity whose members interact on a fairly regular basis in cliques or sometimes as a whole group. The activities of the gang may be regarded as legitimate, illegitimate, and criminal in varying combinations. The term "gang" as used here has certain distinguishing characteristics, mainly the group's emphasis on use of violence to achieve various purposes, including social recognition, group solidarity, and, at times, economic gain. "Street gang," the term preferred by law enforcement agencies, emphasizes the organized character of a group of persons on the street, often engaged in significant illegitimate or criminal activity. Some of the gangs are more street-based than others. The term is generally inclusive of teenagers and young adults. Some authorities report arrests of street gang members in their 30s, 40s and 50s. The term "youth gang," often used as an equivalent to street gang, is preferred by community agencies or organizations, such as youth agencies and schools. It generally refers to mainly adolescent members and/or a youth segment of a gang, mainly between 12 and 24 years old.

HISTORY, CONTEMPORARY SCOPE, AND SERIOUSNESS OF THE PROBLEM

Youth gangs or street gangs are not unique to contemporary urban America. They have existed across time and cultures. Youth gangs tend to develop and become identified as a problem mainly during times of rapid social and economic change, cultural transition, and political instability. Gangs function as residual or interstitial socializing institutions—in somewhat different ways in different communities—when other institutions fail; gangs may provide a certain degree of controlled disorder or temporary stability and economic gain for their members and the surrounding community. The youth gang is most likely to form and develop in those organizational contexts, local communities, and societies that are undergoing extensive and precipitous population change, often under deteriorating or improving but fragmented economic conditions. Social institutions of family, school, church, and employment are weak and unstable; established organizations in the local community may be in conflict with each other and poorly integrated into the larger society. Basic youth-socializing functions, especially social control, social support, and legitimate economic development, cannot be carried out under these circumstances.

Youth gangs existed in urban centers of the United States in the 19th century and earlier (Hyman, 1984). One analyst has written that "nearly every nationality is represented in American gang history" (Haskins, 1974, p. 7). The "Five Points" district of Manhattan, New York City, was a poor but relatively quiet residential area until about 1820, when the first influx of Irish immigrants settled there. These gangs joined together in the face of poverty, squalid conditions, and great prejudice. Some of the gangs numbered in the hundreds; one gang claimed 1,200 members. They had distinctive names and dress, and they usually fought in their undershirts. The weapons used included pistols and muskets, as well as knives, brickbats, bludgeons, brass knuckles, ice picks, and pikes. "The most bitter and lasting feud was between the Dead Rabbits and the Bowery Boys. From the 1830s to the 1860s hardly a week passed that the Dead Rabbits . . . did not engage in battle. Sometimes these battles lasted two or three days [with] endless melees of beating, maiming and murder . . . regiments of soldiers in full battle dress, marching through the streets to the scene of a gang melee, were not an uncommon sight in New York" (Haskins, 1974, pp. 26-29).

Prison gangs existed in Illinois as early as the 1920s. The crimes of these early prison groups were similar to those practiced today and included "intimidation, extortion, homosexual prostitution, and other illegitimate business. Riots and killings were numerous" (Camp and Camp, 1988, p. 57). The gang tradition has been particularly strong in the Southwest in recent decades. Some gangs in Los Angeles date back 60 or more years—at least in terms of name and tradition. One writer reports that "today a Hispanic in Los Angeles may be a fourth generation gang member" (Donovan, 1988, p. 14). It has been estimated that gangs are active in 70 of the 84 incorporated cities in Los Angeles County (Philibosian, 1986, p. 7).

The contemporary gang problem may be described as follows: Youth gangs today are found in almost all 50 states, as well as in the Commonwealth of Puerto Rico and U.S. territories, and the problem of gang delinquency and crime is increasingly prevalent and more serious. Miller estimates that in the late 1970s, gangs were present in almost 300 U.S. cities, or 13 percent of all cities with populations of 10,000 or more (Miller, 1982, chap. 3). Needle and Stapleton report that 39 percent of cities with populations between 100,000 and 250,000 had gang problems (Needle and Stapleton, 1983). In the early 1990s, Curry and his colleagues surveyed 79 of the largest U.S. cities with populations over 200,000 and, on the basis of police information, found that more than 90 percent had a gang problem (Curry et al., 1992, p. 22). In a recent small-scale survey of twelve prosecutors in rural areas of Colorado, Iowa, Michigan, New Hampshire, South Carolina, Texas, and Washington, "gangs were mentioned by one-fourth of the respondents as the prevalent criminal organization" (Justice Research and Statistics Association, 1993, p. 6).

Gangs increasingly exist in smaller cities, suburban communities, small towns, and rural areas that have no recognized history of gang problems. Gangs in these areas usually do not exhibit the same degree of organization, violence, and criminality as in the larger cities. A *Chicago Tribune* report indicates that gangs are not only present "in older poor communities [in or near Cook County], including Joliet, Aurora, Elgin, Harvey, Robbins and Chicago Heights . . . but police say gang activity is also on the rise in such suburbs as Evanston, Calumet City, Bensenville, Glendale Heights, West Chicago and Addison" (Koziol, 1991).

It is not possible to devise precise or even meaningful estimates of the exact or approximate number of youth gangs or gang members in the United States, partly because there is no standard definition of a gang, gang member, or gang incident. Some definitions are inclusive of *all* criminal activities committed by an identified *gang member*; some are limited to *gang-motivated* incidents, that is, strictly related to gang-oriented or gang-determined activities. Often youth gangs, adult criminal organizations, ephemeral street youth associations, and other delinquent groups are confused with one another; these types of groups are overlapping in their activities. In addition, different street gangs that share the same or similar names may be considered one gang, and sometimes factions of the same street gang are reported as separate gangs. Although the police usually provide the figures used in most media or scholarly reports, these estimates are often grossly exaggerated and occasionally minimized for political purposes. Generally, a systematic aging and inflation bias is structured into these estimates based on police lists of gang members, as the names of gang individuals tend not to be removed for at least three to five years after a gang offense is committed.

In many cities, the number of gangs and gang members seems to go up each year. In a smaller number of cities, they seem to go down. In still other cities, the estimates fluctuate up and down within a short period of time. In Los Angeles County, the sheriff's office estimated 600 gangs and 70,000 gang members in 1987; these estimates had grown to 1,000 gangs and 150,000 gang members in 1991 (Spergel and Curry, 1990; Reiner, 1992). In 1992, the Chicago Police Department estimated 41 gangs or major factions and 36,000 hard-core gang members (Herrman, 1992, p. 17). However, a Chicago police analyst has said that gang membership has ranged from "12,000 to as many as 120,000 persons" (Bobrowski, 1988, p. 40). Furthermore, certain racial/ethnic groups are more likely to be represented as gang members. A report of the Los Angeles County District Attorney's Office states that "the police have identified almost half of all black men in Los Angeles between the ages of 21 and 24 as gang members." The report cautiously adds that "a careful professional examination is needed to determine whether police procedures may be systematically over-identifying black youths as gang members" (Reiner, 1992, p. iv).

Figures on gang membership are highly unreliable, inflammatory, and subject to agency exploitation, particularly to frighten the community, mobilize public support for suppression strategies and tactics, and secure additional funds for manpower and equipment. Criteria of gang membership and categories of members are not clear, easily operationalized, or consistently used. Street gangs are usually diffuse structures, and youths move in and out, changing categories of membership rapidly. The far more reliable and valid measure for purposes of public policy should be actual criminal gang-related incidents committed, especially felony violence.

Gang Violence

Serious violence seems to be the most significant characteristic of the gang problem from a community experience, policy, and research perspective. Reasonably adequate data are available on the current nature and scope of violence committed by gang members, in particular cities. Gang-related violence has clearly increased in recent years, and gang members, at least those with arrest records, are responsible for a disproportionate amount of violent crime, particularly homicides, batteries, and assaults. Violent crime generally has increased in the United States over the past several years according to reports of the U.S. Justice Department's National Crime Survey and the Federal Bureau of Investigation (Brody, 1992, p. 13; Associated Press, 1992, p. A12). Much of this increase, particularly homicides in certain cities, has been attributed to gang violence. In the city of Los Angeles, gang homicides were 25.2 percent of the total number of homicides in 1987, but 36 percent in 1991, when gang members committed 771 homicides. In Chicago, gang homicides were 7 percent of the total number of homicides in 1987, but 14 percent in 1991, when gang members committed 133 gang homicides, and 34 percent in 1994 (Mulack and Fuesel, 1995, p. 17). Chicago presently uses a definition of gang incident based mainly on the motivation of gang members or the gang-related circumstances of the crime, whereas Los Angeles uses a broader definition based on whether the person is a gang member in a gang incident, regardless of motivation or circumstances. Thus, Chicago uses a more precise but somewhat less inclusive set of figures of crime, especially violent crime, perpetuated by gang members. Because of the narrower definition of a gang homicide incident in Chicago, one needs to approximately double the Chicago figures to make them equivalent to the Los Angeles figures. Gang homicides in Chicago, as a percentage of total homicides, have ranged from 1.71 percent in 1975 to 34 percent in 1994. "In 1973, 3 percent of the murders were attributed to street gangs; in 1993, that number was 15 percent (Mulack and Fuesel, 1995, p. 17).

The general increase in gang violence in many cities, including Chicago, over the past decade has been attributed to several factors. Gangs have more and better weapons and use them more often. Intergang rumbles comprising large assemblages of youths arriving for battle on foot, which may be easily interdicted, have been replaced by smaller mobile groups of two or three youths in a vehicle shooting opposing gang members, incidents that are more difficult to prevent or control. Spur-of-the-moment decisions to attack targets of opportunity, on street corners or public gatherings, are common (see also Horowitz, 1983). Klein and Maxson add that greater levels of violence among and between gangs may also reflect a growth in the number of gang members, an increasingly violent society, and/or more sophisticated gang intelligence (Klein and Maxson, 1989, p. 218).

In general, older adolescents and young adults are responsible for the highest proportions of violence, in part because they have better access to and can make more sophisticated use of weaponry and violence. In recent years, the median age of the gang homicide offender in Chicago has been 19 years old and that of the gang homicide victim 20 years (Spergel, 1986). Los Angeles data and San Diego police statistics likewise indicate that gang homicides mainly involve older adolescents and young adults (Maxson, Gordon, and Klein, 1985; San Diego Association of Governments, 1982). There is some evidence, however, that the involvement of younger youth in gang homicides has been increasing in recent years, especially in the African-American community in Chicago.

There continue to be important differences in patterns of gang violence based on gender and racial/ethnic characteristics. Street-gang violence is mainly a male phenomenon. Gang homicide offenders in Chicago are more than 98 percent male. While there has probably been a general increase in female membership in gangs and female violence, it is not clear that the female proportion of total gang members or female participation in violence has gone up. There is better evidence of a relative increase in drug offenses by females compared with drug offenses by males.

For the past two decades, street-gang violence has remained a *relatively* greater problem in the Hispanic than in the African-American communities in Chicago and Los Angeles (and probably in many other cities) despite media and some law enforcement reports to the contrary. The media contribute to a distortion of the facts and to public failure to understand the true nature and dimensions of the problem. For example, many reputable newspapers, TV stations, movies, and recording companies project a stereotyped and exaggerated, if not mythical, view of Black gang violence. This is not to deny that crime—particularly robbery, family-related violence, and homicide—is higher in African-American than in Hispanic communities. In Chicago, however, Block reports that "of all identified homicide offenders from 1982 through 1989, the Latino male offenders were by far the most likely to have committed the offense in a street-gang confrontation. Over 40 percent of Latino male offenders, compared to only 12 percent of non-Latino white and non-Latino black male offenders, were involved in a street-gang-related homicide" (Block, 1991, p. 33).

Gang Members as Career Criminals

The relationship between gangs and violence is most evident when patterns of behavior by gang members and non-members are compared. Gang youths engage in more violent crime than non-gang delinquent youths. More than 20 years ago, Klein and Meyerhoff observed that "the urban gang delinquent is different in kind from the urban non-gang delinquent. . . . Gang members have higher police contact rates . . . and become involved in more serious delinquencies than non-members (1967, pp. 1-2). Friedman, Mann, and Friedman found that violent behavior differentiated street-gang members from non-gang members, whether delinquent or not, better than all the other legal, socioeconomic, and psychological factors studied. Gang members were also characterized by more police arrests for non-violent crime, more truancy, and more alcohol and drug abuse (Friedman, Mann, and Friedman, 1975, pp. 599-600). Gang influence on criminality does not stop at the end of the juvenile period. Thus, gang membership appears to prolong the extent and seriousness of criminal careers (Tracy, 1987, p. 19).

However, it is extremely important for the creation of appropriate—and necessarily complex—public policy addressing the gang problem that we be aware that gangs and their members participate in different forms and degrees of violence, crime, and delinquency. Furthermore, significant numbers of gang members may not be involved in delinquency, while many serious delinquents have no relation to gangs. In a recent research of 11-to-15-year-old Hispanic and African-American male youths at four schools, high-crime areas of Chicago, we found that about 14 percent of youths who declared themselves to be gang members in fact had no self-reported or official records of delinquency. We also noted that non-gang delinquents were more common among African-American respondents (19.7%) than Hispanic respondents (5.8%) (Curry and Spergel, 1992, p. 287). This finding supports the conclusion of earlier research that gangs do not exist for the sole purpose of engaging in delinquency and crime, that culture or subculture associated with race/ethnicity and critical age periods, not only early but older adolescence, must be taken into account in prevention, intervention, and suppression policies and programs, particularly at the local community level.

Gang Violence and Drugs

Research suggests a highly variable set of relationships between street-gang membership, drug use, drug selling, and violence. Fagan (1988) found both violent and nonviolent Black and Hispanic youth gangs in inner-city communities of Chicago, Los Angeles, and San Diego, whether the gang engaged in drug trafficking or not. Gang involvement in violent activity is neither cause nor consequence of drug use or drug dealing: "While some incidents no doubt are precipitated by disputes over drug sales or selling territories, the majority of violent incidents do not appear to involve drug sales. Rather they continue to be part of the status, territorial, and other gang conflicts that historically have fueled gang violence" (Fagan, 1988, p. 20).

This is not to deny that there can be a close relationship between gang membership and drug offenses. Bobrowski (1988) states that of 62 street gangs or major factions responsible for street-gang crime in Chicago between January 1987 and July 1988, 90 percent of the gangs showed some membership involvement in vice activities, most of which were drug-related. However, the relationship between arrests for drug dealing and drug possession by gang members, on the one hand, and gang violence, on the other, may be quite tenuous. Bobrowski reports that vice activity was discovered at the gang incident level in "only 3 of 82 homicides, 3 of 362 robberies, and 18 of 4,052 street-gang related batteries and assaults" in the year-and-a-half study period (Bobrowski, 1988, p. 25). He concludes that available data do not support the notion that "street gangs have been enmeshed in some web of violence and contentious criminality" as a result of their involvement in drug-related activities (Bobrowski, 1988, pp. 44-45). The Los Angeles County Sheriff's Department states that only 10 percent of gang homicides have been drug-related (McBride, 1988). Again, it should be noted that the broad definition of gang-related incidents in Los Angeles refers to the arrest of any person involved in almost any crime, regardless of whether the crime is gang-motivated or whether the circumstances indicate a gang connection.

More recently, Block confirms Bobrowski's analysis and also indicates there are important racial/ethnic distinctions in the relationship among gangs, drugs, and violence. She says that "only about 2 percent of Chicago street-gang-related homicides from 1982 to 1989 involved a drug-related motive . . . and fewer still involved an offender or victim who were high on drugs at the time of the incident. In 1989, when Latino street-gang homicides increased, the proportion that were drug-related was even smaller" (Block, 1991, p. 37). Evidence from several cities suggests that Hispanic gangs may still be relatively more involved in traditional turf-related activities, with Black gangs or their members involved in relatively more drug trafficking. Hispanic gang members may be less entrepreneurial when it comes to drug trafficking, but this may be changing. In Chicago, Hispanic gangs (mixed Puerto Rican and Mexican-American) on the Northwest side are reported to be more heavily involved in drug trafficking than Hispanic gangs (mainly Mexican-American) on the Southwest side. However, some gangs in a particular neighborhood may be more involved in drug dealing than other gangs. Established older drug trafficking organizations also may recruit persons who have previous histories of gang violence; gang members, for their part, may seek out drug-selling groups. In any case, gangs socialize members to a pattern of group identification, boldness, and solidarity that can prove useful to a drug or any adult criminal organization.

The relationships between gang membership, drug dealing, and violence at the street level can probably be explained by such factors as city size, the availability of drug supplies, the stability of the drug market, distinctive gang cultures, differential access by youths and young adults to legitimate and illegitimate opportunities, and the organizational development of the gang. The traditional gang structure and alliances among gangs seem to shift or dissolve under the impact of drug use and selling. This is particularly evident in large northeastern cities, in some parts of California, and increasingly in large and small midwestern cities. Traditional turf-related or status-related gang violence is ordinarily not functional to drug selling and criminal business enterprise, which require more rational organization and stability of distribution systems. Nevertheless, violence does occur in the course of drug trafficking competition in Chicago and elsewhere among former gang members, as individuals or in cliques, and may no longer be based on traditional gang allegiances.

CAUSES OF THE GANG PROBLEM

There is extensive theory on the causes of gangs and gang crime. Most of it is untested and developed within particular social science disciplinary frameworks, or partially tested on a case-by-case, small-sample basis. Furthermore, little gang theory or research has been developed that is specifically relevant to policy and program development. Cloward and Ohlin's opportunity theory in the 1960s, however, became the basis for a shift of federal government policy from program initiatives based on psychological or interpersonal causes of the problem to a structural or social opportunity approach (Cloward and Ohlin, 1960). Opportunity theory was a partial basis for the War on Poverty during the Johnson administration, although its focus on the delinquency and youth crime problem was quickly lost.

Recent research on gangs has to some extent been informed by underclass and social disorganization theories. I have integrated various elements of these theories into a framework at societal, community, organizational, and individual levels to explain the problem in such a way that policies of control, prevention, and intervention may be more readily derived. Primary emphasis in the model is on how violent gang crime in its traditional—and still typical—sense arises. Secondary attention is on the connection between violent gang crime and more rational or economically oriented types of criminal organization that may involve gang members or former gang members, especially around drug dealing. Poverty in interaction with social disorganization at neighborhood or local community levels largely accounts for the inception of the problem, which then is sustained and achieves distinctive character based on particular cultural and subcultural traditions. Racism is probably less directly responsible for the gang problem, but it may have strong indirect effects. The failure of social policy as it affects the structure and connectedness of social institutions at national, city, and community levels contributes significantly to the development of the gang problem. Structural and developmental problems at the personal and family levels also make youths more vulnerable to social-institutional problems, especially at school and in the labor market.

Poverty-Related Theory

A series of overlapping poverty-related theories has developed since the middle 1950s to explain youth gang or delinquent subcultures. These theories focus on the social, economic, and cultural environment as a source of strain or pressure on youths to become gang members and to lead them to deviant actions.

Miller's lower-class theory and Cloward and Ohlin's opportunity theory were popular in the 1960s in the explanation of deviant behavior, especially gang behavior or delinquent subcultures (Miller, 1958; Cloward and Ohlin, 1960). William Julius Wilson's current and more comprehensive theory attempts to account for gang problems, as well as other inner-city problems (Wilson, 1987, p. 462). Wilson's formulation does not sufficiently recognize variable local community resources, policies, and programs that may contribute to youth gang subcultures. The theory may be too comprehensive for the development of policy addressing the varieties of gang problems.

Social Disorganization

Social disorganization at societal and community levels is often associated with, or a consequence of, large and rapid population movements of minority, low-income, or working-class groups, as well as major disruptions in labor markets, rapid industrialization or urbanization, wars and revolutions, and the failure of institutions to meet the social needs of a population in appropriate ways, for example, for education, training, and socialization. Social disorganization is indicated by fragmentation or the failure of schools, police, and local community institutions to collectively and interactively mesh their policies and procedures with the interests of newcomer, often minority, low-income populations.

The importance of immigration or emigration, rapidly expanding or contracting populations, the incursion of different racial/ethnic groups, or even different segments or generations of the same racial/ethnic population can readily lead to community problems of safety and security, as well as related problems of gang development. In Chicago, serious gang problems may have developed in those African-American communities that underwent significant population transition and social change, including the movement of Black working-class and middle-class families out of the inner-city ghettos to the suburbs, shifts of population from south to north in the 1950s or back south or west in the 1980s, or simply as the Black population expanded from one neighborhood to another in the inner city.

In the process of community and population change, local agencies and community organizations often fail to meet the needs of newcomer groups. Churches, schools, youth agencies, and other civic groups lose their constituencies. Middle-class groups leave the area. Agencies and organizations suffer a lack of funding and can barely survive with the aid of absentee clientele or parishioners. Social agencies do not immediately or sufficiently reach out to newcomer youths and families. The problem of social distance is particularly severe between schools or police and the local population, usually of a different ethnic/racial or class background.

In these transitional, and often resource-deprived communities, schools, police, youth agencies, and local community organizations tend not to coordinate their efforts, particularly in dealing with gang problems. They may be in conflict with each other for ideological reasons or because of competition for scarce resources. Some of these agencies are large citywide bureaucracies with little concern for the distinctive interests, needs, and problems of local communities or neighborhoods. They are also not coordinated across different types and levels of jurisdictions. In Cook County, for example, "criminal justice is not characterized by a smoothly functioning system, but rather by a fragmented amalgam of agencies which lack central coordination." Juvenile justice and community-based organizations, including mental health agencies, do not share relationships. They become self-contained subsystems, and children are "suspended between warring agencies" (Manikas et al., 1990, pp. 100, 104).

Family and Personal Disorganization

Both the family and the individual youth may contribute to the development of the gang problem. The family may not supply the social support, supervision, and role models to meet the social development needs of youth. Parents of gang youths may lose control of their youths, parents may be present but working long hours without sufficient time to supervise children, and parents may not always be aware that their children are associating with gang members. Problems of communication may exist between parent(s) and socializing institutions such as the schools. Gang youths often manipulate communication between parents and school teachers or officials, and poorly educated parents may become pawns in the games youths play to avoid school attendance and responsibilities.

A key question is why certain youths engage in gang-motivated activity, especially violent behavior, while others, often from the same families, do not. Two general perspectives appear to be insightful. One perspective finds answers in the defects of the social, cultural, economic, or neighborhood environment. Joining a gang can be part of a natural learning process in certain neighborhoods or low-income areas. This classic learning-theory perspective emphasizes the positive reinforcements that youths obtain for deviant gang behavior, as well as punishments for not joining or fully participating in the gang's activities. In the other perspective, mainly social control theory, emphasis is on the characteristics of the individual youth rather than the social environment. It is not external pressures but the strength of internal controls that regulates the individual's behavior and, more important, restrains "the natural impulses to delinquency" (Elliott, Huizinga, and Ageton, 1985, pp. 33-35).

A third, integrative explanation emphasizes the interaction of social disorganization and poverty at social structural and personality levels. The need for order and organization is viewed as critically important, and the lack of an adequate relationship between the two levels may be the critical cause of the problem. More directly, lack of personal identity and isolation stimulated by a lack of adequate social support structure are the distinctive characteristics of the youth who seeks gang membership (Ianni, 1989, pp. 207-211).

APPROACHES TO DEALING WITH THE PROBLEM

Recent decades have produced four basic strategies for dealing with youth gangs. Each of the strategies has assumed some dominance in different historical periods, and each is related to different assumptions about cause and effect and about policy and practice. The strategies, in order of historical development, are (1) local community organization and mobilization; (2) social intervention, including youth outreach or street-gang work; (3) providing social and economic opportunities for inner-city youths; and (4) gang suppression and incarceration. A fifth strategy, organizational change and development, usually modifies or elaborates the four primary strategies. There has been very little systematic evaluation of these approaches. The following discussion examines the nature of these organized responses to the youth gang problem, with special attention to promising policy and program arrangements.

Community/Grassroots Mobilization

The principal response to youth gangs or delinquent groups prior to World War II involved local community groups taking responsibility to deal with immediate neighborhood youth problems and related local community conditions of fragmented agency concerns and lack of services. In Chicago and elsewhere, community and neighborhood groups—for example, the Chicago Area Project—attempted to bind elements of local citizenry, local organization, and the criminal justice system in collaborative responses to the delinquent group problem, which was relatively mild compared with the current youth gang problem (Kobrin, 1959; Schlossman, Zellman, and Shavelson, 1984). Emphasis was on coordination of available local resources, with use of indigenous leadership, including former delinquent group members or ex-convicts. A key idea was to restore a sense of community—to use grassroots leaders and local youth agencies to provide youths support and stimulate citizen involvement in programming that would lead to more conventional youth behavior.

The youth gang problem in the late 1940s and 1950s brought more complex efforts to better coordinate agency and community efforts. Citywide or even statewide special projects and youth authorities evolved. Outreach services were often sponsored by welfare councils or coalitions of agencies, as in Chicago, or by citywide or countywide public agencies, as in New York (Crawford, Malamud, and Dumpson, 1950; New York City Youth Board, 1960; Klein, 1968). These large-scale, often professionalized, youth service and criminal justice programs were introduced into local communities with limited grassroots organizational involvement. The earlier stable base of community organizations characteristic of White ethnic populations also did not exist in newer, rapidly expanding, Black and Hispanic communities in the northern urban centers such as Chicago. Specialized, increasingly non-community-based and individual client service strategies were emphasized. Furthermore, the interests of various agencies, particularly those of police and youth agencies, began to clash (Spergel, 1969).

In the late 1950s and throughout much of the 1960s, foundation and federal resources directed to various social problems inadvertently stimulated a series of uncoordinated, if not clashing, approaches that may have heightened the gang problem. The civil rights movement, local community action organizations stimulated by the Office of Economic Opportunity, and agency and political interests created an increasingly diverse and clashing set of values for addressing social problems, particularly in Chicago. The character of gangs was also changing as the labor market could no longer provide sufficient numbers of unskilled and semi-skilled jobs for low-income youths ready to leave the gang. Youth gangs in Chicago and elsewhere probably grew larger and more complex as a result of rapid changes in the economy, the failure of socializing institutions, and the conflicting social philosophies, policies, and uncoordinated agency programs responding to the gang problem (Moore, 1978; Poston, 1971). In Chicago, some gang members were and still are viewed as local community leaders, and gang organizations were encouraged to participate in or even assume leadership in urban development programs. They became citizen patrols during riot periods. Some gang members ran for elective office, then and now. It was and is not clear today that all such efforts were directed to legitimate community development goals.

In the 1970s and 1980s, the expansion of citizen participation and community-based programs to deal with a whole range of social problems resulted in an emphasis on individualized services and may have shifted interest away from gang member-oriented services. The YMCA, the Boys Clubs, and neighborhood agencies in Chicago ceased to provide detached-worker programs for gang youths. Community mobilization occurred to deal with delinquency and youth gang problems, but more and more to protect the interests of the "good" local citizenry against the interest of the "bad" local citizenry, mainly the youth delinquents. Crime prevention and crime control efforts by grassroots organizations and youth agencies were committed to a frontal attack on crime (Roehl and Cook, 1984; Wilson and Kelling, 1982). Attention turned to collaborative programs by local citizens and police to attack and control crime and violence on the streets and on school grounds and send more gang members to jail (Gottfredson and Gottfredson, 1985; Gottfredson, Gottfredson, and Cook, 1983).

In its most recent evolution in the late 1980s and early 1990s, the idea of community organization or mobilization may be assuming broader scope in Chicago. It stands for the development of coalitions of social service agencies, schools, criminal justice agencies, community groups, and sometimes former gang members (as workers or mentors) in efforts to deal collectively and consensually with the problem of gangs, especially gang violence and drug trafficking. A broad set of strategies is evolving, including a more community-oriented gang suppression strategy. The idea of community mobilization incorporates notions developed in prior historical periods, including local community agency responsibility, interagency criminal justice coordination, grassroots citizen participation, and increasingly community- or problem-oriented policing—a concept in process of formulation and implementation. Recent federal initiatives, involving the Department of Health and Human Services, the Department of Justice, and the Department of Housing and Urban Development, to deal with the problems of juvenile drug gangs and gang violence through a local community-mobilization strategy may be a sign of the invigoration and broadening of traditional agency and community approaches focused on fighting youth or street-gang crime.

Social Intervention/Youth Outreach/Street Work

A stream of social science and social work theory served as a partial basis for the development of outreach services for deviant youths in the 1950s and 1960s (e.g., Cohen, 1955; Miller, 1958;

Spergel, 1966). The assumption of youth agency programs was that youth gangs in lower-class communities were viable and adaptive and could be redirected through certain social relationship principles and techniques to meet the expectations and needs of the larger society. Youth gang norms and values could be changed with the aid of outreach services. Counseling and group activities attempted to persuade youth gang members to give up unlawful behavior. The gang itself was to be the vehicle of its own transformation, and the gang or subgroup was the unit of attention by the street worker. Group meetings, recreation, counseling, and referral of individual members for services were at the heart of efforts to co-opt or redirect gang member values and behaviors. These procedures were and still are characteristic of a range of agencies—in Chicago, Los Angeles, and elsewhere—dealing with gang youths or those at risk of such involvement.

The youth-outreach strategy targeted specific gangs and troublesome youths. It required "hanging out" with gang members on street corners and on their turf. The program was often not part of established youth service programs. Some of the gang workers were ex-gang members and were viewed as highly identified with gang members. The police at times believed that street workers, by their relation with street-gang members, often contributed to an increase in gang crime. Research on the Los Angeles County Probation Department's outreach gang program revealed that street workers may indeed have made gangs more cohesive by their lack of planning and unfocused group programming. When, for various reasons, street workers were removed or key gang member influentials separated from the gang, delinquent *group* activities declined (Klein, 1968, 1971).

In the 1970s, traditional youth-outreach programs were sharply curtailed as gang conflicts seemed to subside or were converted to drug problems in some cities. Youth agencies in Chicago turned their attention increasingly to less violent forms of youth deviancy, such as status offenses, especially runaways. Many of these agencies also were now concerned with services to less serious youth offenders who were no longer placed in correctional institutions. Federal funding was available for such services that were presumed to be cheaper than institutionalization. Also, since older youths and young adults had become a proportionately larger part of gangs, and gangs had become more criminalized, they were not considered amenable to traditional teenage-oriented street-work counseling or recreational strategies.

By the late 1980s and early 1990s, youth agencies in Chicago and elsewhere were increasingly committed to targeting younger youths in efforts to prevent serious gang violence and criminal behavior. The few remaining street-gang programs put less emphasis on crisis intervention and mediation of intergang disputes and were attempting to coordinate their efforts with those of law enforcement and probation. The schools, with the aid of youth agencies and juvenile justice agencies, also slowly became a context for preventive efforts. An implicit division of responsibility developed, with law enforcement taking primary responsibility for dealing with older, core gang members, now increasingly involved in drug trafficking, and youth agencies becoming responsible for work with so-called at-risk youth in their early teens or younger.

Providing Social Opportunities

Rising concerns with delinquency, unemployment, and school failure by inner-city youths in the late 1950s and 1960s were the basis for a series of large-scale efforts to change social institutions and establish new types of school programs, training institutions, and job programs directed to inner-city youths. These efforts focused on increased economic and social opportunities for youths as well as increased participation by local citizens to deal with local community problems. The strategy of the 1960s and early 1970s, however, was not primarily addressed to the youth gang problem. As suggested above, low-income and/or minority populations were generally the principal targets of the newer policies that were supported mainly by federal funds. The Ford Foundation, the President's Committee on Juvenile Delinquency and Youth Crime, the Office of Economic Opportunity, the Labor Department, and private foundations stimulated the development of new alternative educational and special training programs, job projects, and business development to benefit the socially disadvantaged, including a range of youths in both inner-city and low-income rural areas across the nation.

Broad-scale community-based multiservice programs were established. Distinctions between social intervention, opportunity provision, and community-development strategies were not easily made. Client groups were involved sometimes in the development, but more often in the delivery, of services, and they often themselves obtained jobs in these programs. Youth gangs were not ordinarily targeted, but when they were, these programs were a source of great community controversy (Poston, 1971; Spergel, 1972). Some social reformers, federal bureaucrats, and militant grassroots organizations mistakenly believed that gangs, per se, could be used to stabilize volatile communities during the riot-torn 1960s. These innovative local programs were, as a rule, not well designed. Also, as suggested above, the gangs had begun to change in terms of older age composition, more sophisticated organizational structure, and greater commitment to crime. This is not to deny that nationally supported programs such as Head Start and Job Corps were successful, at least over the short term, in the socialization, academic development, and retraining of a general population of inner-city minority young people, and even in reducing delinquency. But, we are less clear how well these programs targeted more serious delinquents and older gang youths, who may well have required special attention and services.

Gang Suppression

In the late 1970s and 1980s, with the decline of community-development and youth-outreach efforts, the inability of opportunity-provision approaches to target gang youths or modify gang structures, and the increased criminalization of now-older gang members, community alarm and political conservatism stimulated a dominant police suppression approach. The gang was increasingly viewed as evil and dangerous, a collecting place for sociopaths and hardened criminals. Gangs were regarded as beyond the rehabilitative reach of most community-based agencies and social programs. Community defense and self-protection became the key goal. Vigorous law enforcement was called for. Gang members were to be arrested, prosecuted, and sentenced to the longest possible prison terms.

Police and prosecutors came to play the primary response roles in cities such as Chicago and Los Angeles. Local, state, and federal information systems, surveillance, tactical patrols, and sweeps by specialized law enforcement agencies were developed or planned. Chicago created the nation's largest, most sophisticated, and most specialized police organization dealing with gang crimes. The office of the Cook County State's Attorney developed a prosecution unit to target hard-core gang members. Cook County did not develop a special probation approach to dealing with gang members until more recently—at the adult probation level. Illinois state legislation increasingly authorized law enforcement agents to seize property and required judges to enhance sentences of gang members participating in serious criminal incidents. Local interagency task forces at the city and county levels were organized involving school, youth agency, public housing, and grassroots organizations, as well as law enforcement to improve intelligence gathering and suppression of gangs. Law enforcement became more involved in youth supervisory roles in schools and community agencies.

The suppression strategy in Chicago has been associated not only with more arrests, convictions, and longer prison sentences for gang members, but also with continued growth and spread of gangs within and across the city, suburbs, the state, and the nation. The dominance of a suppression strategy has also been associated with a rise in gang member-related drug trafficking. Gang youths are also more and more represented in prison populations, where they have created serious problems of custody, especially violence against other inmates. Gangs have become increasingly well organized in prisons, with close and continuing connections and considerable influence over local community street-gang activities. The strategy of suppression, as currently developed and specialized, has not proved sufficient to reduce the gang problem and return "control of the streets" to local citizens.

Finally, in our recent national survey of expert informants from criminal justice, community agencies, and grassroots organizations throughout the United States, we found that suppression alone or social intervention alone appeared not to be sufficient to reduce gang crime. A majority of these informants were from the justice system and believed that the provision of social opportunities in combination with a community-mobilization strategy, particularly in cities with chronic gang problems, was the best approach to the gang problem. A community-mobilization strategy involved joint efforts by criminal justice and community agencies, schools, and grassroots groups in a common perception and definition of the problem with close network relations and reciprocal roles targeting gang members and gang-prone youths. Community mobilization by itself was the most effective strategy in cities with an emerging gang problem, that is, in cities where the gang problem was less serious and had existed over a relatively shorter period of time and where social opportunities were relatively more available than in chronic problem cities. Furthermore, we were able to confirm and establish the validity of these perceptual findings in a supplementary collection of quantitative data from these same cities. These data demonstrated a decrease in the number of gangs, gang members, gang homicides, gang assaults, and gang drug-related incidents in those cities with a primary strategic emphasis on community-mobilization and opportunity-provision strategies (Spergel and Curry, 1990).

RECOMMENDATIONS FOR POLICY AND PRACTICE

Certain policy and program approaches, based on the foregoing analysis, may be useful in controlling and reducing youth gang crime. These approaches include (1) broad social policy sensitive to the social development needs of, yet mainstreaming, gang youths to the extent possible; (2) carefully defining and targeting the local gang problem; (3) creation of appropriate program structures and activities; and (4) prioritizing and interrelating strategies of action in systematically different ways for different kinds of youths in different communities. Policies should be formulated in related ways at federal, state, and local levels to support these varying approaches.

Broad Social Policy

The youth-gang or street-gang problem is related in basic and complex ways to more general social problems affecting youth development. Yet, it is a mistake to assume that as "larger" social issues such as youth education and employment, economic or community development, and criminal justice coordination are resolved, the scope and severity of the youth gang problem will automatically lessen. The gang problem differs depending on a variety of community-level factors, at particular times, and it must be addressed on its own terms as well as in relation to other fundamental or broader social issues.

It is important that the approach to the gang problem be neither too broad nor too narrow. Criminal justice policymakers and administrators must influence decision-makers in other social policy arenas, such as education, training, employment, and social services, to reflect their specific interests in the youth gang problem. General social policy—for example, in the youth employment area—should be developed in terms relevant to the gang problem. This may require creation of policies, programs, and procedures that do not exclude gang members, but rather include youths with prior records of violence. Obviously, special safeguards and social support services will be required in these endeavors, and, to the extent possible, such programs must be guided by the concept of mainstreaming these youths. National or state policy should provide social opportunities for gang and gang-prone youths to escape ghetto conditions yet build in special controls as necessary to safeguard non-gang youths as well as the community. National youth development policy should enable and encourage both mainstream youths and gang youths together to participate in programs that contribute to the social regeneration of inner-city areas. At the local level, special efforts to refer older gang adolescents and young adults for jobs should also be integrally connected to community policing efforts.

Defining and Targeting the Problem

It is important that the problem of gangs be neither denied nor exaggerated. Gang crime neighborhoods, overwhelmed with failing social institutions that deal with, or should be dealing with, gang youths, should be targeted for attention, that is, for appropriate control, support, and additional resources and services. Differences of perception of the problem and the development of specific policies must be reconciled and addressed by local participants through proactive and shared community involvement, planning, and programming processes. These efforts should be supported by state and federal resources, to the extent possible. The development of local programs must be based on a collaborative and sustained approach over many years in which program operators are held accountable for adequately targeting and addressing the problem, without "creaming," making false claims of "prevention," or exaggerating the problem.

The development of relevant, accurate, and accessible information systems is of special importance. At the state and national levels, care must be taken not to label youths as gang members unless reliable and valid confirming information is available. Statewide and national information systems, which are in the process of development, should be careful to primarily include convicted gang members and not simply everyone identified as a gang member, gang associate, or suspect. Juveniles under 17 years of age should be afforded special protection and generally excluded from these systems. At the local level, a narrow gang incident rather than a broad membership definition should be the principal means for assessing the scope and severity of the problem. Special care should be taken not to accumulate names of gang members—who are often no longer active—or to assume that the gang problem is reflected simply by the age, gender, race, ethnicity, or neighborhood characteristics of youths or adults. Furthermore, such information, usually controlled by the police, should be accessible, under appropriate legal and human subject protection conditions, to a range of program providers, planners, and researchers.

Finally, individual youths should be targeted for special supervision, social services, and social opportunities in the following order of priority, yet in interrelated fashion:

> First, leadership and core gang youths, in order to disrupt gang networks, protect the community, and facilitate the reintegration of these youths into legitimate pursuits through community-oriented, proactive law enforcement and educational and social assistance programming;

> Second, high-risk, gang-prone youths who are often younger or aspiring gang members who give clear evidence of beginning participation in criminal gang activities. They should receive intensive supervision and support services;

> Third, regular and peripheral gang members, in order to address their needs for social control and intervention services; and

> Fourth, youths generally in high-risk gang crime communities, particularly those who are in fourth through seventh grade. They should be assisted to develop attitudes and learn ways to avoid gang membership or gang victimization.

Policy and Program Structure

A structure and set of mechanisms must be created for the development of these policy and program strategies and tactics across agencies and community groups or interests at different government and non-governmental levels. Of special importance is the integration of policy among federal agencies that deal or should deal with various aspects of youth policy, including the gang problem. Interagency structures already exist—for example, in the Office of Juvenile Justice and Delinquency Prevention—but are often not sufficiently activated across units within the Justice Department or across the departments of Health and Human Services, Education, Labor, and Housing and Urban Development.

A local community structure should be developed to coordinate and integrate ongoing efforts based on the interests, needs, and resources (present and potential) of the particular community. Mechanisms must be created for the integration of criminal justice, community agencies, and grassroots groups, including those community groups that are most affected by the problem and are usually less well organized or articulate. In jurisdictions with emerging gang-problems, a less formal and more limited structure and set of strategies may be sufficient to deal with the problem. Of special importance, especially in chronic problem communities, is the development of procedures for the collection and sharing of appropriate information about youths to be targeted and the development of explicit standards for reciprocal relations among such key institutions as police, schools, and youth agencies. The police must assume a significant, if not the key, role in such partnership arrangements. Different racial/ethnic, class, organizational, and interorganizational interests as well as different levels of the gang problem must be taken into account in fashioning appropriate local structures of community mobilization.

Interactive and Balanced Strategies

Key strategies that contribute to the reduction and control of the youth gang problem in particular crime contexts must be formulated at both the local and state/national levels. The assumption should be that the gang problem is not simply a "medical-type" problem to be prevented by targeting only younger youths before the social disease becomes advanced. The gang problem is systemic and structural. It reflects basic and rapid changes in modern societies, in which the socialization of teenagers and their transition to mainstream adult life are problematic or defective in certain communities. Key social institutions and programs, as well as gangs and individuals in the environment, must be targeted for change and development. Such change should occur mainly through a community-mobilization approach. Funding for and management of the strategy should be arranged through a consortia of local agencies and community groups with the aid of state and federal resources. No single approach, however, whether social intervention, provision of social opportunities, suppression, or even community mobilization, may be sufficient. A key strategy, nevertheless, in addition to community organization, should be opportunity provision targeted to specific neighborhood youths, with special focus on remedial and specialized education, training, and jobs.

A principal program objective should be the development of appropriate support and control with certain communal or family character over long periods of time directly in the community, whether through school, work, or justice agencies. A high degree of specialization in agency operations or role functioning should be avoided. Ongoing communication must be developed with gang members and gang-prone youths in a manner that contributes to both the social development and social control of youth, as well as the protection of the community's interests and safety. Communication and collaboration among key organizations targeting gang youths, including core gang members, should be developed. Regular meetings and mechanisms must be developed—involving such organizations as police, schools, employment agencies, youth agencies, and community groups—for exchanging information about program efforts for targeted at-risk and hard-core youths.

Planners and administrators should be encouraged, if not required, to develop evaluative research designs to determine which approaches are most effective under different social, economic, and cultural conditions. We know very little about what works in dealing with particular types of gangs and gang youths. We know a little more about what does not work. Sadly, federal, state, and local policymakers remain focused on doing what is politic in the short term but often expensive and ineffective both in the short and long term. Sound evaluative research is essential to any breakthroughs in policies and programs that seek honestly to address gang problems.

Finally, a carefully planned effort to restructure a social context and to change the pattern of relationships of gang youths to each other, as well as to social institutions, is a very large undertaking. It requires modest objectives joined with heroic efforts. At best, we can anticipate only limited success. Our analysis has been focused on the reduction of gang-motivated violence, which can be controlled and prevented to a certain extent. The general reduction of violence is also required and should principally be addressed through effective gun control legislation and enforcement, involving limitation on the manufacture, distribution, and possession of all handguns. We make no claims that our model is as useful in the reduction of drug trafficking and other more organized criminal operations, which, although modestly related to street-gang violence, are a distinctive set of deviancy problems that require modified, if not different, strategies.

REFERENCES

Associated Press (1992). "Violent Crime Rose 5% in U.S. in 1991," *New York Times*, April 27, 1992, p. A12.
Block, Carolyn R. (1991). "Lethal Violence in the Chicago Latino Community." Draft. Chicago: Statistical Analysis Center, Illinois Criminal Justice Information Authority, March 7, 1991.
Bobrowski, Lawrence J. (1988). *Collecting, Organizing, and Reporting Street Gang Crime*. Chicago: Chicago Police Department, Special Functions Group, November 1988.
Brody, Jane E. (1992). "Report Says Rape Leads in Violent Crimes," *New York Times*, April 20, 1992, p. A13.
Camp, Camille Graham, and George M. Camp (1988). *Management Strategies for Combatting Prison Gang Violence*. South Salem, N.Y.: Criminal Justice Institute, September 1988.
Cloward, Richard A., and Lloyd E. Ohlin (1960). *Delinquency and Opportunity: A Theory of Delinquent Gangs*. Glencoe, Ill.: Free Press.
Cohen, Albert K. (1955). *Delinquent Boys: The Culture of the Gang*. Glencoe, Ill.: Free Press.
Crawford, Paul Z., Daniel I. Malamud, and James R. Dumpson (1950). *Working with Teenage Gangs*. New York: Welfare Council of New York City.
Curry, G. David, Robert J. Fox, Richard A. Ball, and Darryl Stone (1992). *National Assessment of Law Enforcement Anti-Gang Information Resources*. Draft. Morgantown, W. Va.
Curry, G. David, and Irving A. Spergel (1992). "Gang Involvement and Delinquency Among Hispanic and African-American Adolescent Males," *Journal of Research in Crime and Delinquency*, vol. 29, no. 3 (August 1992), pp. 273-292.
Donovan, John (1988). "An Introduction to Street Gangs." Paper prepared for the office of Senator John Garamemdi. Sacramento, Calif., August 1988.

Elliott, Delbert S., David Huizinga, and Suzanne S. Ageton (1985). *Explaining Delinquency and Drug Use.* Beverly Hills, Calif.: Sage Publications.

Fagan, Jeffrey (1988). "The Social Organization of Drug Use and Drug Dealing Among Urban Gangs." New York: Criminal Justice Center, John Jay College of Criminal Justice, July 1988.

Friedman, C. Jack, Frederica Mann, and Alfred S. Friedman (1975). "A Profile of Juvenile Street Gang Members," *Adolescence*, vol. 10, no. 40 (Winter 1975), pp. 563-607.

Gottfredson, Gary D., and Denise C. Gottfredson (1985). *Victimization in Schools.* New York: Plenum.

Gottfredson, Gary D., Denise C. Gottfredson, and Michael S. Cook, eds. (1983). *The School Action Effectiveness Study.* Second Interim Report, Part 1, Report No. 342. Baltimore: John Hopkins University, June 1983.

Haskins, James (1974). *Street Gangs: Yesterday and Today.* New York: Hastings House Publishers.

Herrman, Andrew (1992). "Suburbs Map Gang War," *Chicago Sun-Times*, September 18, 1992, pp. 1, 17.

Horowitz, Ruth (1983). *Honor and the American Dream.* New Brunswick, N.J.: Rutgers University Press.

Hyman, Irwin A. (1984). "Testimony before the Subcommittee on Elementary, Secondary, and Vocational Education of the Committee on Education and Labor." U.S. House of Representatives, January 24, 1984.

Ianni, Francis A.J. (1989). *The Search for Structure.* Report on American Youth Today. New York: Free Press.

Justice Research and Statistics Association (1993). *Violent Crime and Drug Abuse in Rural Areas: Issues, Concerns, and Programs.* Washington, D.C.: Bureau of Justice Assistance, Office of Justice Programs, U.S. Department of Justice.

Klein, Malcolm W. (1968). *From Association to Guilt: The Group Guidance Project in Juvenile Gang Intervention.* Los Angeles: Youth Studies Center, University of Southern California, and the Los Angeles County Probation Department.

―――― (1971). *Street Gangs and Street Workers.* Englewood Cliffs, N.J.: Prentice-Hall.

Klein, Malcolm W., and Cheryl L. Maxson (1989). "Street Gang Violence." In Marvin E. Wolfgang and Neil Weiner, eds., *Violent Crime, Violent Criminals.* Beverly Hills, Calif.: Sage Publications.

Klein, Malcolm W., and Barbara G. Myerhoff, eds. (1967). *Juvenile Gangs in Context: Theory, Research, and Action.* Englewood Cliffs, N.J.: Prentice-Hall.

Kobrin, Solomon (1959). "The Chicago Area Project—A Twenty-Five Year Assessment," *Annals of the American Academy of Political and Social Science*, vol. 322 (March 1959), pp. 19-29.

Koziol, Ronald (1991). "16 Seized by Kankakee Police Linked to Chicago Street Gangs," *Chicago Tribune*, November 22, 1991, sec. 2, p. 5.

Manikas, Peter, John P. Heinz, Mindy S. Trossman, and Jack C. Doppelt (1990). *Criminal Justice Policy Making: Boundaries and Borderlands.* Final Report of the Criminal Justice Project. Evanston, Ill.: Center for Urban Affairs and Policy Research, Northwestern University.

Maxson, Cheryl L., Margaret A. Gordon, and Malcolm W. Klein (1985). "Differences Between Gang and Non-gang Homicides," *Criminology*, vol. 23, no. 2 (May 1985), pp. 209-222.

McBride, Wes (1988). Personal Communication. Los Angeles County Sheriff's Department, November 18, 1988.

Miller, Walter B. (1958). "Lower Class Culture as a Generating Milieu of Gang Delinquency," *Journal of Social Issues*, vol. 14, no. 3, pp. 5-19.

_____ (1982). *Crime by Youth Gangs and Groups in the United States.* Washington, D.C.: Office of Juvenile Justice and Delinquency Prevention, U.S. Department of Justice.

Moore, Joan W. (1978). *Homeboys.* Philadelphia: Temple University Press.

Mulack, Donald G., and Robert Fuesel (1995). *Gangs: Public Enemy Number One.* Chicago: Chicago Crime Commission.

Needle, Jerome A., and William Vaughan Stapleton (1983). *Police Handling of Youth Gangs.* Washington, D.C.: National Institute for Juvenile Justice and Delinquency Prevention, Office of Juvenile Justice and Delinquency Prevention, U.S. Department of Justice.

New York City Youth Board (1960). *Reaching the Fighting Gang.* New York: New York City Youth Board.

Philibosian, Robert H. (1986). *State Task Force on Youth Gang Violence: Final Report.* Sacramento, Calif.: California Council on Criminal Justice.

Poston, Richard W. (1971). *The Gang and the Establishment.* New York: Harper and Row.

Reiner, Ira (1992). *Gangs, Crime and Violence in Los Angeles*. Los Angeles: Office of the District Attorney of the County of Los Angeles.

Roehl, Janice, and Royer F. Cook (1984). *Evaluation of the Urban Crime Prevention Program*. Washington, D.C.: U.S. Department of Justice, National Institute of Justice.

San Diego Association of Governments (1982). *Juvenile Violence and Gang-Related Crime*. San Diego: Association of State Governments.

Schlossman, Steven, Gail Zellman, and Richard Shavelson (1984). *Delinquency Prevention in South Chicago: A Fifty-Year Assessment of the Chicago Area Project*. Santa Monica, Calif.: Rand.

Spergel, Irving A. (1966). *Street Gang Work: Theory and Practice*. Reading, Mass.: Addison-Wesley.

─────── (1969). *Problem Solving: The Delinquency Example*. Chicago: University of Chicago Press.

─────── (1972). "Community Action Research as a Political Process." In Irving A. Spergel, ed., *Community Organization: Studies in Constraint*. Beverly Hills, Calif.: Sage Publications.

─────── (1986). "The Violent Gang Problem in Chicago: A Local Community Approach," *Social Service Review*, vol. 60, no. 1 (March 1986), pp. 94-131.

Spergel, Irving A., and G. David Curry, with Ruth E. Ross and Ron L. Chance (1990). *Survey of Youth Gang Problems and Programs in 45 Cities and 6 Sites*. Chicago: School of Social Service Administration, University of Chicago.

Tracy, Paul E. (1987). "Subcultural Delinquency: A Comparison of the Incidence and Severity of Gang and Non-gang Member Offenses." Boston: College of Criminal Justice, Northeastern University.

Wilson, James Q., and George L. Kelling (1982). "Broken Windows: The Police and Neighborhood Safety," *Atlantic Monthly*, March 1982, pp. 29-38.

Wilson, William Julius. (1987). *The Truly Disadvantaged: The Inner City, the Underclass, and Public Policy*. Chicago: University of Chicago Press.

A COMPREHENSIVE APPROACH TO VIOLENCE PREVENTION: PUBLIC HEALTH AND CRIMINAL JUSTICE IN PARTNERSHIP

Howard Spivak
Deborah Prothrow-Stith
Mark Moore[*]

Violence and its consequences of death and disability have become issues of growing concern over the past decade in the United States (U.S. Public Health Service, 1990). Although violence and intentional injury (the major physical consequence of violence) have been serious problems for far longer than that, the public's perception and, in fact, the available statistics suggest a significant increase in the level of violence experienced in this country in recent years (Centers for Disease Control, 1983, 1990). Not only are the consequences of serious injury or death considerable for individuals personally affected, but violence is increasingly taking its toll in terms of fear and frustration for many communities. To date, effective solutions and responses have eluded the nation as a whole. Many law enforcement experts agree that the problem of violence cannot be controlled by the criminal justice system alone. In particular, these experts believe that prevailing social conditions regarding family stability, education, and other societal institutions affect the behavior of juveniles (FBI, 1992, p. 279).

Efforts by the criminal justice system and others to address this problem have been episodic and inconsistent and have lacked a comprehensive and coordinated vision. The growing magnitude of this problem not only demands continued attention but also requires new and creative approaches and partnerships if we are to effectively stem the growing tide of violence.

---

[*] The authors would like to thank Alice Hausman and Renee Wilson for their help and advice in the preparation of this article, Micki Diegel for her invaluable assistance in preparing the manuscript, and Sher Quaday for editing this document.

VIOLENCE IN THE UNITED STATES

Before entering into a discussion of solutions and approaches, it is essential to recognize the extent and the characteristics of violence in the United States (Spivak, Prothrow-Stith, and Hausman, 1988). This country has the fifth highest homicide rate of all nations reporting such data. Not only is the U.S. homicide rate 10 to 25 times higher than most industrialized nations, but our homicide rates rival some less developed countries facing war or considerable social, political, and economic turmoil (Wolfgang, 1986, p. 400).

In 1991, of the 24,703 murder victims in the United States, 93 percent of Black victims were killed by Black offenders, and 85 percent of White murder victims were killed by White offenders. Firearms were used in seven out of ten murders (FBI, 1992, p. 17). Homicide in this country has become the twelfth leading cause of death overall, the second leading cause of death for teenagers and young adults, and the leading cause of death for African-American men and women ages 15 to 34 (Centers for Disease Control, 1990). Each year over 20,000 individuals die by homicide, hundreds of thousands are injured by assault, and millions are fearful of the risks and potential destruction of intentional injury.

ADOLESCENTS AT RISK

Adolescent violence should be a major concern for all Americans. The decade from 1980 to 1990 saw the juvenile violent crime arrest rate for Blacks increase by 19 percent; for Whites it increased 44 percent, while the rates for the "other" race category declined 53 percent (chiefly because of the large increase of Asian youth). Increases in the crime rate are predicted through the next decade. A common misconception of violent crime is that it is just an inner-city, Black problem. But that is simply not so. The recent escalation of adolescent violent crime rates in the past several decades cuts across race, class, and lifestyle (FBI, 1992, pp. 279-289).

There are some children who are more susceptible and more at risk of becoming victims or perpetrators of violence. Those at higher risk tend to be male, be poor, live in urban areas, and have witnessed much violence or been victims of violence during early childhood development. The social condition of poverty wrecks havoc on many communities and is a factor for many adolescent high-risk behaviors (Prothrow-Stith, 1992).

One American child in every five lives in poverty. Among children under age six, one in four is poor. One-third of these children are Black. There are 13.4 million poor American children. Nearly two of three poor families with children had one or more members in the work force in 1990 (Children's Defense Fund, 1992). The economic, political, social, and familial problems that breed violence in very poor neighborhoods are formidable. No single institution can bring about the kind of change needed to restore a sense of safety and order to everyday life. Children and adolescents have little choice in their environment and educational opportunities or in the racism, sexism, and parental upbringing that may have shaped the personal choices that place them at risk in war-torn communities. Inner-city adolescents are often painfully aware of how different their neighborhoods are from their more affluent peers. Most teenagers understand and respond to real opportunity when it is offered. But when there is no hope for a better future, adolescents may by default choose what makes them feel better, what the media portray as glamorous and exciting, and what counteracts the grinding boredom of poverty with few options in sight. Our poorest adolescents have armed themselves and become guerilla fighters against each other in a way that has no name, no political ideology, and no end in sight (Prothrow-Stith and Weissman, 1991).

CHARACTERISTICS OF VIOLENCE

While the statistics of violence may not be surprising to some, the nature of this violence is unknown to many. Contrary to the stereotypes of violence promoted by the media as predominantly involving strangers or occurring in the context of criminal behavior such as racial harassment, robbery, or drug dealing, much of the violence experienced in this country is far more intimate and occurs in the context of personal relationships (Spivak, Prothrow-Stith, and Hausman, 1988). In fact, the typical homicide involves two people who know each other, who, under the influence of alcohol, get into an argument that escalates with the presence of a gun or knife. Only 15 percent of homicides occur in the course of committing a crime, as compared with over 50 percent that stem from arguments among acquaintances (Centers for Disease Control, 1982). This 50 percent takes place in family relationships (e.g., child abuse, elder abuse, spouse abuse) or among friends (interpersonal peer violence). In the remaining 35 percent, the relationship between victim and perpetrator is unknown.

The perpetrator and victim of violence share many traits. They are likely to be young and male and of the same race. They are likely to be poor and to have been exposed to violence in the past—especially family violence. They may be depressed and use alcohol and/or drugs (Prothrow-Stith and Weissman, 1991). This incongruity between public perception and actual circumstances has resulted in demands for resources and solutions that address only part—possibly the smaller part—of the problem. While certainly not discarding established anti-crime and anti-violence strategies, we must recognize the diversity of violent circumstances that exist and must build a broader base of efforts that not only responds to violent events but also focuses on preventive services.

THE CRIMINAL JUSTICE RESPONSE TO VIOLENCE

Historically, American society has relied almost exclusively on the criminal justice system to both respond to and prevent violence. This is rooted in the beliefs that violence is criminal, that those who commit violence should be punished, and that the threat of punishment is a potential deterrent to violent acts. A large, elaborate set of institutions has been developed to achieve these goals. That system includes police, prosecutors, public defenders, judges, probation officers, and prison guards. It is designed principally to respond to crimes after they have been committed by identifying, apprehending, prosecuting, punishing, and controlling the violent offender. It is guided not only by the practical goals of reducing crimes of all types (including violence) but also by the normative goal of assuring justice to victims and the accused.

The public health and criminal justice systems have been historically separate in their conceptualization of approaches to violence and the development of activities to reduce or prevent violence. The public health field has approached the issue through efforts to identify the risk factors related to violent behavior. The field turns to this issue in reaction to the magnitude of intentional injuries that are present in health care settings. The criminal justice system has approached the issue through efforts to identify and assign blame for criminal behavior, maintain public safety, and remove violent offenders from the community.

Viewed from the perspective of those interested in reducing violence, the criminal justice system's responses have had only limited success. Part of the reason is inherent limitations in the overall approach of the criminal justice system. First, it is more reactive than preventive in its basic orientation. True, deterrence may produce some preventive results. True, too, the criminal justice system has sought to rehabilitate offenders through special programs in prisons and to prevent children from becoming violent offenders through the development of the juvenile justice system, whose most fundamental goal is to prevent future criminal activity by children. Nonetheless, the criminal justice system comes into play only after a crime episode has occurred.

Second, the criminal justice system—particularly the police—is focused primarily on the predatory violence that occurs among strangers on the street. The violence that emerges from nagging frustrations and festering disputes and takes place in intimate settings is far more difficult for the criminal justice system to deal with than stranger-inflicted violence that arises from greed or desperate need and that takes place in the open. Robbery and burglary—and the violence that attends them—are more traditional and central to the criminal justice system's business (and consciousness) than aggravated assaults that spring up among friends in bars, lovers in bedrooms, or teenagers at dances.

Despite such limitations, no one seriously questions the importance of these institutions and their approach to the control of violence. Questions, however, do properly arise about the comprehensiveness of this approach.

THE PUBLIC HEALTH RESPONSE TO VIOLENCE

Public health practitioners have recently stepped up to the problem of violence, bringing different orientations and techniques to complement and strengthen the criminal justice approach. The public health system has noted that violence affects the nation's health statistics as well as its crime statistics. As noted earlier, violence is a prominent contributor to mortality and morbidity. In just one year, homicide and intentional injury may represent as much as $60 billion in short- and long-term health care costs and lost productivity for those who are injured or disabled by violence (Rice, Mackenzie, and Max, 1989). These facts alone should warrant attention by public health professionals, as well as the broader spectrum of human services professionals, and give society even more reason to be concerned about violence.

In addition, the public health community has been drawn to this issue by the growing conviction that its techniques of analysis and prevention might be usefully applied to violence. Public health brings an analytic approach to problems that concentrates on identifying risk factors and important causes that could become the focus of preventive interventions. It also brings a record of accomplishment in controlling "accidental" (unintentional) injuries through both environmental manipulations (e.g., seat belts and childproof caps on medicines) and behavioral change (e.g., laws and educational campaigns to reduce drunk driving). These techniques may be valuable in the analysis and prevention of violence as well. This approach seems particularly plausible as we learn more about what occasions violence in society, including what factors put individuals, especially youth, at risk of either committing or being victimized by violence, and as we learn the limitations of the criminal justice system in dealing with some of these contributing factors.

OPPORTUNITIES FOR EFFECTIVE COLLABORATION

On the surface, the predominantly reactive stance of the criminal justice system and the pro-active perspective of the public health community would appear both complementary and potentially productive. There are, in fact, several examples of collaboration between these disciplines that have been substantially effective. Interdisciplinary programs are now standard practice in the areas of child abuse and sexual assault. For example, the recommended plan for treatment of rape victims by criminal justice, medical, public health, and mental health systems is a model collaborative effort: Community groups staff and train hotline volunteers who offer crisis counseling, criminal justice assistance, and information. Trained staff are available to accompany victims to hospital emergency departments and police interviews. Emergency room staff specially trained to deal with rape victims administer the appropriate tests and treat the victim. After the immediate emergency services are complete, a referral is made to a mental health counseling service that offers short- and long-term services to the victim and the victim's family. Trained staff at police departments will handle the rape victim's complaint. The criminal justice system uses victim-witness staff to keep the victim up to date with case information, give the victim an orientation to the courtroom and a description of what to expect in a hearing or a trial, and provide information on parole hearings, escaped prisoners, appeals, and other issues (Rosenberg and Fenley, 1991). Criminal justice interventions and health services together are key in the identification of cases, treatment of victims, possible rehabilitation of offenders, and early identification of at-risk situations prior to more serious injury being inflicted.

In the area of unintentional injury, specifically drunk driving, there has been a very successful partnership between the educational strategies of the public health sector for behavior change and the threats of punitive action and the monitoring practices of the criminal justice system. The public health sector launched a series of preventive interventions in schools and in the media to educate children and adults on the risks of drinking and driving and about strategies to avoid the risks. Concurrently, the criminal justice system imposed stiffer penalties, enhanced enforcement of drunk-driving laws, developed screening techniques such as roadblocks, placed more responsibility on establishments that serve alcohol, and increased treatment requirements for those arrested for drunk driving. Together, these approaches not only have changed the behaviors of at least some individuals but also have substantially influenced public attitudes with respect to the unacceptability of drinking and driving. Scientific evaluations of the efficacy of drunk-driving legislation, enforcement, and health education indicate that the legal and social sanctions met with some success. Between 1980 and 1984, the number of fatal crashes involving alcohol declined by 20 percent (Hingson, Howland, and Levenson, 1988).

CHALLENGES TO EFFECTIVE COLLABORATION

Unfortunately, the collaboration of public health and criminal justice in the area of violence prevention has been wrought with tension. Some of this may stem from a basic failure to effectively reduce the problem of violence that has put both disciplines on the defensive: criminal justice for its failure to bring the problem under control and meet societal expectations; public health for the slowness with which it has recognized and taken on the problem. However, much of this tension probably comes from the divergence of perspective of the two disciplines and the fact that there are inadequate resources directed to addressing violence, which has forced the disciplines to compete rather than collaborate.

Public health is primarily focused on identifying causality (or its approximation) and intervening to control or reduce risk factors. It has little interest in assigning blame or meting out punishment and does not discriminate between victim and offender. The public health community may agree that justice must be done, but it is not professionally committed to the process. The criminal justice system, by contrast, is deeply and morally rooted in "justice" and criminal offenders being properly identified and punished. There is less emphasis on the precursors or factors that may have led to the violent event. The criminal justice system is less likely to consider external factors that might have motivated the offender to engage in violence because it sees these issues as largely irrelevant to judgment of guilt and innocence. At worst, the claims that these other factors were causally important in the particular instance seems like a rationalization or an apology for what was a criminal deed. This rift is further exacerbated by the fact that the criminal justice profession continues to develop preventive agendas, such as first offender programs and community policing initiatives, and probably feels that its "thunder" and leadership are in jeopardy of being stolen by the arrival of another professional player onto its turf.

This tension is clearly unproductive. It threatens effective collaboration and frustrates the opportunity to pool resources and expertise at a time when resources are seriously inadequate and the problem is increasing. Healing this rift requires a more collaborative spirit from both disciplines. The public health "purists" must get beyond their science and recognize the invaluable contributions and practical experiences of the criminal justice professionals. The criminal justice "moralists" must, in turn, recognize the limitations of a primary agenda of assigning blame and assuring justice is done.

If we are to get past these initial reactions and successfully exploit the complementary qualities of these two approaches to violence, it is essential to put aside professional jealousies. More important, we must better define the perspective, roles, and expertise both groups bring to the issue. This will lead not only to a more creative process but also to establishing productive working partnerships. The history of positive interaction between the two disciplines, as noted earlier, establishes an experiential base on which future collaboration can be built.

A CONCEPTUAL APPROACH TO ORGANIZING THE COLLABORATION

One conceptual framework that can alleviate this interprofessional tension, facilitate definitions of roles in addressing the problem, and assist in developing a broader perspective on programmatic strategies involves breaking the spectrum of violence into levels that reflect different points of intervention. This framework, used frequently in public health circles, structures approaches to problems into three stages: primary prevention, secondary prevention (or early intervention), and tertiary prevention (or treatment/rehabilitation). These distinctions have proved valuable in thinking about intervention efforts even though their boundaries are a little fuzzy. In this discussion, it might be best to think of these distinctions in terms of concentric circles that widen out in space and time from a central point, which is the occurrence of some violent event.

Tertiary prevention is distinguished from secondary and primary prevention in that it lies on the opposite side of the violent event from the other two. Its focus is on trying to reduce the negative consequences of a particular event after it has occurred or on trying to find ways to use the event to reduce the likelihood of similar incidents occurring in the future. Thus, one might think of improved trauma care, on the one hand, and increased efforts to rehabilitate or incapacitate violent offenders, on the other hand, as tertiary prevention instruments in the control of or the response to violence.

Primary prevention, which by definition addresses the broadest level of the general public, might seek to reduce the level of violence that is shown on television or to promote gun control. This would be an effort directed toward dealing with the public values and attitudes that may promote or encourage the use of violence.

Secondary prevention is distinguished from primary prevention in that it identifies and focuses attention on relatively narrowly defined sub-groups or circumstances that are at high risk of being involved in or occasioning violence. Thus, secondary prevention efforts might focus on urban poor, young men who are at particularly high risk of engaging in or being victimized by violence, educating them in non-violent methods of resolving disputes or displaying competence and power.

Of course, the relative risk level of groups or circumstances is a continuum—with some people and circumstances at very high risk (say, a person who has been victimized by violence in his or her own home, also surrounded by violence in school, entering a bar in which members of a rival gang are drinking), and others at relatively low risk (say, a happily married professor, who owns no weapon more lethal than a screwdriver, writing on his computer at home). Moreover, it is generally true that the higher-risk groups are smaller than the lower-risk groups.

Primary prevention instruments are those that can affect larger and larger populations, ideally at relatively low cost. Indeed, the need to reach very large populations requires primary prevention efforts to have low costs per individual reached. Thus, primary prevention instruments tend to involve providing information and education on the problem of violence through the popular media rather than providing non-violence training to the entire population. Examples of the former approach include the recruitment of Bill Cosby to the cause of using the media to prevent adolescent violence (*USA Weekend*, 1992) and Sarah Brady's efforts to advocate for gun control laws and educate the public about the risks of handguns. There are, of course, the ultimate long-term primary prevention goals that have to do with eliminating some of the root causes of violence such as social injustice and discrimination.

This public health model can be very useful when applied specifically to the issue of interpersonal violence. In the past, the criminal justice system has addressed each of the three points of intervention to varying degrees, as represented in Figure 1 (panel A). However, the bulk of criminal justice efforts have focused on the response to serious violent behavior, with moderate attention to early identification and intervention and limited efforts in the area of primary prevention.

The major activities of the criminal justice system have historically involved the roles of the police, the courts, and the prison system in responding to criminal or violent events. Most resources have been directed to investigating and punishing criminal behavior. Tertiary prevention has generally involved incarceration. In the area of secondary prevention, the police have focused efforts on "situational" crime prevention, and the juvenile justice system has made attempts at early intervention with youthful offenders, although youth were frequently ignored by the courts and probation system until their criminal behavior reached a relatively high level of concern. Primary prevention efforts have focused on controlling "criminogenic" commodities such as guns, drugs, and alcohol or on elementary school drug and violence prevention education by police.

FIGURE 1:
Model for Violence Prevention Activities

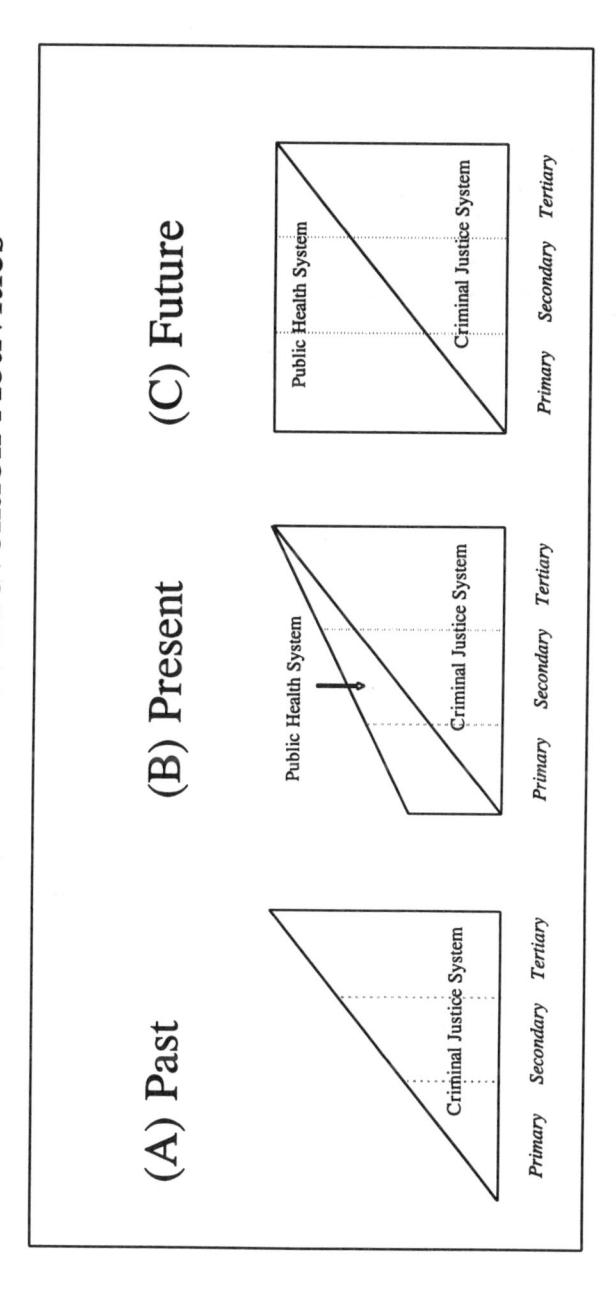

(A) Past   (B) Present   (C) Future

Primary Secondary Tertiary   *Primary Secondary Tertiary*   *Primary Secondary Tertiary*

Criminal Justice System

Public Health System / Criminal Justice System

Public Health System / Criminal Justice System

Adapted from Deborah Prothrow-Stith, with Michaele Weissman, *Deadly Consequences* (New York: Harper Collins, 1991), p. 226. Used with permission of the authors.

With the more recent involvement of the public health system, attention has been broadened with enhanced efforts in the preventive arena. The public health agenda has focused primarily on prevention and early intervention, playing only a small role in the treatment of individuals with serious violence-related problems. As reflected in Figure 1 (panel B), the role and activities of the public health system are newer, less extensive, and, therefore, less evolved than those of the criminal justice system. Traditionally, public health has responded by treating the violence-related injury in the emergency setting.

Today, a new generation of committed health practitioners, community violence-prevention practitioners, social workers, and community activists have devised numerous intervention programs to serve medium- to high-risk adolescents. At the primary prevention level, efforts have focused on gun control and safety and on enhanced public awareness of risk factors and the true characteristics of most violence to dispel myths and modify societal values around the use of violence. Additionally, some educational interventions (e.g., violence prevention curricula) have been applied in broader, less high risk settings. Again, much of this work is relatively recent and therefore has not yet established a long track record to fully assess its effects. Finally, public health has applied its analytical expertise to greatly enhance the understanding of risk factors, allowing for a broader vision in the planning and development of preventive approaches (Spivak, Prothrow-Stith, and Hausman, 1988; Prothrow-Stith and Weissman, 1991).

In the area of secondary prevention, public health has been involved in the development of educational interventions specifically focused on behavior modification of high-risk individuals, particularly children and youth. A number of curricula are currently in use addressing both the risks of violence in solving problems and conflict resolution techniques (Spivak, Prothrow-Stith, and Hausman, 1988; Prothrow-Stith and Weissman, 1991).

It is important to note that the criminal justice system has, more recently, increased its involvement with primary and secondary prevention efforts. For example, some criminal justice professionals have become involved in gun control initiatives. The Juvenile Justice and Delinquency Prevention Act of 1974 gave the Justice Department primary responsibility for delinquency prevention programs. The Office of Juvenile Justice and Delinquency Prevention was designed in part to encourage the development of model delinquency prevention programs. One such initiative is the Targeting Program for Delinquency Intervention, sponsored by the Boys Clubs of America. At-risk boys are referred to the targeting program by other community groups. Early evaluations of the program seem promising. Data indicate that 39 percent of the boys did better at school and that 93 percent who completed the program did not become reinvolved with the juvenile justice system (Boys Clubs of America, 1986). These types of interventions reflect an important interface between the criminal justice and public health professions.

With further attention and the dedication of resources of the public health system to this issue and the broadening vision of criminal justice, a more reasonable balance between prevention and treatment can be achieved in the future. As represented in Figure 1 (panel C), efforts can be broadened to reflect more fully the range of efforts needed to both reduce the extent of violent behavior and respond to the violence that does occur. The emphasis of the public health system will be on prevention, with the criminal justice system prioritizing the response to violence, but with both disciplines working together across the spectrum.

THE MODEL ILLUSTRATED IN OTHER AREAS

To illustrate the advantages of this approach, it is useful to review how it has worked successfully in other areas. One example, which on the surface appears to be a considerable stretch from violence, is the multi-disciplinary approach that has been developed to deal with tobacco use. It is important to note that while this example illustrates a collaboration between public health and the medical care system, it represents a useful analogy to the possible collaboration between public health and criminal justice.

Smoking is a major contributing factor to death and disability in this country. Significant inroads have been made in turning the tide on this major health threat. What was once a valued, sexy, and socially acceptable behavior is now viewed as a disgusting, unhealthy, and socially unacceptable behavior. Heroes in the media used to smoke all the time; now they rarely do. Nationally, the number of people who smoke has declined dramatically. And smoking was and still is a learned behavior, one that can be unpleasant or distasteful to start but is extremely difficult to stop.

The strategy to deal with smoking involved a three-pronged approach: (1) primary prevention for those not yet smoking to teach the reasons for not starting and to support the decision not to start; (2) secondary prevention to encourage stopping or reducing use for those who already started smoking, which often involves helping individuals to identify alternative behaviors to replace smoking behavior; and (3) treatment in the form of surgery, chemotherapy, or other medical interventions for those smokers who have developed cancer or other health consequences of their behavior. Broad public initiatives to alter the societal values that encouraged smoking were also established to support the above efforts. This was done through legislation (e.g., package labeling, advertising constraints, restrictions on sales to minors, establishment of smoke-free environments), public education, and pressure on media to change images and role models. Although, as stated earlier, this is an example of a public health/medical care interface, it represents an important success that suggests possibilities for a public health and criminal justice collaboration in addressing violence.

A similar approach could and should be taken with respect to violence. Primary prevention strategies and more targeted secondary prevention efforts need to be applied that pro-actively value and teach non-violent behaviors in response to anger and conflict. This is particularly important given the growing evidence that violence is a *learned* behavior.[1] Well-child health visits in neighborhood health centers provide an ideal window of opportunity for early intervention. Peter Stringham, a pediatrician at the East Boston Neighborhood Health Center, incorporates a violence prevention protocol for families, from the newborn visit through the teenage years. Teaching our children social skills is as important as teaching them the academic subjects that we now emphasize in our society. This will in no way eliminate the underlying societal stresses that influence violent behavior but can affect and direct responses to these stresses toward a pro-social and productive outcome. Curricula that emphasize decision-making, non-violent conflict resolution, and development of self-esteem do currently exist, but they are terribly underutilized and are viewed as an "add-on" in academic settings rather than as a basic component of education. A move to place more emphasis on the use of such curricula, with enhanced investment in social

---

[1] See Prothrow-Stith and Weissman, 1991; Allen, 1981; Bandura, Ross, and Ross, 1963; Eron and Huesmann, 1984; Liebert, Neale, and Davidson, 1973; Slaby and Quarfoth, 1980; Straus, 1991; Vissing et al., 1991.

and support services for families and youth, would be an important step in countering the learned use of violence by our youth. Such a move would also require that the education, human service, and public health institutions play major roles in effecting these changes in our communities.

Indeed, the recognition that education designed to teach nonviolent behaviors might be an important part of a combined public health/criminal justice response to the problem of violence helps to remind us that the modern view of how the law operates on behavior in society has become far narrower than it once was. In our modern conceptions of the law, we imagine it operating on individual behavior primarily through its incentive effects—the promise of punishment for misconduct made concrete and credible through individual prosecutions. In the classic writings on law, however, a great deal of attention was devoted not only to the passage of laws and to their application to individual cases, but also to their *promulgation* throughout the society (Friedman, 1975). Extensive efforts to educate citizens as to why the laws were necessary helped to ensure both their justice and their efficacy. Unless citizens knew about the law—its spirit as well as its letter—they could not reasonably be held accountable for failures to obey it. If the purposes of the law were not made clear, then voluntary compliance, which was crucial to the law's effect, could not be assured.

The public health community's interest in non-violence education can be viewed as the modern rediscovery of the importance of explaining to and educating the public about violence, as well as simply having laws and applying them. It also incorporates an important modern discovery about the promulgation of obligations: Persuading people to comply with an important obligation is often far easier when one can show individuals that it is in their best interests to do so and when one can help them comply with the law. Persuasion and assistance are often more effective tools than accusation and blame. Still, it often helps in persuading and assisting if there is a broad social rule against violence that becomes part of the context for the education. Thus, behavioral change may depend on a combination of education and laws that used to be called promulgation.

Gun control legislation efforts represent an important example of the interconnection between education and laws. Although there is growing support for increased handgun ownership restrictions as a primary prevention strategy, legislation alone is unlikely to create great change in violent injury rates in the foreseeable future. With over 60 million handguns in circulation in the United States, an understanding and acceptance of the risks of handgun ownership and carrying are as important as legislative restrictions to reducing intentional handgun injuries (Bureau of Alcohol, Tobacco, and Firearms, 1991).

A secondary-level strategy requires a more targeted effort. It requires early identification of individuals who are at high risk for violence or are already beginning to exhibit violent behavior, as well as the development of treatment services for such individuals. Secondary prevention represents an important interface between the human service and the criminal justice systems because the early identification of individuals at high risk for violence requires considerable collaboration. Points of early identification occur in schools, health facilities, police departments, courts, and a variety of other community institutions. Professional training in early identification and appropriate evaluation and treatment is necessary. This is not an easy process. Professional definitions and institutional boundaries have been established that encourage limited, one-dimensional approaches.

Treatment interventions (tertiary prevention) for the most seriously affected individuals represent a key focal point for the criminal justice system. Violent behavior cannot be condoned; punishment is an appropriate response to violent crimes or episodes, and some individuals with serious pathology are not able to live in the general society. While it is essential that we understand how violent behavior evolves, we must deal with it firmly to maintain safety within our communities.

Although tertiary prevention falls most extensively into the criminal justice realm, with incarceration as the major strategy, public health needs to work along with the prison system in the area of rehabilitation. Without increased attention to rehabilitative efforts, including supportive services for those returning from prison to the community, most will continue to leave the prison system without the skills to avoid violence in the future. Public health must advocate for and support drug and alcohol treatment services, job training efforts, conflict resolution, and violence prevention skills. In addition, the development of more extensive behavior change interventions must be addressed. To date, successful rehabilitative efforts have been limited, further reinforcing the need for more attention focused on this area.

Finally, the broader societal context that promotes and inadvertently encourages violence needs to be addressed. Again, this is clearly an area requiring collaboration. Changing societal values is an enormous undertaking that requires a broad base of energy and support. Legislatively, measures such as gun control and media guidelines on violence must be drafted, advocated, and passed. Prevention directed at individuals and communities must be supported and reinforced by professional associations and advocacy efforts that cross traditional boundaries. Resources for children and families must be identified that allow adequate investment in schools, health care, employment opportunities, human service supports, mental health, and, yes, police and courts. This requires a unified vision.

CONCLUSION

Table 1 outlines various strategies that can be used to address violence in each of the three prevention areas—primary, secondary, and tertiary. Some of the activities listed are specific to either the criminal justice profession or the public health profession; others reflect areas of collaboration and overlap between the two disciplines.

Public health focuses on prevention by addressing underlying causes; criminal justice focuses on responding to criminal behavior with the expectation that prevention will grow from the threat of punishment. Both of these systems have important roles to play, and their different perspectives are both complementary and reflective of the continuum necessary to reverse the pattern of growing violence. A process of building communication and collaboration between the fields is essential. Increased communication can be facilitated and enhanced through conferences that recognize the need for cross-disciplinary dialogue, efforts to synthesize perspectives in joint publications, and collaborative research projects that integrate the skills of both professional disciplines.

Collaborative programmatic efforts will move this process even further and will help to establish concrete working relationships between the disciplines of public health and criminal justice. An example of concrete collaboration could be accomplished in joint community training efforts. As part of a violence prevention curriculum in the schools, police officers could provide training on safety behavior to low- to moderate-risk children and adolescents. This has already been accomplished in other programmatic areas described earlier in this chapter.

TABLE 1: Classification of Preventive Strategies

Primary Prevention
- reduced availability of guns (gun control)
- reduced use of alcohol and drugs
- reduced media violence
- behavioral education, anger and conflict resolution
- promulgation of laws
- threat of punishment
- parent education
- street safety measures
- social support services
- community awareness
- risk-factor identification and reduction

Secondary Prevention
- early identification and screening
- behavior modification
- early intervention in schools, emergency rooms, juvenile justice system
- counseling, family support services
- risk-factor reduction

Tertiary Prevention
- jail/prison
- rehabilitation services

Essential to such programmatic collaboration is a closer, more cooperative interface at the federal level between the Department of Health and Human Services and the Department of Justice. Similarly, collaboration at the state and local levels must occur among educators, public health professionals, law enforcement agencies, the legal justice system, and human services systems. Continued fragmentation of funding will thwart collaboration; joint funding and promotion of interdisciplinary program development will greatly enhance collaboration. Some individuals within each of these professions have recognized the need for a comprehensive agenda and have begun this important dialogue. More individuals need to enter this process, and the institutions that greatly influence the bigger picture and provide the resources for all of our work must create the opportunities for this to happen. There is so much to be gained.

REFERENCES

Allen, Nancy H. (1981). "Homicide Prevention and Intervention," *Suicide and Life Threatening Behavior*, vol. 11, no. 3 (Fall 1981), pp. 167-179.
Bandura, Albert, Dorothea Ross, and Sheila A. Ross (1963). "Vicarious Reinforcement and Imitative Learning," *Journal of Abnormal and Social Psychology*, vol. 67, no. 6 (1963), pp. 601-607.
Boys Clubs of America (1986). *Targeted Outreach Newsletter*, vol. II-1, 1986.
Bureau of Alcohol, Tobacco, and Firearms (1991). *Firearm Census Report*. Washington, D.C.: U.S. Department of the Treasury.
Centers for Disease Control (1982). "Homicide—United States," *Morbidity and Mortality Weekly Report*, vol. 31, no. 44 (November 12, 1982), pp. 596-602.
_____ (1983). *Homicide Surveillance: High-Risk Racial and Ethnic Groups — Blacks and Hispanics, 1970 to 1983*. Washington, D.C.: U.S. Department of Health and Human Services, Public Health Service.
_____ (1990). "Homicide Among Young Black Males—United States, 1978-1987," *Morbidity and Mortality Weekly Report*, vol. 39, no. 48 (December 7, 1990), pp. 869-873.

Children's Defense Fund (1992). *An Opinion Maker's Guide to Children in Election Year 1992, Leave No Child Behind.* Washington, D.C.: Children's Defense Fund.

Eron, Leonard D., and L. Rowell Huesmann (1984). "Television Violence and Aggressive Behavior." In Benjamin B. Lahey and Alan E. Kazdin, eds., *Advances in Clinical Child Psychology.* Vol. 7. New York: Plenum Press.

FBI (1992). *Uniform Crime Reports for the United States, 1991.* Washington, D.C.: Federal Bureau of Investigation, U.S. Department of Justice.

Friedman, Lawrence M. (1975). *The Legal System: A Social Science Perspective.* New York: Russell Sage Foundation.

Hingson, Ralph, Jonathan Howland, and Suzette Levenson (1988). "Effects of Legislative Reform to Reduce Drunken Driving and Alcohol-Related Traffic Fatalities," *Public Health Reports*, vol. 103, no. 6 (November-December, 1988), pp. 659-667.

Liebert, Robert M., John M. Neale, and Emily S. Davidson (1973). *The Early Window: Effects of Television on Children and Youth.* New York: Pergamon Press.

Prothrow-Stith, Deborah (1992). "Can Physicians Help Curb Adolescent Violence?" *Hospital Practice*, vol. 27, no. 6 (June 15, 1992), pp. 193ff.

Prothrow-Stith, Deborah, with Michaele Weissman (1991). *Deadly Consequences: How Violence Is Destroying Our Teenage Population and a Plan to Begin Solving the Problem.* New York: Harper Collins Publishers.

Rice, Dorothy P., Ellen J. Mackenzie, and Wendy Max (1989). *Cost of Injury in the United States: A Report to Congress 1989.* San Francisco: Institute for Health and Aging, University of California, and Injury Prevention Center, Johns Hopkins University.

Rosenberg, Mark L., and Mary Ann Fenley, eds. (1991). *Violence in America: A Public Health Approach.* New York: Oxford University Press.

Slaby, Ronald, and Gary R. Quarfoth (1980). "Effects of Television on the Developing Child," *Advances in Developmental and Behavioral Pediatrics*, vol. 1 (1980), pp. 225-266.

Spivak, Howard, Deborah Prothrow-Stith, and Alice J. Hausman (1988). "Dying Is No Accident: Adolescents, Violence, and Intentional Injury," *Pediatric Clinics of North America*, vol. 35, no. 6 (December 1988), pp. 1339-1347.

Straus, Murray A. (1991). "Discipline and Deviance: Physical Punishment of Children and Violence and Other Crime in

Adulthood," *Social Problems*, vol. 38, no. 2 (May 1991), pp. 133-154.

USA Weekend (1992). "Cosby's New Cause." October 2-4, 1992.

U.S. Public Health Service (1990). *Healthy People 2000: National Health Promotion and Disease Prevention Objectives*. Washington, D.C.: U.S. Department of Health and Human Services, Public Health Service.

Vissing, Yvonne, Murray A. Straus, Richard J. Gelles, and John W. Harrop (1991). "Verbal Aggression by Parents and Psychological Problems of Children," *Child Abuse and Neglect*, vol. 15 (1991), pp. 223-238.

Wolfgang, Marvin E. (1986). "Homicide in Other Industrialized Countries," *Bulletin of the New York Academy of Medicine*, vol. 62, no. 5 (June 1986), pp. 400-412.

COMMENTS

Margaret K. Rosenheim

The chapter by Howard Spivak, Deborah Prothrow-Stith, and Mark Moore presents a forceful case for incorporating a public health perspective into today's responses to violence and for encouraging collaborative arrangements for its prevention and control between criminal justice and public health officials. My remarks will address the implications of the authors' approach for dealing with interpersonal violence among children and adolescents.

While admittedly young adults, not children and young adolescents, claim first place in the honors for peak violent crime rate, the record of the juvenile population is nonetheless worrisome. Juvenile arrests for violent crime have been rising. Recent arrest data point to an unprecedented level of juvenile violence, with crimes of violence a more significant component of overall juvenile arrests than previously. As the authors point out, homicide is the leading cause of death for African-American men and women ages 15 to 34. At the same time, the authors note, violent crime is not just another inner-city problem but one that cuts across race, class, and lifestyle.

A second reason for concern about trends affecting the juvenile population relates to society's expectations for prevention, as well as reform, of lawbreaking among this age group. Society's response to crime committed by young people, symbolized for about 100 years by the existence of a juvenile justice system, rests on its beliefs in the malleability and rehabilitative potential of juveniles, beliefs having far less potency in the criminal justice system. These views can be summed up in the widely held belief that kids should be given "room to reform" (Zimring, 1982).

In my judgment, the public health approach can substantially enhance our understanding of the antecedents and consequences of violence and, by enlarging the focus of inquiry, suggest new strategies for prevention according to the traditional schema of primary, secondary, and tertiary prevention. My comments will emphasize two aspects of this approach: the emergence of certain preventive measures, on the one hand, and the implications of the public health model for the juvenile justice system, on the other. I will not attempt to identify systematically the levels of prevention as primary, secondary, and tertiary because, as the authors themselves note, the boundaries of these intervention efforts "are a little fuzzy."[1]

PREVENTIVE MEASURES

Two recent efforts seem particularly promising. One is the introduction of community- and school-based programs to impart skills in negotiating various life events. Some programs are broadly conceived, such as those that focus on life-skills training; others focus specifically on violence. With regard to the latter, as the authors note, programs rest on the assumption that violence is a learned behavior for resolving conflict, and they seek to demonstrate that alternative, pacific ways of channeling and confronting disputes are rewarding (Deutsch, 1991). The Violence Prevention Project of Boston, for example, includes a media campaign, prevention training, intervention in schools, and clinical services (Hamburg, 1992). In addition, several curricular models appropriate to different grade levels have been designed and tested. Particular attention may be given to middle-school curricula because the middle school, an institution composed of young adolescents, represents a dramatic shift from the familiar confines of elementary school for an age group coping with dramatic changes in their biological, social, and cognitive capacities. This is an age group ripe for exploration of new means of dealing with interpersonal conflict, and the new curricula seek to take advantage of this fact. As many of these initiatives have sprung up independently of one another, it is welcome news that the creation of a national network is underway. It is predicated on the idea that "exchanges of knowledge and professionals and the development of a common language are sorely needed," and it is seen as an early step toward systematizing and evaluating such efforts for the reduction of violence (Education Development Center, 1992, p. 9).

Another big push focuses on the media's representations of violence. Increasingly, a case can be made for links between

---

[1] For an outline of interventions arrayed according to the traditional grid, see Table 1 of their chapter.

television viewing of violence on screen and heightened levels of aggressive behavior on the part of child viewers (Comstock and Paik, 1990). The concern that this has generated is echoed by expressions of alarm over the content of other forms of mass media—such as film and videotapes—and the frustration felt by parents in obtaining information about their content. Parents feel impeded in their efforts to identify objectionable content by lack of efficient techniques of monitoring media materials. Additionally, these very media exemplify the intrusion of the commercial marketplace into various aspects of family life, which makes parental control difficult, especially given the changing patterns of parent-child supervision that accompany the dramatic increase in mothers employed in the workplace. New initiatives seek to increase parental information and influence related to national and local media, at low cost in terms of money and time, so as to enable parents to file objections to program content or propose more appropriate story lines (Carnegie Council on Adolescent Development, 1987a, 1987b; Hechinger, 1992).

A proposal of long standing should also be noted—gun control. Although curtailing access to guns does not in itself necessarily reduce the number of acts of violence, it does substantially affect both the type of violence and its consequences. One policy thrust within public health circles is minimizing unsupervised access by children to loaded guns, a non-controversial side of the gun control debate in the United States that has so frustrated proponents of controls related to access and type of weaponry available to adults. In the current scene, it is scarcely misplaced to speak of the availability of guns in terms of "epidemic." But to date, congressional resistance to statutory restrictions has been so strong that some gun-control advocates are concentrating on the less controversial subject of curbing access to, and rendering less "user-friendly," handguns held by children (Rosenberg, O'Carroll, and Powell, 1992; Fulginiti, 1992).

JUVENILE JUSTICE SYSTEMS

For those of us who live in major metropolitan areas, experience with local juvenile courts is discouraging because of their history of overwhelming caseloads and the demonstrable seriousness of some of the crime on their dockets. We should remind ourselves, however, that there are over 2,000 juvenile courts in the nation and that our own experiences should not determine our reactions to what particular juvenile justice systems might be able to accomplish under the influence of the public health agenda. One can believe, as I do, that, in the short term, the contribution of this approach to juvenile justice will be modest, and still believe in its ultimate value. Indeed, at the level of theory, the goals of the juvenile justice system and of public health overlap and reinforce each other to a substantial degree. Behavioral and parent education are long-standing goals of juvenile justice; the introduction of social support services was a raison d'être of juvenile justice; and certainly early identification and screening and early intervention in the child-related systems of schools, youth organizations, and juvenile courts are hallmark objectives.

At the level of practice, however, I suspect that juvenile justice and public health diverge; here, however, the authors have less to say. Although it is clear that they focus their concerns on the juvenile population and favor interventions that would have an impact on juvenile court practice, they do not indicate what specific changes in the juvenile justice system they would advocate to conform to their public health approach. Does this approach offer fresh perspectives on such nettlesome issues as strategies of juvenile policing, decisions regarding detention, or screening of petitions at intake? Can it help us in thinking about the exercise of discretion within the agencies of juvenile justice? How, in the opinion of public health specialists, should information on patterns of violent crime be used by the courts at the point of disposition?

It may be that the authors envisage a limited contribution from public health officials in the juvenile justice context, directing instead these potentially valuable resources to other points in adolescents' careers and to different institutional settings.[2] I can see an important role for education by public health officials in tandem with juvenile justice personnel and an equally valuable contribution in epidemiological terms. The proposal for a firearm fatality reporting system illustrates one data-gathering effort of potential usefulness (Teret, Wintemute, and Bailenson, 1992), and I am sure there are many others.

---

[2] See, for example, the review of strategies for prevention of delinquency in Dryfoos, 1990.

CONCLUSION

In closing, I would like to raise the issue of corporal punishment as it relates to violence. Evidence has been accumulating as to an association between child abuse and later aggressive behavior by victims of child abuse (Widom, 1989). While this association should be regarded as a hypothesis requiring further testing, it leads to speculation that reliance on violence as part of the arsenal of child disciplinary practices influences children's attitudes toward recourse to violence and gives them a limited repertoire of conflict resolution techniques.

Should we, as a society, give serious consideration to reducing reliance on corporal punishment? It will not be easy to bring it about. A recent survey of pediatricians and family physicians, those critically situated dispensers of advice to parents, showed that most of these physicians still believe that "corporal punishment is appropriate" (McCormick, 1992). But public health officials have led protracted and ultimately successful campaigns on other fronts involving change of ingrained behavior patterns: smoking and seat-belt use come quickly to mind. The question here is whether altering patterns of discipline is more closely akin to these successes than to campaigns to reduce school dropouts and teen pregnancy, which have produced less dramatic results. The answer is that we will never know until we try.

REFERENCES

Carnegie Council on Adolescent Development (1987a). *Adolescence and the Media: Collaborations to Support Healthy Adolescent Development*. Report of meeting of the council, April 1987.

––––––– (1987b). *Creating New Television Programs for and about Adolescents*. Report of meeting of the council, June 1987.

Comstock, George, and Jaejung Paik (1990). "The Effects of Television Violence on Aggressive Behavior: A Meta-Analysis." Preliminary report presented to the National Research Council for the Panel on the Understanding and Control of Violent Behavior, September 1990.

Deutsch, Morton (1991). "Educating for a Peaceful World." Presidential address to the Division of Peace Psychology, presented at the Annual Meeting of the American Psychological Association, San Francisco, August 8, 1991.

Dryfoos, Joy G. (1990). *Adolescents at Risk*. New York: Oxford University Press.

Education Development Center (1992). "EDC Launches National Violence Prevention Network," *EDC News* (Newton, Mass.), vol. 2, no. 2 (Fall 1992), p. 9.

Fulginiti, Vincent A. (1992). "Violence and Children in the United States," *American Journal of Diseases of Children*, vol. 146, no. 6 (June 1992), pp. 671-672.

Hamburg, David (1992). *Today's Children: Creating a Future for a Generation in Crisis*. New York: Times Books.

Hechinger, Fred M. (1992). *Fateful Choices: Healthy Youth for the Twenty-first Century*. New York: Carnegie Council on Adolescent Development, Carnegie Corporation of New York.

McCormick, Kenelm F. (1992). "Attitudes of Primary Care Physicians toward Corporal Punishment," *Journal of the American Medical Association*, vol. 267, no. 23 (June 17, 1992), pp. 3161-3165.

Rosenberg, Mark L., Patrick W. O'Carroll, and Kenneth E. Powell (1992). "Let's Be Clear: Violence Is a Public Health Problem," *Journal of the American Medical Association*, vol. 267, no. 22 (June 10, 1992), pp. 3071-3072.

Teret, Stephen P., Garen J. Wintemute, and Peter L. Bailenson (1992). "The Firearm Fatality Reporting System: A Proposal," *Journal of the American Medical Association*, vol. 267, no. 22 (June 10, 1992), pp. 3073-3074.

Widom, Cathy Spatz (1989). "Does Violence Beget Violence? A Critical Examination of the Literature," *Psychological Bulletin*, vol. 106, no. 1 (July 1989), pp. 3-28.

Zimring, Franklin E. (1982). *The Changing Legal World of Adolescence*. New York: Free Press.

COMMENTS

Darnell F. Hawkins

Howard Spivak, Deborah Prothrow-Stith, and Mark Moore propose that the growing epidemic of violence in America demands immediate attention and action. They suggest that violence in our society can be alleviated by a targeted, cohesive, collaborative effort from a variety of disciplines, including public health, criminal justice, education, social services, business, health care, and others. Most of the chapter describes the theoretical and practical foundations for a potential violence prevention collaboration between public health and criminal justice.

In order to appreciate fully the significance of the authors' call for cooperation between public health and criminal justice professionals, we must first examine several related developments of the last two decades. During this period, the injuries that result from violent and aggressive behavior (intentional injury) have come to be seen increasingly as a public health problem. In 1980, the U.S. Department of Health and Human Services identified homicide among young Black males as a health concern. Among its objectives was the reduction of the homicide rate for 15-to-24-year-old Black males from 72.5 per 100,000 persons in 1978 to 60 per 100,000 in 1990 (U.S. Department of Health and Human Services, 1981). In 1985, a report by the National Research Council and the Institute of Medicine, *Injury in America*, gave additional impetus to the inclusion within the public health domain of all forms of accidental and intentional injury (National Research Council and the Institute of Medicine, 1985). The report noted the extent to which homicide contributed to the reduced life expectancies of Americans, especially minorities. The report recommended the establishment of a federal center for injury control. In 1986, an injury-control unit was established within one of the existing centers of the Centers for Disease Control in Atlanta; that unit became an independent center in 1992.

The chapter by Spivak, Prothrow-Stith, and Moore responds to many of the issues that have emerged as public health and medical professionals have moved increasingly into an area of research and public policy once considered the exclusive domain of social/behavioral scientists and criminal justice practitioners. Noting the potential for "turf battles" between public health and criminal justice professionals, the authors suggest that the public health community has been drawn to this issue by the growing conviction that its techniques of analysis and prevention might be useful for the successful control of violence. The proactive, preventive/rehabilitative stance of the public health community is contrasted to the more reactive, punishment/justice orientation of the criminal justice system. This disciplinary contrast has also been presented by other recent advocates of a public health approach to the analysis and control of violence (Mercy and O'Carroll, 1988; Rosenberg and Fenley, 1991).

As a proponent of new and creative ways to study and attempt to prevent violent behavior, I applaud the authors' call for a comprehensive, multi-disciplinary approach. Their juxtaposition of criminal justice and public health modes of response to violence is an effective heuristic device and call for action. At the same time, this approach in some instances leads to oversimplification. The authors often tend to overstate the uniqueness and potential effectiveness of public health approaches to the study and control of violence. The authors' advocacy orientation also sometimes leads to an uncritical assessment of the complexity of violence in American society.

For example, the authors' depiction of the criminal justice community in the United States is only partially accurate. They seem to be concerned primarily with the administration of justice, that is, police, courts, and prisons. Criminal justice is a multidisciplinary enterprise and, like public health, consists of both academic and applied components. Law, as well as many social and behavioral sciences, has contributed to the study of crime and justice. Analysts within these disciplines, like their public health counterparts with an interest in violence, have attempted to identify risk factors and causes of violent behavior. Indeed, most of the "epidemiologic" studies of homicide conducted during the past several decades have been conducted by criminologists. Some social scientists who study deviant and criminal behavior have noted the increasing "medicalization" of deviance/crime, as the medical profession assumes the role of an agent of social control (Zola, 1972; Conrad, 1975). Some propose that medicine and public health bring few new insights to the study of these social problems. Aside from this criticim, my observation suggests that the kind of collaboration called for by the authors must include not only those persons employed within the criminal justice system but also those academic researchers outside of the public health community who study violence, including the system's response to violence.

The authors also fail to acknowledge many of the potential problems involved in achieving a major reduction in the rate of violence within the context of modern American society. These include a consideration of the difference between violence and other forms of injury and disease, as well as the diversity of forms and sources of violent behavior. They also include the effects of race and class inequality. In regard to the first concern, the authors might have asked whether traditional public health modes of intervention/prevention need to be modified to respond to the task of reducing intentional injury. Further, although violence is ubiquitous in American society, there are special problems that may be encountered in its prevention among minorities and the poor.

The authors note the relatively successful reduction of death and physical harm due to various forms of unintentional injury (e.g., auto accidents and tobacco-related disease) and specific categories of intentional injury (sexual assault). They provide a convincing argument that these improvements are attributable to the use of proven public health modes of intervention. They are less convincing when providing evidence that these same models can be successfully applied to the reduction of violence, or that groups currently at highest risk (the poor, young males, minorities) will benefit from such interventions. For instance, it may be suggested that even when model interventions (primary, secondary, and tertiary approaches) have been implemented, the effects of race, class, and other sources of inequality are evident. Disadvantaged segments of the population show less progress than more privileged sectors.

As I have noted earlier, the problems involved in preventing violence, especially among disadvantaged American minorities, may call for more than the application of public health models or interdisciplinary cooperation (Hawkins, 1987, 1989). Many of the same class, racial, political, and ideological divisions/inequalities that contribute to higher rates of violence among some sectors of the population also impede prevention and intervention efforts. The failure of both traditional medicine and the criminal justice system to achieve reductions in the incidence of violence may partly reflect their disciplinary orientations (involvement primarily in tertiary prevention/treatment). It is also true that these limited, traditional prevention and treatment efforts are currently more effective at reducing violent injury and death among the affluent and Whites than among the poor and non-Whites.

Finally, violence represents a very complex set of phenomena. No single etiological factor predicts all forms of violence. Some forms of violence may be less susceptible to prevention/intervention than others. Violence associated with drug trafficking among minority youth may pose different intervention problems than the violence that stems from gang activities where no drugs are involved. An appropriate preventive response to the former may require a re-examination of public policies and laws regulating drugs, while school-based anti-violence programs may help respond to the latter. A fight among drunken bar patrons in their late twenties may stem from different causes and require interventions unlike those for fights among the same population that occur in the home. Whether trained in public health or any other discipline, those who hope to reduce the rate of violence must consider the relevance for prevention of these differences.

Despite these shortcomings, the chapter by Spivak, Prothrow-Stith, and Moore represents a path-breaking effort. It systematically lays out a framework for cooperation between criminal justice and public health professionals that is both theoretically and organizationally grounded. Beyond theory and strategy, the authors provide a comprehensive vision for responding to the human and economic costs of violence in American society.

REFERENCES

Conrad, Peter (1975). "The Discovery of Hyperkinesis: Notes on the Medicalization of Deviant Behavior," *Social Problems*, vol. 23, no. 1 (October 1975), pp. 12-21.

Hawkins, Darnell F. (1987). "Devalued Lives and Racial Stereotypes: Ideological Barriers to the Prevention of Family Violence among Blacks." In Robert L. Hampton, ed., *Violence in the Black Family: Correlates and Consequences*. Lexington, Mass.: D.C. Heath.

───── (1989). "Intentional Injury: Are There No Solutions?" *Law, Medicine, and Health Care*, vol. 17, no. 1 (Spring 1989), pp. 32-41.

Mercy, James A., and Patrick W. O'Carroll (1988). "New Directions in Violence Prediction: The Public Health Arena," *Violence and Victims*, vol. 3, no. 4 (1988), pp. 285-301.

National Research Council and Institute of Medicine (1985). *Injury in America: A Continuing Public Health Problem.* Committee on Trauma Research, Commission on Life Sciences. Washington, D.C.: National Academy Press.

Rosenberg, Mark, and Mary Ann Fenley (1991). *Violence in America: A Public Health Approach.* New York: Oxford University Press.

U.S. Department of Health and Human Services (1981). *Health—United States: 1980.* Washington, D.C.: U.S. Government Printing Office.

Zola, Irving Kenneth (1972). "Medicine as an Institution of Social Control," *Sociological Review*, vol. 20, no. 4 (November 1972), pp. 487-504.

THE POLITICS OF STREET CRIME AND CRIMINAL JUSTICE

Stuart A. Scheingold

This chapter examines a largely neglected problem: the tendency of street crime to become a political issue. While considerable attention has been given to particular instances in which street crime and politics intersect, there has been very little systematic research on the links between them. For example, much has been made of the notorious 1988 Willie Horton campaign commercial, but only as a single discrete event. Is that event typical or aberrational? What conditions are conducive to campaigning on crime? Are such conditions more, or perhaps less, likely in presidential campaigns than in elections at other levels? What are the policy consequences of making crime into a political issue? Two themes will play prominent roles in my efforts to answer these questions.

First, it is impossible to understand the politics of street crime without coming to terms with the politics of race. Consider Rodney King and Bernhard Goetz, as well as Willie Horton. Each episode was at least as much about race as about street crime. As Lillian Rubin put it in her eloquent analysis of the Goetz trial: "We worry about crime in our streets, on our subways and buses, in our homes. And because young black men between the ages of fifteen and twenty-four commit a disproportionate number of those crimes, when we fill in the outlines of the phrase 'crime in the streets,' we tend to color it black" (Rubin, 1988, p. 260). To narrow the focus to street crime alone is, therefore, to misconceive politicization and to play into the hands of politicians who would prefer to evade both problems by playing them off one another.

Second, one of the more surprising findings of my research on the politics of street crime was how poorly the issue fares in *local* politics. I had expected street crime to be continually salient—albeit with ascertainable ups and downs. What I discovered instead was that campaigning on street crime was rather a hit-and-miss proposition. The evidence indicates that local political leaders have strong incentives for avoiding street crime as a political issue. This stands in sharp contrast to national politics, where the incentives run in the other direction.

POLITICS AND STREET CRIME: WHO CARES?

For the most part, criminologists, journalists, and public officials do not concern themselves with the political dimensions of street crime. Their premise is that street crime is a serious social problem and that it is essential that steps be taken to deal with the problem in a responsible fashion. Accordingly, they focus on measuring the extent of street crime, on assessing its causes and consequences, and on developing more effective crime reduction policies. From this perspective, the relationship between street crime and politics seems something of a sideshow that diverts attention from the core problem, which is the threat of street crime itself.[1]

My research leads me to believe that analysis of the relationship between street crime and politics can be both revealing and rewarding. As has already been suggested by my reference to race, my view is that the politics of street crime is only loosely linked to crime rates and victimization. Not only is this coupling loose, it is also perverse—tending to privilege primarily punitive responses to crime despite evidence indicating that these responses are inadequate.[2] The objective of this chapter is to present my findings on these matters and to make a case for this being a topic worthy of careful attention principally because of the way in which it tends to distort the policy process.

The term "politicization" seems to me the most economical way of describing this enterprise. Politicization is simply a way of characterizing the tendency of street crime to become a political

---

[1] It might also be worth pointing out that these issues lie in something of a scholar's limbo—i.e., calling on the skills of criminologists, sociologists, and political scientists without being a core concern of any of these disciplines.

[2] Even a conservative such as James Q. Wilson rejects purely punitive responses to street crime. This emerges both in the policy analysis he offers in *Thinking About Crime* (1985) and in his more purely criminological inquiry with Richard Herrnstein into *Crime and Human Nature* (1985). For an extended analysis of the latter, see Scheingold, 1991, chap. 1.

issue—most notably when candidates campaign on street crime. My interests in politicization and the focus of this chapter involve two basic questions: (1) How, why, and to what extent has street crime become a political issue at the local, state, and national levels? (2) What are the effects, if any, of politicization on law enforcement policy? The answers to these questions are surprising and, taken together, suggest that our conventional understanding of the relationships among street crime, politics, and policy need to be reexamined.

The conventional view of politicization, as elaborated most prominently in the work of James Q. Wilson, is that street crime becomes a political issue when an increasingly victimized and frightened public demands action from its political leaders (Wilson, 1977, 1985). It is further believed that there is a natural tendency for these demands to develop in a punitive direction—toward cracking down on offenders by means of tougher sentences. When things work correctly, officials then swing into action—appropriating money and initiating anti-crime programs. Of course, the government may be slow to respond. Ultimately, however, in our democratic polity, politicians will get the message and work out effective crime control policies, or so the theory goes.

Findings in Cedar City, the pseudonymous site of my research, as well as data from other sources, suggest that the conventional wisdom is misleading in fundamental ways. First, politicization and the punitive values associated with it are only loosely linked to street crime and victimization. Second, politicization is very much a reciprocal process, with political leaders at least as likely to take the initiative as to respond to the grass roots. Finally, politicization has only an indirect and unpredictable impact on policy. It is for these reasons that I argue that politicization has a life of its own, linked only tenuously to street crime and to street crime's often tragic impact on the lives of victims and on neighborhoods.

LOOSE CONNECTIONS: STREET CRIME, PUNITIVE ATTITUDES, AND POLITICIZATION

The conventional wisdom assumes a straightforward process of politicization: victimization generates fear and anger, thus fueling punitive attitudes and demands for political action to reduce street crime. But a variety of aggregate empirical indicators reveal a different picture. There is simply no reliable relationship between victimization and punitive attitudes or between victimization and demands for political action. Grass-roots reactions are driven at least as much by how we *think about victimization* as by victimization as such. These reactions, moreover, vary according to race, gender, and geography. Accordingly, politicization emerges as a less democratic, less predictable, and much more interesting process than is suggested by the conventional wisdom.

Contradictions, Complexities, and Surprises

Available data indicate that the ups and downs of the crime rate and of politicization do not have much to do with one another. Consider, for example, the findings of the Governmental Responses to Crime Project, conducted in ten cities and covering the period between 1948 and 1978. According to this research, the peak period of politicization was between 1974 and 1978, well after the U.S. crime rate had plateaued in 1973. It is true that street crime became a salient issue in the 1960s, when the crime rate rose precipitously: "From the middle 1960s—when official crime rates were rising most markedly—the political agendas of cities were crowded with issues. . . . Crime thus had stiff competition from other issues. Only during the last period (1974-78) did crime reach the number one position; budget and tax problems and the economy continued to rank near the top" (Jacob, 1984, pp. 20-21). Similarly, I found that campaigning on crime in Cedar City was most frequent and most successful between 1975 and 1978—not a particularly high crime period locally (Scheingold, 1991, pp. 40-46). Thus it would seem that something other than rising crime rates was moving urban America toward the politicization of street crime.[3]

---

[3] This is not to argue that the crime rate is irrelevant to politicization. Since the 1960s, however, politicization has responded to a variety of other forces that will be considered in subsequent portions of this chapter. It is perhaps worth noting the dispute among criminologists about the implications of an increased crime rate during the prosperous decade of the 1960s—what James Q. Wilson refers to as "crime amidst plenty: the paradox of sixties" (1985, chap. 1). This "paradox" leads Wilson to discount the impact of poverty on crime. Elliott Currie responds with an incisive analysis of the impact of unemployment and underemployment on crime (1985, pp. 104-141). Moreover, the crime

Nor does there seem to be much correlation between victimization and fear, although according to conventional wisdom, politicization is rooted in the fear and anger engendered by victimization. National data reveal that fear of crime rose fairly steadily through the 1970s and into the 1980s, although crime rates tended to plateau in the mid-1970s (Scheingold, 1984, pp. 38-45). Similarly, Wesley Skogan and Michael Maxfield's research in Chicago, Philadelphia, and San Francisco revealed that the level of fear cannot be adequately explained by victimization. They discovered that only about 6 percent of their respondents were recent victims of personal crimes, and of these, only 3 percent reported injury—with less than 2 percent seeking medical treatment. This compares with more than 30 percent of respondents who expressed concern for their safety. Skogan and Maxfield concluded that the frequency of victimization is "quite disproportionate to the number of persons in these cities who indicated that they were fearful of personal attack in their neighborhoods" (1981, pp. 45, 60).

Punitive attitudes, the third piece in the politicization puzzle, do not seem to flow from victimization or from fear. Thus, support for capital punishment rose fairly steadily, from 38 percent in 1965 to 67 percent in 1980, despite the above-mentioned leveling off of crime rates (Scheingold, 1984, p. 46). Consider also the work of Arthur Stinchcombe and his associates, who began with the conventional idea that the punitive drift in public attitudes could be traced to the heightened fear and to the increased political salience of street crime. What they found, however, was a more contingent picture. African-Americans, although more victimized and more fearful, have not been more punitive. Women have been more fearful but neither more victimized nor more punitive: "In general, black people are more afraid (and, it might be added, more victimized than whites) but not more punitive; in general, Southerners are less afraid than Northerners but not less punitive; and women are generally more afraid than men and somewhat less punitive" (Stinchcombe et al., 1980, p. 67). Indeed, punitive preferences are strongest among males who live in rural areas, own guns, and are involved in, or exposed to, the hunting tradition—dubbed by Stinchcombe, "the rural hunting cul-

---

rate tended to rise among those excluded from the plenty of the 1960s. As Samuel Walker puts it, "Although the economy as a whole was prosperous, young blacks did not share in the prosperity and in fact were becoming steadily worse off in relation to whites" (1989, p. 260).

ture." These people are punitive, although as a result of their distance from urban street crime, they are less likely to be victimized and, therefore, less frightened. Stinchcombe also points out that fear is not considered an appropriate response in the rural hunting culture (Stinchcombe et al., 1980, pp. 104-105).

My research in Cedar City provides the first glimpse of race in this analysis, while casting still more doubt on the conventional wisdom that attributes politicization to the fear and anger stemming from victimization. A comparison of two areas of the city *with comparably high crime rates* indicated heavy support for two law-and-order initiatives in one of these areas and equally strong opposition in the other. These initiatives dealt with capital punishment and with shooting policies of the police and thus were good indicators of the intrusion of punitive attitudes into the political process. The predominantly Black Central Area voted strongly against punitive policies, thus rebuffing efforts to politicize those issues. Conversely, voters in Crystal Valley, a neighborhood in transition with a poverty rate rising faster than the citywide average and an increasing influx of Blacks, responded positively and enthusiastically to law-and-order initiatives.

Learning About Street Crime

How are we to explain these anomalies—these departures from what the conventional wisdom tells us about the linkages among victimization, fear, and punitive attitudes? At the heart of the matter is Skogan and Maxfield's insight that most of us learn about street crime not from our direct experiences with it, but rather from what we are told by others—principally by people we know and by the media. The available evidence and the logic of these mediated responses is that they converge to provide a misleading message about the nature of street crime and about how best to respond to it.

I call this message the *myth of crime and punishment*—a simple morality play that dramatizes conflict between good and evil: because of bad people, this is a dangerous and violent world. The myth helps us make sense of this precarious situation by signaling the dangers of, and revealing the solutions to, the problems posed by street crime. We learn how to identify criminals, who are portrayed as predatory strangers. We are led to think of them as persons fundamentally different in character (and appearance) from law-abiding members of society: street criminals are unknown predators awaiting their opportunity to attack persons and property. This frightening image triggers a second and more reassuring feature of the myth of crime and punishment: the idea that the morally justified and realistically effective response to street crime is punishment. The moral case can be found, among other places, in the Old Testament, with its prescription of an eye for an eye. In more practical terms, punishment is defended as a realistic way to deter some criminals and keep others behind prison walls.

The available evidence suggests that the myth of crime and punishment offers, at best, a very restricted view of the world of street crime. Surely, the image of the predatory stranger is misleading and exaggerated. Most street crimes are not committed by predatory strangers. Some of the most violent crimes—murder, rape, and assault—are committed most frequently by acquaintances. A systematic study of felony arrests in New York City confirms this and further indicates a prior relationship between defendants and victims in almost 40 percent of most other crimes (Vera Institute, 1981, p. 19). Nor is it accurate to think of brutal and malicious crimes or criminals as typical. The most frightening crimes—robbery, rape, and murder—amount to only about 5 percent of the total crime committed in any given year. Similarly, criminals come with a great variety of proclivities, and for many of them violence is seen as only the last resort—something to be avoided whenever possible (Silberman, 1978, chap. 3).

Basic questions may also be raised about the crime control and moral messages of the myth of crime and punishment. Available data on deterrence and incapacitation are, at best, inconclusive. Moreover, before taking too much solace from the stern morality of the Old Testament, ought we not pause to consider moral codes that stress forgiveness and look to redemption? And ought we not be sensitive to the life circumstances of those benighted segments of society from which street criminals are disproportionately drawn? Rather than being so quick to condemn them as morally deficient people who are unable to rise above the obstacles of poverty and racism, we might be better advised to marvel at those who are not overpowered by the burdens they must bear (Scheingold, 1984, pp. 24-27).

If the myth of crime and punishment skates on such thin ice, how does it come to so dominate our thinking? Skogan and Maxfield's research reveals that the vicarious victimization that fires the public's imagination and indignation feeds quite nicely into the misconceptions of the myth of crime and punishment: "[P]ersonal neighborhood communication networks substantially magnify the apparent volume of local violence. . . . Like media coverage of crime, the processes which lead victims' stories of their experience to 'get around' seem to accentuate the apparent volume of personal as opposed to property crime" (Skogan and Maxfield, 1981, pp. 157-158). With respect to the media, George Gerbner and Larry Gross's research on prime-time television further underscores the point.

> Geared for independent action in loosely knit and often remote social contexts, half of all characters are free to engage in violence. Violence on television, unlike real-life, rarely stems from close personal relationships. Most of it is between strangers, set up to drive home lessons of social typing. Violence is often just a speciality—a skill, a craft, an efficient means to test the norms and settle any challenge to the existing structure of power (Gerbner and Gross, 1976, p. 184).

The correspondence between Gerbner and Gross's summary of their findings and the myth of crime and punishment is readily apparent. All the elements are present: a threatening environment disproportionately populated by predatory strangers, their victims, and their adversaries; punitive solutions to the problems of criminal violence; and society's predators getting their just deserts.

Of course, it is one thing to say that the myth of crime and punishment is all around us and another thing to explain its cultural presence and our receptivity to it. Lillian Rubin's explanation has more to do with race and class conflict than with street crime. Her argument is that our society is increasingly "frightened and insecure" as a result of economic decline. Our economic fears are compounded by a fundamentally new sense of vulnerability: "For the first time in our history, it is the white pulse that quickens in fear at the sound of footsteps on a darkened street; it is white feet that hurry across to the other side at the sight of blacks ahead. Suddenly, we have no way to protect ourselves; we are no longer in control" (Rubin, 1988, p. 240).[4] Because this loss of control is intolerable, "we defend against it with our rage. . . . A rage that has no easy target, therefore finds

---

[4] For an extended look at this theme, see Silberman, 1978, chap. 5.

expression in a script that pits the dark barbarians against the brave, blond knight" (ibid., p. 239).[5]

Thus, street crime and street criminals, along with welfare cheaters and drug addicts, become legitimate targets of our anxieties and code words for our racial antipathies. Moreover, the myth of crime and punishment offers not only scapegoats but easy answers that are not available to the complex problems of economic decline and racial justice. Serious answers to these problems not only are elusive but also require us to take responsibility for both causes and solutions. Better then the comfortable moralizing of the myth of crime and punishment.

The simple message of this section is that the politicization process is at least three times removed from street crime, per se: first, by vicarious victimization; second, by the myth of crime and punishment; and third, by the social and economic malaise that plagues this country. But, as we will see in the next section, the political process itself further distances politicization from street crime, as enterprising political leaders attempt to put our misconceptions about crime and our broader anxieties to their own uses.[6]

---

[5] The circumstances in the Bernhard Goetz trial were strikingly similar to the first Rodney King case. In both proceedings, the jurors had conclusive evidence of the defendants' gratuitous violence but nonetheless acquitted them of virtually all charges. The jurors in the Goetz case knew from Goetz's own words that he did not act in self-defense and that his intention was to murder the unarmed Black youths. Although Goetz did not testify, the jurors saw his taped confession, and it was just as damaging as was the tape of the police officers' assault on King. Nonetheless, Goetz was acquitted of all crimes except carrying a concealed weapon. Rubin concludes that the jurors (and much of the rest of White America) are so imbued with the criminal threat posed by young Black males that, putting themselves in Goetz's place, they believed that it was reasonable to feel threatened in those circumstances, irrespective of his own statement to the contrary (Rubin, 1988, p. 261).

[6] This argument is, of course, speculative and in need of much more attention than it has so far received. For more extended and systematic, albeit equally speculative, explorations of these elusive issues, see Scheingold, 1984, chap. 3; 1991, pp. 173-181.

PUZZLING PATTERNS OF POLITICIZATION

In the local elections in Cedar City, there were a few candidates, mostly from outside the established political elite, who campaigned on street crime, and some of their campaigns were successful. But neither the frequency nor the success rate suggests that such campaigning was particularly inviting. Over the 15 years covered by my research, the success rate was about 50 percent for the small number of "law-and-order" candidates (38) and ballot issues (13). It is also worth noting that well over half of this campaign activity and these successes were confined to the single four-year period of high politicization from 1975 through 1978. Finally, efforts to parlay occasional victories into successful political careers did not work very well.

The ten cities researched in the Governmental Responses to Crime Project provide some data that tend to confirm my Cedar City research. Once again, there were law-and-order success stories—perhaps most notably the mayoral victories of police chiefs Frank Rizzo in Philadelphia and Charles Stenvig in Minneapolis. More generally, the data, presented in Table 1, suggest that there were a number of cities, such as Boston and Minneapolis, where crime was more consistently a significant issue than it was in Cedar City. There were other cities, such as Newark, Philadelphia, and Indianapolis, where crime was, for limited periods of time, a more intense issue than it was even at the high point of Cedar City politicization in the mid-to-late 1970s. But the overall message of Table 1 is that most of the time in most of the ten cities, moderation was the rule rather than the exception.

While there are no comparable data on national politics, street crime has been a prominent factor in presidential politics—especially in the campaigns of Republicans seeking a first term in the White House. George Bush's success in 1988 with the Willie Horton television spots echoed messages of previous Republican candidates—most notably Barry Goldwater in 1964, Richard Nixon in 1968, and Ronald Reagan in 1980. Democrats have not been immune from the crime issue, although they have inflected it in a slightly less punitive way. Similarly, Congress has frequently become embroiled in the issue over the past several decades, beginning with the 1968 Crime Control and Safe Streets Act, which created the Law Enforcement Assistance Administration. Congress continues to be engaged in a variety of anti-crime measures dealing with such matters as capital punishment, gun control, prison construction, and putting more police on the streets.

TABLE 1: Salience of the Crime Issue in Local Elections, 1948-1978

	1948-62	1962-78	1974-78	1948-78	N
Atlanta	1.00	3.50	5.00	3.25	4
Boston	5.50	4.00	4.00	4.75	4
Houston	1.50	1.00	5.50	2.57	7
Indianapolis	3.57	2.67	6.00	3.57	7
Minneapolis	3.50	4.33	3.50	3.86	7
Newark	3.00	5.00	6.00	4.67	3
Oakland	1.50	1.00	4.00	1.80	5
Philadelphia	1.67	1.00	6.00	2.40	5
Phoenix	4.50	2.00	3.50	3.63	8
San Jose	1.00	1.00	4.00	1.75	4
Ten cities	2.87	2.61	4.62	3.20	54

Note: N = number of mayoral incumbencies.

Key: 1 = Crime was not a salient election issue at all.
7 = Crime was a very salient election issue.

Source: Herbert Jacob, Robert L. Lineberry, with Anne M. Heinz, Janice A. Beecher, Jack Moran, and Duane H. Swank, *Governmental Responses to Crime: Crime on Urban Agendas* (Washington, D.C.: National Institute of Justice, 1982), p. 32.

So much for the national and local levels. What can be said about politicization at the state level? Research on California in the 1960s revealed that street crime played rather well in legislative and gubernatorial politics. Indeed, Ronald Reagan's 1966 law-and-order campaign for governor set the tone for much of what was to follow in presidential politics (Berk et al., 1977, p. 59). More broadly, the legislature seemed inclined to invoke criminal law indiscriminately. "[T]he almost universal response to a wide spectrum of perceived social problems was increased criminalization" (Berk et al., 1977, p. 300). Recent research, again in California, indicates the continued salience of street crime in state politics (Rhodes, 1989). Throughout the country, sentencing and prison construction data suggest that legislators see street crime as a priority issue and that they see it in largely punitive terms. From 1984 to 1990, the capacity of state prisons rose by 52 percent and the number of prisoners increased by 67 percent (Bureau of Justice Statistics, 1992). Affinities between state and national politicization, I will argue below, distinguish them from politicization in urban areas.

To make sense out of the puzzling patterns of politicization that emerge from the data, we must look at both the *opportunities* and the *incentives* for politicians to politicize street crime. The evidence as well as the logic of politicization strongly suggest that these opportunities and incentives vary inversely with proximity to street crime and with responsibilities for the institutions of the criminal justice system. In other words, I shall argue that politicization is increasingly attractive as one moves up the line from local to state to national politics. And running through the analysis of both opportunities and incentives is, once again, the issue of racial conflict.

Opportunities to Politicize Street Crime

While the public is clearly involved in the policy process in the United States, there is substantial agreement among policy analysts that political leaders have more to say about what is on our political agenda than does the general public (see Cobb and Elder, 1983; Eyestone, 1978). What is true for the broad range of policy issues may be especially true for street crime (Berk et al., 1977, p. 280). What gives political leaders so much leeway with respect to street crime is the abstract and vicarious way that the issue presents itself to most Americans.

In partial confirmation of these assertions about the opportunities that politicians have to lead the public astray on matters of crime and punishment, consider the contrast between the public's response to forced-choice and open-ended questions about crime. As Table 2 indicates, when the Gallup Poll asked an *open-ended* question ("What do you think is the most important issue facing the country today?"), the political salience of crime fluctuated widely during the 1970s, with no apparent relationship to the crime rate (Scheingold, 1984, pp. 43-45). However, Table 3 reveals that during this same period, the public, when presented with a series of policy issues in *forced-choice* questions, consistently ranked crime at the top of the list—with the related issue of drugs a close second.

TABLE 2: The Political Salience of Crime in the United States, 1968-1980, Open-Ended Questions

Question: "What do you think is the most important issue facing the country today?"

Percentage responding "crime" or crime combined with such related matters as "lawlessness," "law enforcement," "juvenile delinquency," and "immorality":

	Pct.	Rank Order
1968	29%	2
1969	17	2
1970	5	5
1971	7	4
1972	10	3
1973	17	2
1974	4	3
1975	5	5
1976	8	3
1977	15	4
1978	3	5
1979	8	2
1980	2	8

Sources: Compiled from *The Gallup Poll: Public Opinion, 1935-1971*, 2 vols. (New York: Random House, 1972); *The Gallup Poll: Public Opinion, 1972-1977*, 2 vols. (Wilmington, Del.: Scholarly Resources, 1978); *The Gallup Opinion Index*, Report no. 157 (August 1978), Report no. 172 (November 1979), Report no. 181 (September 1980).

TABLE 3: The Political Salience of Crime in the United States, Selected Years, 1973-1980, Forced-Choice Questions

Question: "We are faced with many problems in this country, none of which can be solved easily or inexpensively. I'm going to name some of these problems, and for each one I'd like you to tell me whether you think we're spending too much money on it, too little money, or about the right amount."

Percentage Responding "Too Little"

	1973	1975	1977	1980
Halting the rising crime rate	64	65	65	69
Dealing with drug addiction	65	55	55	59
Improving/protecting the nation's health	61	62	56	55
Improving/protecting the environment	61	53	47	48
Improving the nation's education system	49	49	48	53
Solving the problems of the big cities	48	47	40	40
Improving the conditions of Blacks	32	27	25	24
Welfare	20	23	12	13
The military, armaments, and defense	11	17	24	56
Space exploration program	7	7	10	18
Foreign aid	4	5	3	5

Source: *General Social Surveys, 1972-1980: Cumulative Codebook* (Storrs, Conn.: Roper Center, July 1980), pp. 71-74.

Taken together, these findings signal a powerful current of suggestibility within the public when it comes to crime. According to the data from open-ended questions, crime is occasionally an issue of great immediacy to Americans—something that comes spontaneously to mind—but most of the time other things (probably economic matters or questions of war and peace) weigh more heavily on our minds. In contrast, the response to forced-choice questions suggests that concern about crime is just below the surface and may, therefore, be easily politicized by an enterprising candidate.

That generalization does not, however, hold true for all Americans. Those living closest to street crime, the residents of our most heavily populated urban areas, have a much more concrete sense of its causes and consequences. The closer one is to the dead-end lives of the underclass, the less likely one is to be taken in by the oversimplifications of the myth of crime and punishment.[7] Punishment entails pointing the finger of blame at someone else—a relatively easy thing to do when the culprit is the stereotypical predatory stranger. Perhaps this helps explain why "the rural hunting culture" has tended to be the most punitive element of the society. Conversely, one of the reasons that African-Americans, although more victimized, seem to be less punitive may well be that they better understand the forces that drive marginalized Americans toward crime.

In addition, despite their multiplicity of problems, our urban areas are seldom, if ever, so jungle-like as they are portrayed by the media. Insofar as life in one's own city thus appears reasonably normal, one may be less receptive to the threatening imagery evoked by a politics of law and order in local political campaigns. At the same time, this imagery may be so much a part of our culture that many of us may be prepared to believe that somewhere beyond our home terrain predatory strangers do imperil our laws and our social order. Accordingly, presidential candidates making vague allusions to a national crisis or state legislators feeding rural, small town, and suburban fears may be able to campaign successfully against street crime.

---

[7] The exceptions to this rule are victims of predatory violence who do seem to accept the myth of crime and punishment and are prepared to participate in and, indeed, to lead the politicization process (Scheingold, Olson, and Pershing, 1994; Elias, 1986). But as was established in the previous section, it is not victimization but vicarious victimization that accounts for the high levels of fear in the society.

But there are also racial factors that influence the opportunities for politicization in urban America. Recall the contrasting responses to politicization by the Central Area and Crystal Valley residents of Cedar City. Central Area African-Americans, like other African-Americans, have been estranged from hard-line wars against street crime, drugs, and urban disorder. Although minorities have been disproportionately victimized by criminal violence, they have been similarly afflicted by police violence. More fundamentally, as Rubin's analysis of the Goetz case clearly suggests, these campaigns are often largely covert expressions of racial antagonism. Their most concrete consequences have often been to make African-Americans and other minorities fair game for police violence. Indeed, there is evidence that those residents of Crystal Valley who supported politicization associated increasing crime and economic decline with the growing Black presence in their neighborhoods (Fleissner et al., 1991, pp. 88-89).

Incentives to Politicize Street Crime

There are fewer incentives, as well as fewer opportunities, to politicize street crime in local urban settings than at the state and national levels. First of all, urban political leaders and criminal process professionals must to some extent answer for a failure to control street crime. Because they realize that crime is a largely insoluble problem, they are reluctant to make promises for which they may be held accountable. Second, politicization of street crime is bad for business—it is likely to drive people from the inner city to suburban shopping malls, housing developments, and business parks. Finally and most fundamentally, many political leaders in urban areas are reluctant to play the crime card because, as I have argued above, they cannot do so without playing the race card. Politicization of street crime tends to exacerbate racial tensions and to make governance more difficult—particularly once racial minorities have gained a substantial political voice, as is increasingly the case in urban America. It is thus more prudent to cool down the issue of street crime than to heat it up.

In Cedar City, the struggle to politicize street crime was led by politicians who were not drawn from or connected to the civic elite—the rank-and-file police officers' organization and some small business people from crime-ridden and racially polarized Crystal Valley. While they did win an occasional battle (most notably when they unseated two liberal judges), over the long haul, the forces driving politicization were no match for the established elites who worked actively against most law-and-order candidates (Scheingold, 1991, pp. 55-65).[8]

National politicians, in contrast, have strong incentives to politicize street crime. For them, street crime is an almost entirely symbolic issue. Because they have virtually no policy responsibility for dealing with crime, national leaders never have to live up to their extravagant promises. Indeed, as has already been suggested, street crime offers national leaders a way to divert attention from economic problems and to identify scapegoats and easy answers to social tensions. In presidential campaigns, being tough on street crime is particularly good politics for Republicans, who do not look to conflicted inner-city voters for support. For Democrats, who depend more heavily on inner-city voters, street crime is a more precarious issue.

At the state level, the picture is somewhat more complex. State governments are rather distant from the harsh realities of street crime and from most of the institutional responsibilities it imposes on the criminal justice system. Moreover, although urban minorities are, of course, represented at the state level, their influence is seriously diluted by a wide variety of other interests. Accordingly, the incentives to politicize street crime probably outweigh the drawbacks. But ultimately, legislators must face up to the costs of politicization—namely, the tax dollars required to house ever greater numbers of prison inmates. Thus, in the long run, fiscal realities impose some constraints on state-level politicization of crime.

---

[8] My tracking of newspaper reporting of street crime revealed that at the period of peak politicization from 1975 to 1978, the proportion of local crime reporting diminished to the point where it actually fell beneath reports of crime elsewhere in the country (Scheingold, 1991, pp. 53, 64). I do not know whether this was intentional, but the diversion of public attention from the immediate crime problems of Cedar City was surely consistent with the depoliticizing objectives of established elites.

POLICY CONSEQUENCES OF POLITICIZATION

For all of these reasons, it would certainly be a mistake to take the rhetoric of politicization at face value. In policy terms, what we see is by no means what we will get. At the national level, the politicization of street crime is frequently a symbolic exercise without serious policy objectives or capabilities. In state and urban jurisdictions, where virtually all of the policy responsibility resides, there are moderating forces at work.

The Symbolic Character of National Politicization

There is good reason to believe that the federal government's well-publicized wars against crime and drugs are little more than symbolic engagements. Consider the Bush administration's largely punitive but modestly funded war on drugs. Critics complain that the program was predominantly punitive, with very little support for drug prevention activities programs directed at reducing demand. Even taken on its own terms, the funding was grossly inadequate to take the steps to reduce supply (Scheingold, 1990). The discontinuity between dramatic rhetoric and limited commitment of resources is a clear tip-off that the war on drugs is more about getting elected, reinforcing flagging political authority, or enhancing federal law enforcement prerogatives than about serious policymaking. Indeed, the major achievement of these moral crusades that pit good against the evils of crime and drugs has probably been to divert attention from the underlying social and economic problems that plague this nation. To face up to these problems directly would cost a great deal of money and would therefore be hard to sell politically. Nor is there any guarantee of success. It is much easier to fall back on the simple truths of the myth of crime and punishment—a much easier sell and ultimately the responsibility of state and local law enforcement officials.

Even with the best of intentions, however, the transmission lines from national to local institutions are not very dependable. This was the essential lesson of the original war on street crime, launched by the Crime Control and Safe Streets Act of 1968 and conducted by the Law Enforcement Assistance Administration (LEAA) during the 1970s. Efforts by the LEAA to develop a coherent anti-crime program foundered on the ad hoc quality of the legislative mandate and on conflicts between the state planning agencies that distributed funds and well-entrenched local law enforcement officials (Feeley and Sarat, 1980). The LEAA did, however, fund a wide variety of demonstration projects and thus became one of the primary sources of innovative law enforcement (Feeley, 1983). Community policing, for example, originated this way. But whether such projects take root and, if so, how they develop are determined locally. The character, direction, and pace of policy reform are, in short, primarily a function of local conditions.[9]

Policy Ambivalence at the State and Local Levels

While policy at the national level is purely punitive and largely symbolic, at the state and local levels things are more complex. In the first place, the stakes of politicization are more concrete and less symbolic because state and local government officials have to answer for the policy shortcomings of the police and the criminal courts.[10] Second, there is a strong, yet not unchallenged, moderate counterpoint to the punitive values that dominate politicization of street crime at the national level. Accordingly, there are meaningful changes in policy according to which way the political winds are blowing. The ambiguity, the complexity, and the variation are all readily apparent in an examination of two of the principal policy reforms of recent years: determinate sentencing and community policing.

---

[9] Generally speaking, LEAA funds were not used as intended. Instead, the programs served as targets of opportunity: write as much hardware as possible into the proposal, go through the motions of implementing programs, and then terminate them when the funds run out (Feeley, 1983, pp. 220-221). The LEAA thus tended to become just another source of funds. In Cedar City, for example, the mayor and the city council tended to use LEAA money as an alternative to local funding rather than as a crime-fighting supplement (Scheingold, 1991, chap. 3).

[10] The inertial tendencies and substantial insulation of the agencies of criminal process mean that even at its most concrete, the politicization of criminal process has a significant symbolic dimension. Although policy change does occur, the course of change tends to be sluggish and unpredictable. For a detailed analysis of this process as it works in the police department and criminal courts of Cedar City, see Scheingold, 1991, chaps. 3-4.

Determinate sentencing is a reform designed to severely curtail the discretion of judges and prison officials. Under traditional sentencing practices, judges have wide latitude to set minimum and maximum terms or to release convicts under probationary sentencing schemes. Prison officials could, within those judicially established limits, hold prisoners until they were deemed to be rehabilitated. Sometimes referred to as mandatory or presumptive sentencing, depending on how it is structured, determinate sentencing imposes guidelines on judges and fixed terms on prison officials. These sentencing standards are established by the legislature and/or by a sentencing commission and are to be based primarily on the seriousness of the offense and the criminal record of the offender.

Determinate sentencing managed to strike responsive chords among both liberals and conservatives—with their convergent objections to the discretionary model. Liberals and conservatives agreed that discretion was unjust and arbitrary, albeit for different reasons. To conservatives, the discretionary model was permissive and counterproductive: Soft-hearted judges and the use of plea-bargaining allowed criminals—especially the savvy, hardened criminals—to escape punishment, thereby robbing the criminal justice system of its capability to deter and to incapacitate criminals. To liberals, the discretionary model tended to be coercive and especially unfair to defendants at the margins of society—those who are poorer risks for probation and parole programs. In addition, indeterminate sentences put convicts at the mercy of prison officials, who could decide whether and when to release inmates.

Accordingly, a rare if somewhat fragile consensus developed around determinate sentencing (Greenberg and Humphries, 1980). It is more just, so the argument goes, to mete out punishment strictly in proportion to the offense and the criminal record—according, in other words, to the offender's behavior rather than his or her identity. The point is to punish offenders for what they have done rather than for who they are (Von Hirsch, 1976, 1987). Moreover, this desert-based approach is also said to promote deterrence without being gratuitously punitive: deterrence theory gives precedence to certainty rather than severity, thus validating moderate sentencing practices (Wilson, 1977, pp. 194-204).

In practice, the fragile consensus between liberals and conservatives quickly broke down. The consensus was fragile because conservative support for determinate sentencing had more to do with an eagerness to curb the discretion of "soft" judges, whereas liberals were more interested in curbing the power of government. By and large, conservatives have gained control of legislatively mandated sentences and have proceeded to ratchet up initially moderate sentences—especially, but not exclusively, for drug and sex offenses (Zimring and Hawkins, 1991, pp. 162-171).

Community policing, like determinate sentencing, is rooted in a belief that traditional practices are ineffectual and inequitable, with minorities—African-Americans in particular—being unfairly burdened by police violence and harassment. Accordingly, the goal of community policing is to effect a reconciliation between accountable police departments and the citizens they serve. Measures to achieve these objectives include decentralizing command and control to the precinct level, incorporating the police into neighborhood networks and institutions, establishing mechanisms to insure police accountability to the community, and otherwise maximizing opportunities for constructive interaction between police officers and the citizenry. The assumption is that these steps will not only improve relationships between the police and the community but will also contribute to more effective law enforcement by mobilizing the public against crime and, indeed, by bringing the public into the crime-control process.

Community policing's moderate side is most apparent and most publicized. It is presented as a corrective to the confrontational and often alienating styles of policing that have prevailed in the past. As problem-solvers who develop close relationships with their neighborhoods and who work through neighborhood organizations, community police officers are to become more like service providers and less like what James Baldwin once referred to as "soldiers of occupation in a hostile country" (1961, pp. 65-66). The broader aspiration is that a collective struggle against street crime will revitalize afflicted communities by bringing people together in the service of a common objective.

There may, however, be a darker side to community policing. The focus of community policing is much more on order maintenance than on law enforcement. The goal is to take back the streets and the neighborhoods, not just from the predatory, but from the unruly as well. Taking back the streets is justified on the dual assumptions, articulated most prominently by James Q. Wilson and George Kelling, that disorder inhibits the access of law-abiding citizens to parks and other public spaces and that disorder invites and frequently leads to crime (Wilson and Kelling, 1982).

The appropriate response to disorder, according to this way of thinking, is to enhance the discretion of police officers to decide whether to arrest and prosecute offenders or to treat them in an ad hoc fashion. Maintaining order, according to Wilson and Kelling, may frequently lead police officers to "kick ass"—thus validating a kind of "consensual" police violence (Wilson and Kelling, 1982, p. 35). But will it be consensual? In cracking down not only on criminal activity but also on such incipient criminality as graffiti, disorderly conduct, and the like, the police may end up mobilizing some portions of the neighborhood against other portions of the neighborhood—for example, an apprehensive older generation against youth.

Moreover, in reaching out to the community and participating in neighborhood organizations, community policing provides the state, Stanley Cohen warns us, with access to "the family, the school, and the neighbourhood" (Cohen, 1985, p. 83). He suggests, in other words, that our strong tradition of limited government is jeopardized by inviting the coercive power of the police into social and family life. At the very least, Cohen implies that we should think seriously about the costs of extending the reach of the state beyond its traditional boundaries.

PROSPECTS FOR MODERATION

The major lesson of my own work and the work of others is something of a paradox: there has been an inverse relationship between politicization of and proximity to street crime. Except for victims, the closer people have been to street crime, the less receptive they have been to the simplistic remedies suggested by the myth of crime and punishment. The result has been a standoff between hard-line and moderate law enforcement policies. It remains to be seen how relevant this finding, even if accepted for other times and other places, will be to Chicago and other urban areas. Let me offer some brief concluding speculation on what I take to be the modestly promising prospects for policy moderation.

Community Policing and Local Politics

Until recently, local political leaders have had considerable leeway to pursue moderate versions of community policing that have as an underlying objective the incorporation of marginalized minorities into the broader community. Increasing levels of violence and racial polarization *may or may not* be changing all that. Available evidence cuts both ways, but my impression is that the forces of moderation will prove stronger *for the time being*.

First, the bad news. Gang- and drug-related violence combined with interracial tensions may well be driving both minorities and Whites toward the politics of law and order. In the worst case scenario, Whites and minorities will clash over high-profile incidents such as the Rodney King beating and its aftermath in Los Angeles or the Bernhard Goetz shooting and the Bensonhurst murder in New York. But it is also possible that the fight against street crime will bring Whites and minorities together. *Either way, I see this as bad news because moderate policies are likely to be sacrificed.*

In 1992, the *Chicago Tribune* reported racial conflict in the Chicago City Council over a new anti-loitering ordinance. The Chicago law, like similar laws in other cities, was directed at gang activities and at the threat they pose to law-abiding citizens in areas of the city where gangs and drug dealing flourish. Here we have a classic illustration of the case for order maintenance leading to a law that authorizes the police to, among other things, "disperse or arrest groups as small as two people if one of them is a known gang member" (*Chicago Tribune*, 1992b). This ordinance was, in short, an invitation to "kick ass."

At first glance, what we seem to have here is an example of racial conflict spawning and condoning punitive policies: "In a vote that centered *more on race than on crime*, opponents of the ordinance were led by Ald. John Steele (6th), who charged that the law, drawn up by several white aldermen and enthusiastically endorsed by Mayor Richard Daley, was aimed primarily at blacks and Hispanics" (*Chicago Tribune*, 1992a; emphasis added). The newspaper went on to point out, however, that at least one Black alderman, speaking for constituents whose neighborhood had been "struck most severely by violence and looting in the wake of the Chicago Bulls' championship victory, supported the measure" (ibid.). This would suggest that minorities as well as Whites may be reaching the boiling point. Note also that Mayor Daley had opposed a similar ordinance three years earlier. The *Tribune*, therefore, may have put the wrong gloss on this controversy. The ordinance may have less to tell us about racial conflict than about which way the wind is blowing. Still, the news is bad, because the forces of moderation would seem to be on the run. And Chicago is not the only city that is increasingly inclined to "kick ass." Certainly, in my own city, Seattle, there is a new willingness to empower police to engage in a variety of preemptive, and constitutionally suspect, activities designed to make it difficult for gangs to gather, for drug deals to take place, for crack houses to function, and so on.

There is, however, another way of looking at these same trends and events—a way that I find somewhat more persuasive. Policy moderation in the past, I argued above, has depended on a coalition between civic elites and newly empowered minorities—or at least a resolve by civic elites to discourage a racially polarizing politics of law and order. There is reason to believe that this coalition still has some staying power. Surely, the Chicago anti-loitering ordinance can be reinterpreted along these lines. Black aldermen were, in the first place, divided on the issue. Morever, the police superintendent, a Hispanic, instructed the police to be moderate in enforcing the ordinance and to avoid making neighborhood sweeps with multiple arrests (*Chicago Tribune*, 1992b). Punitive policies alienate minorities who think of themselves as more the victims than the beneficiaries of law-and-order campaigns. Thus politicization of street crime is racially divisive—often inflaming Whites and intimidating minorities. At the same time, politicization is bad for business in that it may well frighten people away from shops, restaurants, and other commercial property.

Minorities have been particularly insistent on police accountability, and community policing seems to provide a consensual answer to this long-standing problem. Of course, police accountability need not go in the direction of community policing. But none of the obvious alternatives is so generally acceptable. Civilian review boards have been exceedingly unwelcome among both police administrators and rank-and-file police officers.[11] Conversely, minority communities are inclined to see promises to beef up the internal affairs offices within police departments as window dressing. In this context, community policing looks attractive. It is all things to all people: more effective crime control, neighborhood accountability, and rapprochement between the police and minority communities.

---

[11] A recent controversy in New York over a police review board resulted in an unruly, racially sullied public protest by rank-and-file police officers (*New York Times*, 1992).

In the long run, if and when a relationship of trust is forged between the police and minorities, support could build for punitive policies. But that kind of trust is still a long way off, and there is ample evidence from urban areas throughout the country that relationships between the police and minority communities remain explosive. Accordingly, when the police start "kicking ass," confrontations regularly erupt. Enlightened police leaders are sensitive to these tendencies, and this may account for the lukewarm response of Chicago police officials to the anti-loitering ordinance (*Chicago Tribune*, 1992b). More broadly, cracking down on street crime continues to be perceived among both Whites and minorities as a code for cracking down on minorities and thus is inherently divisive. Because the future of American cities depends on a continuation of cooperation between civic elites and ever-growing blocs of minority voters, there are, to put it simply, very strong incentives for the middle to hold and for moderate policies to prevail.

Sentencing Practices and State Politics

To begin again with the bad news, legislative opportunities and incentives continue to favor politicization of street crime and "get tough" sentencing. First, the moderating impact of minorities is diluted in a sea of suburban and rural voters.[12] Nor is there any force that I know of at the state level comparable to civic elites in urban areas, who have a substantial stake in opposing hard-line politicization. All other things being equal, it would thus be reasonable to expect a continuation of punitive sentencing legislation.

But things are not equal, and a kind of moderation appears to be in the cards. The tidal wave of offenders flowing into prisons and jails as a result of punitive policies is outstripping fiscal resources, especially under current circumstances. My own interviews with state legislators in Washington make it clear that they are looking for ways to avoid expensive prison construction and to ease the heavy custodial costs of forever more inmates.

---

[12] I am inclined, by the way, to suspect that the hard-line policing that has prevailed in Los Angeles for so long can be attributed at least in part to the way in which the minority vote is diluted by the broad geographic boundaries of the city.

Accordingly, states are beginning to think about, and experiment with, alternatives to incarceration for non-violent offenders—especially drug offenders, who account for much of the overcrowding (Zimring and Hawkins, 1990, pp. 134-136). Of course, there continue to be calls for boot camps and heavier sentences, but at least in Washington even the hard-liners see the fiscal handwriting on the wall.[13]

In closing, I should make more explicit my policy objections to the politicization of street crime. As was suggested above, the inertial forces of politicization lead in a purely punitive direction. As a consequence, the complex problems posed by street crime become reduced to a game of cops and robbers. Punitive policies certainly have their place, but not to the exclusion of other ways of coping with crime. Politicization, in other words, leads to law-and-order populism that heavily discounts the pragmatic responses that criminal process professionals are likely to favor. By pragmatic responses, I have in mind—in addition to community policing and more moderate sentencing—such things as drug treatment programs, job skills training, diversion programs, community dispute-resolution schemes, and selective decriminalization of victimless crimes, including some drug offenses, gambling, and prostitution. Insiders certainly do not have all the answers to the problems of street crime, but they are much more likely to see through the demagogic formula provided by the myth of crime and punishment.

To take this argument one step further and to conclude on a broader, more personal, and less optimistic note: while the moderate center may hold in the near future, there is reason to believe that it will not hold indefinitely. If we cannot stem our economic and social deterioration, the prospects for policy moderation and for social peace are bleak. Pragmatic tinkering with law enforcement policy provides what is, at best, symptomatic relief. To stop there, or to not even go that far as the hard-liners would have it,

---

[13] It is possible to argue, as does criminologist Stanley Cohen, that the moderation of these reforms is more apparent than real because of the tendency to apply these alternative sentencing programs to an increasing number of minor offenders who formerly would not have been caught in the criminal justice net at all. In other words, because these penalties appear benign and inexpensive, there is less reluctance to use them.

is to contribute to social crisis and, accordingly, to our own anxiety. We cannot with impunity turn our backs on the conditions that are producing economic insecurity throughout the society—in particular among the unemployed, the underemployed, and the unemployable, who struggle against one another and are without a stake in, or commitment to, civility and mutuality.

REFERENCES

Baldwin, James (1961). *Nobody Knows My Name.* New York: Dial.
Berk, Richard A., Harold Brackman, and Selma Lesser (1977). *A Measure of Justice: An Empirical Study of Changes in the California Penal Code, 1955-1971.* New York: Academic Press.
Bureau of Justice Statistics (1992). *National Update*, vol. 2, no. 1 (July 1992). Washington D.C.: U.S. Department of Justice.
Chicago Tribune (1992a). June 18, 1992, sec. 1, p. 1.
―――― (1992b). June 19, 1992, sec. 2, p. 5.
Cobb, Roger W., and Charles D. Elder (1983). *Participation in American Politics: The Dynamics of Agenda-Building.* 2nd ed. Baltimore: Johns Hopkins University Press.
Cohen, Stanley (1985). *Visions of Social Control.* Cambridge, England: Polity Press.
Currie, Elliott (1985). *Confronting Crime: An American Challenge.* New York: Pantheon Books.
Elias, Robert (1986). *The Politics of Victimization: Victims, Victimology, and Human Rights.* New York: Oxford University Press.
Eyestone, Robert (1978). *From Social Issues to Public Policy.* New York: John Wiley.
Feeley, Malcolm M. (1983). *Court Reform on Trial: Why Simple Solutions Fail.* New York: Basic Books.
Feeley, Malcolm M., and Austin D. Sarat (1980). *The Policy Dilemma: Federal Crime Policy and the Law Enforcement Assistance Administration, 1968-1978.* Minneapolis: University of Minnesota Press.
Fleissner, Dan, Nicholas Fedan, Ezra Stotland, and David Klinger (1991). "Community Policing in Seattle: A Descriptive Study of the South Seattle Crime Reduction Project." Unpublished Final Report to the National Institute of Justice. Seattle: Seattle Police Department, 1991.

Gerbner, George, and Larry Gross (1976). "Living with Television: The Violence Profile," *Journal of Communications*, vol. 26 (1976), pp. 173-197.

Greenberg, David F., and Drew Humphries (1980). "The Cooptation of Fixed Sentencing Reform," *Crime and Delinquency*, vol. 26, no. 2 (April 1980), pp. 206-225.

Jacob, Herbert (1984). *The Frustrations of Policy: Responses to Crime by American Cities*. Boston: Little, Brown.

New York Times (1992). September 18, 1992, p. A1.

Rhodes, Susan L. (1989). "State Policy-Makers and the 'Get Tough' Movement: The Politics of Prison Building and the Prison Overcrowding Crisis in California." Unpublished paper prepared for delivery at the 1989 Annual Meeting of the Law and Society Association, Madison, Wisc., June 9-11, 1989.

Rubin, Lillian B. (1988). *Quiet Rage: Bernie Goetz in a Time of Madness*. Berkeley: University of California Press.

Scheingold, Stuart A. (1984). *The Politics of Law and Order: Street Crime and Public Policy*. New York: Longman.

——— (1990). "The War on Drugs in Context: Crisis Politics and Social Control." Unpublished paper prepared for delivery at the 1990 Annual Meeting of the Law and Society Association. Berkeley/Oakland, Calif., May 31-June 3, 1990.

——— (1991). *The Politics of Street Crime: Criminal Process and Cultural Obsession*. Philadelphia: Temple University Press.

Scheingold, Stuart A., Toska Olson, and Jana Pershing (1994). "Sexual Violence, Victim Advocacy, and Republican Criminology: Washington State's Community Protection Act," *Law and Society Review*, vol. 28, no. 4 (December 1994), pp. 729-763.

Silberman, Charles (1978). *Criminal Violence, Criminal Justice*. New York: Random House.

Skogan, Wesley G., and Michael G. Maxfield (1981). *Coping with Crime: Individual and Neighborhood Reactions*. Beverly Hills, Calif.: Sage.

Stinchcombe, Arthur L., Rebecca Adams, Carol A. Heimer, Kim Lane Scheppele, Tom W. Smith, and D. Garth Taylor (1980). *Crime and Punishment—Changing Attitudes in America*. San Francisco: Jossey-Bass.

Vera Institute of Justice (1981). *Felony Arrests: Their Prosecution and Disposition in New York City's Courts*. Rev. ed. New York: Longman.

Von Hirsch, Andrew (1976). *Doing Justice: Report of the Committee for the Study of Incarceration.* New York: Hill and Wang.
⎯⎯⎯⎯ (1987). *Past or Future Crimes: Deservedness and Dangerousness in the Sentencing of Criminals.* New Brunswick, N.J.: Rutgers University Press.
Walker, Samuel (1989). *Sense and Nonsense About Crime.* 2nd ed. Pacific Grove, Calif: Brooks/Cole.
Wilson, James Q. (1977). *Thinking About Crime.* New York: Vintage.
⎯⎯⎯⎯ (1985). *Thinking About Crime.* Rev. ed. New York: Vintage.
Wilson, James Q., and Richard J. Herrnstein (1985). *Crime and Human Nature.* New York: Simon and Schuster.
Wilson, James Q., and George L. Kelling (1982). "Broken Windows: The Police and Neighborhood Safety," *Atlantic Monthly*, March 1982, pp. 29-38.
Zimring, Franklin E., and Gordon Hawkins (1991). *The Scale of Imprisonment.* Chicago: University of Chicago Press.

COMMENTS

Peter M. Manikas

According to the prevailing view, street crime becomes a political issue when an outraged public, responding to rising crime rates, demands action from public officials. Stuart Scheingold's chapter challenges this conventional wisdom. Based largely on his research on Cedar City (the pseudonym for a medium-sized urban community in the western United States), Scheingold argues that (1) the politicization of street crime is only loosely based on the level of crime; (2) often, political leaders—rather than victimized communities—initiate street crime as an issue; and (3) the further policymakers are from areas with high crime rates (e.g., at the national and state levels), the more likely they are to favor punitive policies. The following discusses criminal justice activity in the Chicago area in light of the issues Scheingold raises.

CRIME RATES AND CRIMINAL JUSTICE POLICIES

Violent Crime

Since 1984 (the year the Chicago Police Department revised its crime reporting system), reports of violent crime in Chicago have risen 48 percent (ICJIA, 1992b). Violent crimes—such as murder, aggravated assault, and robbery—rose moderately during the decade until 1989, when they began to soar.

The number of reported homicides declined by almost 11 percent from 1984 through 1988 (although there was considerable annual variation). In 1989, the murder rate increased 12 percent over the previous year. Between 1989 and 1991, the number of murders in Chicago increased by approximately 25 percent. In 1991, there were 927 murders reported to police (ICJIA, 1992b; Chicago Police Department, 1984-1991). Chicago's highest number of murders were committed in 1974, when the record was set at 963. However, since the population of the city declined by over 300,000 persons in the intervening years, the murder rate is higher today. In 1974, the murder rate peaked at 30.5 per

100,000 persons. That rate was equaled in 1990; it was exceeded in 1992 when Chicago's murder rate reached 33.2 (Block, 1992).

City Policies

As crime rates and civil strife increased in the mid-1960s and early 1970s, city officials responded by expanding police budgets and personnel. From 1960 to 1975, the Chicago Police Department's budget increased from $72.8 million to $283 million. This spending increase far exceeded the growth in inflation, which was 82 percent during the same period. Between 1975 and 1985, police expenditures grew by 70 percent, but this growth fell behind cost-of-living increases, which rose 97 percent over that decade (Manikas, Trossman, and Doppelt, 1989). After 1970, the Chicago Police Department's budget declined as a percentage of total city spending, falling from 47 percent in 1970 to 40 percent in 1985. Between 1960 and 1975, the number of police officers per 100,000 population increased from 282 to 420. However, between 1975 and 1985, the number of police officers in relation to population declined by 6 percent (Manikas, Trossman, and Doppelt, 1989). In recent years, the ratio has increased because the number of police officers has remained stable and the city population has declined.

State and County Policies

In the late 1970s, Illinois, like several other states, passed determinate sentencing legislation (the legislation also created a new "Class X" offense for serious crimes) that dramatically increased the length of time offenders served in prison (Shane-DuBow, Brown, and Olsen, 1985). When these policies were implemented in 1978, there were fewer than 11,000 adult prisoners in the state. In 1989, the prison population had more than doubled to 22,500 inmates (ICJIA, 1990). By 1991, Illinois prisons held 28,941 inmates in a prison system designed to hold fewer than 19,975 (ICJIA, 1991). This overcrowding has occurred despite the construction of 14 new prisons since 1978 at a total cost of $408.3 million (ICJIA, 1992a).

The dramatic increases were not solely the result of the sentencing reform that occurred in the late 1970s. Throughout the 1980s, the Illinois General Assembly (often at the urging of the

Cook County State's Attorney and other county prosecutors) adopted "get tough" crime measures that increased penalties for many offenses (e.g., residential burglary, sexual assault), created new offenses (e.g., drug-induced infliction of great bodily harm), and gave law enforcement officials stronger investigative powers (e.g., electronic eavesdropping in drug investigations) (Boehmer, 1992). In addition, in 1986 Illinois voters approved an amendment to Illinois's constitution permitting the "preventive detention" of suspects posing a threat to the community. In the late 1980s and early 1990s, this legislative activity accelerated, particularly regarding drug crimes. In what Illinois Appellate Justice Robert Steigman has termed a "legislative frenzy," the legislature adopted 27 substantive amendments to the state's drug laws in the previous four and a half years (Steigman, 1992).

At the county level, because of prosecutorial policies and tougher penalties, plea bargaining has declined—at least at the earliest court stages (Manikas, Trossman, and Doppelt, 1989). Throughout the 1980s, the county's jail population increased, leading to severe overcrowding. Despite a federal district court order and the threat of fines, officials have failed to comply with the terms of a consent decree agreed to in 1982 (Manikas, Trossman, and Doppelt, 1989). In 1992, Cook County jail held over 9,000 prisoners, approximately 1,800 more than it was designed to handle (*Chicago Tribune*, 1992). To deal with the jail crisis, an addition to the jail has been built, and two more are under construction. The total cost is estimated to be approximately $240 million. Efforts to alleviate jail crowding by establishing interagency task forces and the like have so far been ineffective in reducing the jail population.

DISCUSSION

The Chicago-area experience seems to confirm much of Scheingold's argument. Throughout the 1970s and most of the 1980s, for example, the level of resources (such as police expenditures) local officials committed to criminal justice seems to have had little relation to the level of violent crime. There are also many examples of the "politicization" of crime by candidates for public office. In 1992, a candidate for the U.S. Senate proclaimed that he worried about the safety of his home neighborhood in Kenilworth—one of the nation's wealthiest suburbs that has one of the lowest crime rates in the state (Zorn, 1992). Interestingly, crime has seldom been a key issue in Chicago's mayoral campaigns. Factors such as the ethnic composition of the police force and selection of police superintendent have received more attention than the efficacy of police policies (Green and Holli, 1991; Kleppner, 1985; Holli and Green, 1984). Legislation, such as that aimed at "stalkers" or "carjackers," appears to be prompted by highly publicized, particularly brutal crimes. Public support for these measures seems to follow rather than to spur initiatives by public officials.

There are, however, some interesting departures from Scheingold's findings: (1) In the late 1980s and early 1990s, community concern about crime increased dramatically. Streetside drug sales and drug-related violence, as well as gang violence, have lead to escalating concern over public safety. In areas of the city that have the greatest victimization rates, elected officials and community leaders have called for a greater police presence, and some officials have called for intervention by the National Guard. City officials have increasingly been challenged by citizens groups to respond to the escalating murder rate (Kass and Gregory, 1992). Support for severe measures, such as capital punishment, has grown most steeply in the African-American community, rising from 40 percent in 1973 to 60 percent in 1992 on a nationwide basis (Goering, 1992).

(2) It is apparent that there are structural forces that militate against moderation at the local and state levels. The fragmentation of authority permits officials to evade responsibility for the practical consequences of their policies. Thus, the jail overcrowding crisis in Cook County remains unresolved. At the state level, the opening of two recently constructed prisons was deferred as a result of high operating costs. Whether such fiscal realities will impose a brake on the expanding prison population remains to be seen.

(3) Issues such as Willie Horton and capital punishment are potent ideological symbols. However, the politics of symbols sometimes evolve into policies that have practical consequences. Since 1987, when the U.S. Congress approved a broad anti-drug program, tens of millions of dollars have flowed into Illinois, influencing the enforcement of drug laws at the local level (Dowse, 1987). The street-level drug arrests that have flooded Cook County's narcotics courts have been financed, in part, with federal dollars.

The criminal justice policies that have been adopted over the past 15 years have led to high rates of incarceration, but they have failed to prevent growing violence in the area's poorest communities. The political rhetoric of conservatives and liberals is stale, with the right offering more laws but continued disorder and the left offering sweeping visions of reform but few short-term or intermediate remedies. The politics of street crime have not served us well.

REFERENCES

Block, Carolyn Rebecca (1992). "The Murders That Can Be Prevented," *The Compiler* (Illinois Criminal Justice Information Authority), Spring 1992, pp. 8-10.
Boehmer, Robert (1992). "Drugs, Corrections, and Financing: A Review," *The Compiler* (Illinois Criminal Justice Information Authority), Winter 1992, p. 5.
Chicago Police Department (1984-1991). *Annual Reports*, 1984-1991. Chicago.
Chicago Tribune (1992). "Who's to Blame for Jail Crisis," Editorial, August 30, 1992, sec. 4, p. 2.
Dowse, Sarah M. (1987). "State Submits $30.6 Million Drug Enforcement Plan," *The Compiler* (Illinois Criminal Justice Information Authority), Spring/Summer 1987.
Goering, Laurie (1992). "U. of C. Study Finds Attitudes of the '70s Alive in the '90s," *Chicago Tribune*, October 12, 1992, sec. 2, p. 3.
Green, Paul M., and Melvin G. Holli, eds. (1991). *Restoration 1989: Chicago Elects a New Daley*. Chicago: Lyceum Books.
Holli, Melvin G., and Paul M. Green, eds. (1984). *The Making of the Mayor: Chicago 1983*. Grand Rapids, Mich.: William B. Eerdmans.
ICJIA (1990). *Trends and Issues 90: Criminal and Juvenile Justice in Illinois*. Chicago: Illinois Criminal Justice Information Authority.
───── (1991). *Trends and Issues 91: Education and Criminal Justice in Illinois*. Chicago: Illinois Criminal Justice Information Authority.
───── (1992a). *Background Information: A Report to the Illinois Task Force on Crime and Corrections*. Chicago: Illinois Criminal Justice Information Authority, March 1992.
───── (1992b). "Drugs and Crime: Chicago Sets New Records," *The Compiler* (Illinois Criminal Justice Information Authority), Spring 1992, p. 5.

Kass, John, and Ted Gregory (1992). "Daley to Strike Back," *Chicago Tribune*, October 19, 1992, sec. 1, p. 1.

Kleppner, Paul (1985). *Chicago Divided: The Making of a Black Mayor*. DeKalb, Ill.: Northern Illinois University Press.

Manikas, Peter M., Mindy S. Trossman, and Jack C. Doppelt (1989). *Crime and Criminal Justice in Cook County: A Report of the Criminal Justice Project*. Evanston, Ill.: Center for Urban Affairs and Policy Research, Northwestern University.

Shane-DuBow, Sandra, Alice P. Brown, and Erik Olsen (1985). *Sentencing Reform in the United States: History, Content, and Effect*. Washington, D.C.: National Institute of Justice, August 1985.

Steigman, Robert (1992). Concurrence in *People v. Liberman*, No. 4-91-0038, Illinois Appellate Court, Fourth District, April 30, 1992.

Zorn, Eric (1992). "Crime Only a Fear for Williamson," *Chicago Tribune*, October 15, 1992, sec. 2, p. 1.

NOTES ON CONTRIBUTORS

Carolyn Rebecca Block is senior research analyst at the Illinois Criminal Justice Information Authority. She holds a doctorate in sociology from the University of Chicago. Her current projects include the Chicago Homicide Dataset, the Early Warning System for Street Gang Violence Crisis Areas, and organization of the Homicide Research Working Group.

Paul J. Goldstein is associate professor in the School of Public Health at the University of Illinois at Chicago. He was formerly deputy director for criminal justice research at Narcotic and Drug Research, Inc., in New York City.

Darnell F. Hawkins is professor of African-American Studies and Sociology at the University of Illinois at Chicago. His publications include *Ethnicity, Race, and Crime: Perspectives Across Time and Place* (editor) and *Homicide Among Black Americans* (editor).

Karen N. Hoover is a resident of Rogers Park, a community on the northeast side of Chicago. She is a co-convener of the Coalition for a Crime-Free Rogers Park, an affiliation of block clubs, social service agencies, business interests, and police, which is working to develop proactive problem-solving partnerships. In her "real" life, she is a psychotherapist.

Lawrence B. Joseph is senior research associate in the School of Social Service Administration and associate director of the Center for Urban Research and Policy Studies at the University of Chicago. He is also program director of the Chicago Assembly.

Paul J. Lavrakas is professor of communication studies, journalism, statistics, and urban affairs at Northwestern University and director of the Northwestern Survey Laboratory. He was the principal investigator on the national evaluation of the Eisenhower Foundation Neighborhood Program and has published widely on citizen crime prevention and fear of crime.

Laurence E. Lynn, Jr., is professor in the School of Social Service Administration and in the Irving B. Harris Graduate School of Public Policy Studies at the University of Chicago. He is also director of the Center for Urban Research and Policy Studies and project director of the Chicago Assembly.

Arthur J. Lurigio is associate professor in the Department of Criminal Justice at Loyola University of Chicago. He is co-editor of *Victims of Crime: Problems, Programs, and Policies*; *AIDS and Community Corrections: The Development of Effective Policies*; and *Smart Sentencing: The Emergence of Intermediate Sanctions*.

Peter M. Manikas is senior fellow at the International Human Rights Law Institute at DePaul University College of Law. He has served as executive director of the Illinois Supreme Court Special Commission on the Administration of Justice and as director of administrative operations for the Cook County Public Defender's Office.

Patrick D. McAnany is professor in and head of the Department of Criminal Justice at the University of Illinois at Chicago. His publications include *Introduction to Juvenile Delinquency: Youth and the Law* (with James T. Carey) and *Probation and Justice: Reconsideration of Mission* (co-editor).

Mark Moore is Guggenheim Professor of Criminal Justice Policy and Management at Harvard University's Kennedy School of Government. His publications include *Dangerous Offenders: The Elusive Target of Justice* and *Beyond 911: A New Era for Policing*.

Norval Morris is Julius Kreeger Professor Emeritus of Law and Criminology at the University of Chicago Law School. His publications include *Between Prison and Probation: Intermediate Punishment in a Rational Sentencing System* (with Michael Tonry) and *The Brothel Boy and Other Parables of the Law*.

Deborah Prothrow-Stith, M.D., is assistant dean of government and community programs and professor of public health practice at the Harvard School of Public Health. She has served as commissioner of public health for the Commonwealth of Massachusetts and is the author of *Deadly Consequences* and *Violence Prevention Curriculum for Adolescents*.

Notes on Contributors

Margaret K. Rosenheim is Helen Ross Professor in the School of Social Service Administration at the University of Chicago. Her current research activity includes the Public World of Childhood Project, which is investigating the changing socio-cultural context of public policy toward children. Her recent publications include *Early Parenthood and Coming of Age in the 1990s* (co-editor).

Robert J. Sampson is professor in the Department of Sociology and the College at the University of Chicago. His publications include *Crime in the Making: Pathways and Turning Points through Life* (with John H. Laub).

Stuart A. Scheingold is professor of political science at the University of Washington, Seattle. He is author of *The Politics of Law and Order: Street Crime and Public Policy* and *The Politics of Street Crime: Criminal Process and Cultural Obsession*.

Irving A. Spergel is George Herbert Jones Professor in the School of Social Service Administration at the University of Chicago. His publications include *The Youth Gang Problem: A Community Approach* (1995).

Howard Spivak, M.D., is vice president for community health programs and chief of general pediatrics and adolescent medicine at New England Medical Center. He is also associate professor of pediatrics and community health at Tufts University School of Medicine.

Deborah C. Stone is executive director of the Metropolitan Planning Council in Chicago.

Randolph N. Stone is clinical professor of law and director of the Mandel Legal Aid Clinic at the University of Chicago Law School. He has served as the Public Defender for Cook County, Illinois, and as chair of the Criminal Justice Section of the American Bar Association.

Frances Kahn Zemans is executive vice president of the American Judicature Society, an independent, national, non-for-profit organization of lawyers and non-lawyers devoted to improving the American justice system. Her publications include *The Making of a Public Profession* and articles in numerous scholarly journals.

CHICAGO ASSEMBLY PARTICIPANTS
"CRIME AND COMMUNITY SAFETY"
NOVEMBER 19-20, 1992

Mary Appelt
Manager, Partnership Development/
 Volunteer Operations
Chicago Cities in Schools

Joseph P. Beazley
Chief of Police
Joliet Police Department

Joseph Bella
Staff Representative
American Federation of State,
 County, and Municipal
 Employees, Council 31
(Chicago)

Larry Bennett
Associate Professor
Department of Political Science
DePaul University
(Chicago)

Ilene R. Bergsmann
Associate Director for Planning
 and Development
Cook County Judicial
 Advisory Council
(Chicago)

Carolyn Rebecca Block
Senior Research Analyst
Illinois Criminal Justice
 Information Authority
(Chicago)

Eduardo Camacho
Manager of Urban Lending
St. Paul Federal Bank
(Chicago)

JoAnn Chiakulas
Chief, Center for Minority Health
Illinois Department of
 Public Health
(Chicago)

Katherine Kaufer Christoffel
Professor of Pediatrics
 and Community Health
Northwestern University
 Medical School
(Chicago)

Nancy Cobb
Deputy Director of Development
Chicago Roseland Coalition for
 Community Control

William P. Cowhey
President
The Civic Federation
(Chicago)

Raymond Curran
Executive Director
Safer Foundation
(Chicago)

Kenneth B. Ehrensaft
Associate Professor of Sociology
 and Management & Business
Barat College
(Lake Forest)

James M. Field
Executive Director
Northwest Neighborhood
 Federation
(Chicago)

Hon. Thomas R. Fitzgerald
Presiding Judge
Criminal Division
Circuit Court of Cook County
(Chicago)

Warren Friedman
Executive Director
Chicago Alliance for
 Neighborhood Safety

Rita Aliese Fry
Cook County Public Defender
(Chicago)

Thomas G. Fuechtmann
Associate Vice President
Loyola University of Chicago

William A. Geller
Associate Director
Police Executive Research Forum
(Wilmette)

Hon. Michael Brennan Getty
Judge, Criminal Division
Circuit Court of Cook County
(Chicago)

Kenneth L. Gillis
First Assistant
Cook County State's
    Attorney's Office
(Chicago)

James W. Graham
Special Assistant for Public Safety
Office of the Governor
State of Illinois
(Chicago)

Melody Heaps
President
Treatment Alternatives for
    Special Clients (TASC, Inc.)
(Chicago)

John P. Heinz
Professor
Northwestern University
    Law School
(Chicago)

Doris B. Holleb
Professorial Lecturer
Social Sciences Collegiate
    Division and Committee
    on Geographical Studies
University of Chicago

Karen N. Hoover
Co-convenor
Coalition for a Crime-Free
    Rogers Park
(Chicago)

Hi Howard
Policy and Planning Specialist
The Neighborhood Institute
(Chicago)

Candice Howell
Board Member
Community Policing Task Force
(Chicago)

Mark Iris
Executive Director
Chicago Police Board

Esther J. Jenkins
Associate Director for Research
Community Mental Health
    Council
(Chicago)

Suzanne E. Jones
President
John Howard Association
(Chicago)

Wayne Kerstetter
Senior Research Fellow
American Bar Foundation
(Chicago)

Richard Lindberg
Executive Administrator
Combined Counties
    Police Association
(Barrington)

Arthur J. Lurigio
Associate Professor
Department of Criminal Justice
Loyola University of Chicago

Monica C. Mahan
Executive Director
Youth in Crisis, Inc.
(Berwyn)

Michael J. Mahoney
Executive Director
John Howard Association
(Chicago)

Peter M. Manikas
Executive Director
Illinois Supreme Court Special
  Commission on the
  Administration of Justice
(Chicago)

LeRoy Martin
Director of Public Safety
Chicago Housing Authority

Nancy Martin
Chief Probation Officer
Cook County Adult
  Probation Department
(Chicago)

Patrick D. McAnany
Professor and Head
Department of Criminal Justice
University of Illinois at Chicago

John McDermott
Community Organizer
Edgewater Community Council
(Chicago)

Jay A. Miller
Executive Director
American Civil Liberties Union
  of Illinois
(Chicago)

Cora Moore
President
CHA Tenant Patrol
(Chicago)

Norval Morris
Julius Kreeger Professor
University of Chicago
  Law School

Jane Mortell
Associate General Counsel
Illinois Department of Alcoholism
  and Substance Abuse
(Chicago)

Laurence Msall
Associate Director
Civic Committee of
  the Commercial Club
(Chicago)

Joseph D. Murphy
Logan Square Neighborhood
  Association
(Chicago)

Dennis E. Nowicki
Executive Director
Illinois Criminal Justice
  Information Authority
(Chicago)

LeRoy O'Shield
Commander, 15th Police District
Chicago Police Department

Howard A. Peters III
Director
Illinois Department of Corrections
(Springfield)

Virgil M. Poole, Sr.
Chief of Police
City of Harvey

Mary D. Powers
Coordinator
Citizens Alert
(Chicago)

Charles H. Ramsey
Deputy Chief of Patrol
Chicago Police Department

Thomas A. Regulus
Assistant Professor
Department of Criminal Justice
Loyola University of Chicago

Dennis P. Rosenbaum
Director, Center for Research in
 Law and Justice
University of Illinois at Chicago

Margaret K. Rosenheim
Helen Ross Professor
School of Social Service
 Administration
University of Chicago

Howard Saffold
Positive Anti-Crime Trust
(Chicago)

Frances Sandoval
President
Mothers Against Gangs
(Chicago)

Stuart Scheingold
Professor
Department of Political Science
University of Washington
(Seattle, Washington)

Barbara M. Schleck
Executive Director
Cook County Court Watchers
(Chicago)

Thomas Schumpp
Deputy Director, Division of
 Criminal Investigation
Illinois State Police
(Springfield)

Bambade H. Shakoor
Executive Director
Leadership Development Institute
(Calumet City)

James R. Simmons
Senior Staff Associate
Institute for Metropolitan Affairs
Roosevelt University
(Chicago)

Irving A. Spergel
George Herbert Jones Professor
School of Social Service
 Administration
University of Chicago

Marlene E. Stern
Executive Director
Citizens' Committee on
 the Juvenile Court
(Chicago)

Nikolas Theodore
Project Director
Chicago Urban League

Ron Tonn
Director, Training Division
Safer Foundation
(Chicago)

Cathy Vates
Vice President
North River Commission
(Chicago)

John P. Weiss
Executive Director
Center for Conflict Resolution
(Chicago)

Wim Wiewel
Director
Center for Urban Economic
 Development
University of Illinois at Chicago

Frances Kahn Zemans
Executive Vice President
American Judicature Society
(Chicago)

Observers

Paul Cuadros
The Chicago Reporter

Kent Lawrence
President
M. R. Bauer Foundation
(Chicago)

James M. O'Rourke
Executive Director
Cook County Judicial
 Advisory Council
(Chicago)

****

Project Director

Laurence E. Lynn, Jr.
Director
Center for Urban Research
 and Policy Studies
University of Chicago

Program Director

Lawrence B. Joseph
Associate Director
Center for Urban Research
 and Policy Studies
University of Chicago

Project Associate

Deborah C. Stone
Executive Director
Metropolitan Planning Council

Staff

Amy Keller
School of Social Service
 Administration
University of Chicago

Courtenay Savage
School of Social Service
 Administration
University of Chicago

Joel Werth
Metropolitan Planning Council

****

Drafting Committee

Joseph P. Beazley
Larry Bennett*
Carolyn Rebecca Block*
Eduardo Camacho**
Thomas R. Fitzgerald
Warren Friedman
Thomas G. Fuechtmann*
William A. Geller
Michael Brennan Getty
John P. Heinz*
Karen N. Hoover**
Suzanne E. Jones**

Wayne Kerstetter
Peter M. Manikas
Nancy Martin
Dennis E. Nowicki
Margaret K. Rosenheim
Barbara M. Schleck
James R. Simmons**
Ron Tonn**
Wim Wiewel*

Lawrence B. Joseph (Chair)
Courtenay Savage (Staff writer)

* Discussion leader
** Recorder

CHICAGO ASSEMBLY PROGRAM COMMITTEE
"CRIME AND COMMUNITY SAFETY"

Carolyn Rebecca Block
Senior Research Analyst
Illinois Criminal Justice
 Information Authority

Warren Friedman
Executive Director
Chicago Alliance for
 Neighborhood Safety

Thomas Fuechtmann
Associate Vice President for
 Government and Community
 Affairs
Loyola University of Chicago

Melody Heaps
President
Treatment Alternatives for
 Special Clients (TASC)

John Heinz
Professor
Northwestern University
 Law School

Karen Hoover
Convenor
Coalition for a
 Crime-Free Rogers Park

Suzanne Jones
President
John Howard Association

Benjamin Kendricks
Executive Director
Marcy-Newberry Association

Jesse Madison
President and CEO
Abraham Lincoln Center

Peter Manikas
Executive Director
Illinois Supreme Court
 Special Commission on the
 Administration of Justice

James O'Rourke
Executive Director
Judicial Advisory Council
 of Cook County

Randolph Stone
Clinical Professor
University of Chicago
 Law School

Nikolas Theodore
Economic Development Specialist
Chicago Urban League

Ron Tonn
Director, Basic Skills
 Training Division
Safer Foundation

CHICAGO ASSEMBLY ADVISORY BOARD

Marcus Alexis
Professor of Economics
Northwestern University

Mark A. Angelini
Vice President
The Shaw Company

David E. Baker
Vice President for
  External Affairs
Illinois Institute of Technology

Michael Belletire
Executive Assistant to
  the Governor
State of Illinois

Larry Bennett
Associate Professor
Department of Political Science
DePaul University

Pastora San Juan Cafferty
Professor, School of Social
  Service Administration
University of Chicago

Eduardo Camacho
Manager, Urban Lending
St. Paul Federal Bank

Barbara Flynn Currie
State Representative
26th District

James Fletcher
President
South Shore Bank

Kirsten A. Gronbjerg
Professor, Department of
  Sociology and Anthropology
Loyola University of Chicago

Donald Haider
Professor, Kellogg Graduate
  School of Management
Northwestern University

Doris B. Holleb
Professional Lecturer, Social
  Sciences Collegiate Division
  and Committee on
  Geographical Studies
University of Chicago

Lewis Manilow
Chairman of the Board
Darome Teleconferencing

Jeffrey Miller
Associate Dean for
  Administration and Planning
Northwestern University
  Medical School

Laurence Msall
Associate Director
Civic Committee of the
  Commercial Club

Michael Newman
Assistant Director, Council 31
American Federation of State,
  County, and Municipal
  Employees

David Ramage, Jr.
President
McCormick Theological Seminary

Elizabeth Ruyle
Executive Director
South Suburban Mayors and
  Managers Association

Kenneth B. Smith
President
Chicago Theological Seminary

Nancy A. Stevenson
Executive Director
Voices for Illinois Children

Nikolas Theodore
Economic Development
  Specialist
Chicago Urban League

Carole J. Travis
Central States Regional
  Coordinator
Service Employees International
  Union

Wim Wiewel
Special Assistant to
  the Chancellor
University of Illinois at Chicago

Timothy W. Wright III
Senior Vice President
Pryor, McClendon, Counts & Co.